Creating
GENDER

Creating GENDER

The Sexual Politics of Welfare Policy

Cathy Marie Johnson
Georgia Duerst-Lahti
Noelle H. Norton

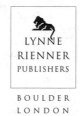

LYNNE
RIENNER
PUBLISHERS

BOULDER
LONDON

Published in the United States of America in 2007 by
Lynne Rienner Publishers, Inc.
1800 30th Street, Boulder, Colorado 80301
www.rienner.com

and in the United Kingdom by
Lynne Rienner Publishers, Inc.
3 Henrietta Street, Covent Garden, London WC2E 8LU

Library of Congress Cataloging-in-Publication Data
Johnson, Cathy Marie.
    Creating gender : the sexual politics of welfare policy / by Cathy Marie
Johnson, Georgia Duerst-Lahti, Noelle H. Norton.
        p. cm.
    Includes bibliographical references and index.
    ISBN-13: 978-1-58826-488-6 (hardcover : alk. paper)
    1. Public welfare—United States. 2. Family policy—United States.
3. Sex role—Government policy—United States. 4. Gender identity—United
States. 5. United States. Personal Responsibility and Work Opportunity
Reconciliation Act of 1996. I. Duerst-Lahti, Georgia, 1955–   II. Norton,
Noelle H., 1958–   III. Title.
HV95.J65 2006
361.6082'0973—dc22
                                                                 2006022406

British Cataloguing in Publication Data
A Cataloguing in Publication record for this book
is available from the British Library.

Printed and bound in the United States of America

    The paper used in this publication meets the requirements
∞   of the American National Standard for Permanence of
    Paper for Printed Library Materials Z39.48-1992.

    5 4 3 2 1

To our children:
Elena Krysten Duerst Lahti
Alexander Kyle Duerst Lahti
Hannah Marie Johnson Gais
Joseph Allen Johnson Gais
Ellen Margaret Willis-Norton

Contents

Tables

■ **Tables**

Preface

"WHERE WERE THE FEMINISTS WHEN WELFARE REFORM PASSED?" demanded Cathy Johnson over lunch, not long after the Personal Responsibility and Work Opportunity Reconciliation Act (PRWORA) became law. "Hoisted on liberal feminism's petard," Georgia Duerst-Lahti answered, more than a little defensively. Thus began the odyssey of this book and this collaboration. When Noelle Norton signed on, we had laid the basis for a truly enjoyable and productive scholarly collaboration. Because we were scattered across the country from east to west—Massachusetts, Wisconsin, and California—the collaboration could have been difficult. Although a few week-long home visits and annual conference lunches were part of the writing, mostly, we e-mailed. In the thick of things, our messages flew nearly as fast as our teenagers' IM-ing.

Instead of being difficult, our work together proved fruitful because we had the perfect mix of expertise and temperament. In order to answer Cathy's question adequately, we needed to cross our respective fields of gender theory (Georgia), social policy (Cathy), legislative behavior (Noelle), and political ideology (all of us). In addition, Cathy writes calmly with unusual clarity, Georgia pushes the boundaries of convention in great bursts of energy, and Noelle possesses superior quantitative skills and an ability to tackle daunting mounds of data while retaining her sanity. We became our own best and worst reviewers—if one of us couldn't understand it, we knew others would not either. By triplechecking and constant e-mailing, we can now claim that we bring "intercoder reliability" to every assertion we make. The process often crawled at a snail's pace, but never once did we argue or otherwise exude negativity, a remarkable feat. Our respect for each other's distinct talents abound.

As we launched this project, we quickly discovered that our combination of subfields would not fit neatly into any of the categories familiar to political science. Nonetheless, we persisted, and with plenty of help from scholarly friends we have designed an approach that, we hope, brings coherence to much of the work related to gender, ideology, welfare, and policymaking. We developed an original framework that helps to make sense of a complicated and nuanced set of ideas used to make policy. In the process of creating welfare policy, lawmakers also create gender. Gender is regularly created through policy, but seldom is that process of gender creation either explicit or tacitly acknowledged. Therefore, legitimated gender is established without scrutiny or debate. We hope this book provides the tools to analyze gender's legitimation in future policy debates.

The particular catalyst for this work was the observation that, in making PRWORA, legislators had destroyed the last vestige of standing given to care work by mothers. No longer would work as mothers—to foster children into able citizens—be recognized by the government as a public contribution. Instead, yet another masculine norm had been elevated—work in paid employment, or breadwinning. Even feminists in Congress seemed not to notice that motherhood had been made masculine. Maybe even more pernicious, but certainly intriguing as an academic puzzle, was that odd alliances and new oppositions arose during the PRWORA debate about motherhood. Our inclination to research and understand the politics behind these fascinating relationships and new bedfellows was made urgent by the fact that this new gender policy carries the force of law. It allocates values about which mode of gender—for women and for men—is to be sanctioned and rewarded with resources, and which will be discouraged and punished. This disciplining of gender is no small matter. It deserves to be brought to the fore of policymaking scholarship.

Our question, "Where were the feminists?" suggested that feminists should have taken a very public stand against PRWORA and that doing so would have made a difference for the value of mother-work. It also suggested that the feminist policymakers abdicated their responsibility to protect and advance the interests of women and children, which then begged the question of why only feminists had this responsibility. Our answer needed to avoid blaming feminists for something everyone should care about, even if they do not, and to attend to the fact that policymaking was ultimately in the control of elite men rather than feminists. Still, we could not let the feminists in legislatures entirely off the hook for participating in a reform effort that clearly had detrimental effects on poor women and their children. So our question expanded to, "Who were these feminists, who else was involved, and how were they involved?"

Clearly, feminists are not a monolithic political force, so we needed to approach this project with sensitivity about hyphenated feminisms and the diversity of ideological orientation across feminism. We also needed to incorporate the ideas of nonfeminist women, recognize men as gendered beings, and sort out the gender ideological variation both among and about men. Georgia had been working on such a project already, spawned by a colleague who casually equated feminism to Marxism. With the late Rita Mae Kelly, she had spelled out the basic notion of gender as protoideological, but quite clearly more nuance was required. Among other things, a new term was needed. Women are not more "liberal" than men, as they often are labeled; instead, they care about things associated with women. They have a feminalist orientation (for a definition, see Box 1.1), and that's why we saw Republican and Democratic women working together to mute the excesses of welfare reform proposals. Men are not more "conservative"; instead they care about things associated with men. They have a masculinist orientation, and that's why we often saw men working across the aisle to offer bipartisan reform proposals by men and about men. Nonetheless, conservative women and men held similar ideas, as did liberal women and men. So we needed a way to show convergence between the sexes. In the end, we developed a framework of compound ideology to help explain the shared and divergent ideas of women and men making policy—the compound gender ideology we outline here.

Cathy brought her expertise and passion for social policy, especially for children's policy. Her knowledge of the history of welfare policy helped her to take charge of the gender paradigms and to apply them to welfare policy as it evolved. In the process, she anchored our contemporary ideology in the paradigms that proponents dispute.

Noelle provided expertise on analyzing legislative behavior to demonstrate quantitatively that we could make the claims we wanted to make. She also teased out quantitative proof from a survey of Wisconsin state legislators, who passed the welfare policy that became the model for federal reform.

We owe an intellectual debt to many scholars who came before us. Their contributions are written through us and onto the pages that follow. Cathy J. Cohen's *The Boundaries of Blackness* served as a model. We strove to theorize meaningfully about gender much as she did about secondary marginalization. For her, the main question was AIDS; for us, it was welfare reform. Mark Kann has written more (and better) about masculinity than anyone else in political science. Joan Tronto has written masterfully about care work, and Christine Di Stefano showed us the place of (m)others in political thought. Gwendolyn Mink has led scholars to think critically about race in social policy. The late Rita Mae Kelly inspired us with the reach of her ideas and her capacity to cross scholarly boundaries. Her memory was with us throughout. We also owe an intellectual debt to several legislative scholars. Richard Fenno and Richard Hall have inspired us to look deep inside the recesses of the legislative committee to find the real players and policymakers. Eric R.A.N. Smith has helped guide us through the measurement of ideological legislative behavior. Sue Carroll, Sue Thomas, Debra Dodson, and Cindy Simon Rosenthal, among others, have written extensively about female members of Congress, providing us with the support to make our claims about female legislators. Michael Cohen taught us to look beyond the obvious. Deborah Stone's creative work on policy analysis inspired us to connect the rhetoric of politics to the goals of policy. The work of many historians, including Linda Gordon, Alice Kessler-Harris, and Rickie Solinger, reminded us that we care about politics because the actions of government have a lasting impact on people's lives.

We also owe a debt of gratitude to those who helped us hone our ideas and who willingly subjected themselves to earlier versions of this book. Some were official discussants who reviewed our papers with care, whereas others were professional colleagues. We thank five anonymous reviewers whose ideas strengthened the book immeasurably. We apologize in advance for missing some who have helped us. Georgia would especially like to thank Susan Carroll, Jane Bayes, Mary Hawkesworth, Wendy Sarvasy, Kenneth Hoover, Tony Affigne, Julia Jordon-Zachery, Ann Davies, John Rapp, Barbara Burrell, and Dorothy Stetson. She also owes an enormous debt to Virginia Sapiro and Dennis Dresang, who continue to mentor her, even now. Noelle would like to thank many of the same colleagues and would like to add Barbra Morris, Sonia Garcia, and Del Dickson to the list of those who provided sage guidance and moral support from beginning to end. Cathy would like to thank Alison Case for reading an entire draft of the manuscript and giving excellent advice about narrative, and the Political Science Department at Williams College for lively feedback and conversation. David Heesen is commended for outstanding work in formatting the manuscript, and a debt of thanks is owed to Arno Damerow for his ability to solve word-processing problems.

This book took longer to complete than we would have liked. Through it all, Leanne Anderson of Lynne Rienner Publishers always showed enthusiasm for the project. We should have listened to her from the beginning; she is a delight to work with. Her insistence that we not write as boring social scientists has improved the book immensely, although we suspect we never quite reached the creative flow of her dreams. We also thank Lynne Rienner, who did double duty as our editor while Leanne was on maternity leave. Her wisdom shone brightly through the many details she covered to make this book better.

This book would not have been possible without financial support. Georgia is grateful to Beloit College and its Professional Development Fund, whose generous support has been crucial. It has funded a host of student research assistants, whom Georgia also thanks for their diligence and for demonstrating that undergraduates can do remarkable work. They include Samir Goswami, who secured the survey of legislative staff, as well as Caty Wyly, Becky Burnett, Beth Drummet, Olivia Garcia, and Sarah Bryner. She also is grateful for the Sanger Summer Scholar Program, which funded Jusztina Traum to undertake interviews with staff members of conservative women's organizations in Washington, D.C. Noelle is grateful to the University of San Diego (USD) Faculty Development Research Grant program and to Patrick Drinan, dean of the College of Arts and Sciences at USD. She would also like to thank several graduate and undergraduate students, including Abigail Parta and Catherine Quizon, who were especially diligent in their attention to this project. Cathy thanks Williams College for its generous support of research at an undergraduate institution and Paola Gentry, Yolanda Davila, Kristen Wikelius, and Nalo Jackson for their remarkable research assistance. She also thanks Tom Gais at the Rockefeller Institute for sharing its data with us.

With all this help, one could hope we have expunged all the inconsistencies and mistakes. Alas, such a feat seldom occurs, and we likely are not to be exempt from such failures. We accept responsibility for any mistakes we have made in using others' ideas, or developing our own.

Finally, no one undertakes a project of this magnitude without the support of family and friends. Cathie Duerst Schroeder continues to inspire Georgia with a positive attitude and willingness to try new things. Cyndi Taylor is a friend beyond compare, who helps with the kids and otherwise keeps Georgia sane. Carol McPhee Norton and Ann FitzGerald were critical to Noelle and this project as her lifelong editors, mentors, and counselors. Beth Norton, Claire Norton, Barbara Morris, Helen Westcott, Deborah Sundmacher, and Jane Beck, all mothers, friends, and sisters, not only keep Noelle sane but all continue to talk through the meaning of mothering, whether on the beach, in the park, or over a lemon-ginger muffin. For Cathy, Scott Wong is a source of good jokes, support, and companionship through the long working days; Gretchen Long and Alexandra Garbarini remind her to breathe and help her unpack comments she does not understand; Cheryl Shanks goes shoe shopping when a break is needed; and Monique Deveaux has delightful conversations about life and politics over a glass of wine.

Finally, to our spouses and life partners, good guys all—Tris Lahti, Tom Gais, and Erwin Willis—we say thanks for your patience when we got cranky, for being a sounding board as we worked through both substance and strategy, for helping to keep the computers running, and for all the many, many things done to make this project go smoothly. Most important, we thank all of you for being good fathers and for inspiring us to think about fatherhood through your example.

— Cathy Marie Johnson,
Georgia Duerst-Lahti,
and Noelle H. Norton

1

Making Gender, Making Policy

DAVID OAKLEY IS A BEWITCHING LADY'S MAN. IT SEEMS HE charmed the pants off at least four women, two of whom he married and two others he impregnated while he was married.[1] Fathering nine children by these four women, he has "always been there" for some of his children but not for others, who claim that he gave them "no nothing." Two of his mates support him still; two do not. His current girlfriend, Rachel Ward, says he does not want more children, but that "he's just a very potent guy" and, by other accounts, proud of it. All four agree that he has not paid child support, so under the law, he is a deadbeat dad, a scofflaw, who owes at least $25,000. Despite that, one defends him because well-paying jobs are hard to find, and another says it should be left to God. His grandfather gave up on him because he has always been in trouble, but his uncle considers him a hard worker who is good-hearted; he just needs a car to get to work. The county sheriff sees him as a "regular customer" at the jail; a city police captain suggests he likes the security and structure of prisons and jails, a roof over his head, and no worry about his next meal.

In a decision in which the justices split 4–3, along gender lines, the Wisconsin Supreme Court ruled that Oakley could be barred from having more children unless he could provide financially for them all. Because he does not provide for the children he has fathered, he should not be allowed to father again. Such prohibitions have been directed toward women, too. For example, after the death by dehydration of Andrea Goetz's nineteen-day-old infant, Judge Dane Morey ordered her not to have more children without permission.[2] Like many pregnant women jailed because they were abusing drugs or alcohol, Goetz did not care for her child as is expected of a mother. Much as the law requires fathers to provide, it requires mothers to give adequate care.

A myriad of important strictures, norms, and policies are packed into the Oakley case. They include not only the laws in question but also conventional understandings about what defines a father, the social roles a good father and husband are to play, and the policy enforcement of those roles. The case incorporates a desirable element of masculinity—potency—and circumstances that may or may not be beyond the man's control. Religious beliefs about parenting are evoked, and explanations of his predicament include a need to punish and to lend him a hand. Given their own expectations, his wives, girlfriends, and children express a range of reactions—from disgust to gratitude—in the way he has comported himself as a man, mate, husband, and father. Most of all, differences in perspective abound, not only between men and women on the court, but also among female justices, the men involved in the justice system, his extended family, and the children and women in his life. All these elements point to the jumbled ambiguity surrounding "proper" gender roles and behavior and the laws that try to hold this propriety in place.

As proper gender roles and behavior are debated, disputes also arise over whether biology should define parenting. Most states deem a husband to be the legal father of any child born during a marriage, even though marriage is not needed for a man to be declared a father. All he needs to do is accept paternity. In these cases, relationships and a willingness to accept responsibility, not biology, matter most. Through a marriage relationship with the mother or a legal relationship with the child, the man legally and socially takes on provider responsibility. However, new technology—DNA testing—threatens the legal and relationship basis for the provider role, raising questions about who should be obliged by the state to act as a father. "Duped Dads" in Massachusetts, Florida, Texas, Georgia, and Ohio claim that a man should not have to provide for children—regardless of whether he loves them as a father—if those children are not biologically his.[3]

Even though biological parenthood is more obvious with mothers, relying on biology cannot always provide simple answers to questions about who is a mother. On November 19, 2003, Danielle Bimber gave birth to triplets she had carried as a surrogate mother. The triplets were conceived from eggs from a donor and sperm from the father, who had arranged the surrogate contract with Bimber. When the father and his fiancé, who had no biological connection to the triplets, failed to pick up the children at the hospital after they were born, Bimber took the children home with her. The case ended up in court, with Bimber suing for custody and the agency responsible for arranging the surrogacy trying to protect the original contract. Despite the fact that neither the eggs nor sperm belonged to Bimber's biological family, the triplets from her womb became her children when a Pennsylvania court granted custody to Bimber. For that court, the gender role of bearing children in a biological womb weighed heavily, as it did in Bimber's desire to become their mother. The court granted the biological father visitation rights, but despite his intentions to marry, recognized no legal relationship between his fiancé and the children.[4] An Ohio appeals court has contested this conclusion and ordered a new custody hearing in which the female donor would have the opportunity to claim parental rights.[5]

That aspects of family law put the government in the position to define gender roles is hardly surprising. But these definitions play out even in unexpected policies, such as the right to bury a child who died in battle or a challenge to inclusion of the words "one nation under God" in the Pledge of Allegiance. In 2005, the Superior Court of Santa Cruz County, California, heard a dispute between divorced parents over a federal regulation that affected the burial of their son, Jason Hendrix, a soldier killed in Iraq. His mother and caretaker until he was eighteen, Renee Amick, wanted to bury her son in Watsonville, California, where Jason was born and raised. Contrary to her wishes, her ex-husband, Russell Hendrix, wanted to bury Jason in Oklahoma, where he finished high school. Because a little-known Defense Department rule grants custody to the eldest parent or the next of kin based on seniority, the father's wishes stood, and Jason is now buried in Oklahoma.[6] Although this rule does not sanction a gender relationship on its face, in 70 percent of marriages in the United States, husbands are older than wives, and the Defense Department assumes that husbands are older than wives in its planning for pensions.[7] Hence, the rule has hidden gender sanctions: whether deliberately or not, the rule confers an advantage on fathers and men, even divorced ones, by reinforcing the male role as head of household and decisionmaker and by potentially limiting the reach of mothers and women, even when they continue to be primary caregivers for children.

Another surprising venue for a dispute about gender roles involves the legal battle over the inclusion of the phrase "one nation under God" in the Pledge of Allegiance. Understood by many as a suit concerning the separation of church and state, behind this battle lies a complicated, tangled question of fatherhood, motherhood, and the privileges of parental status. At issue is whether an unmarried biological father who does not have legal custody of his daughter has standing to bring a lawsuit against the state as a parent or as the child's "next friend." Michael Newdow never married the girl's mother, Sandra Banning. He developed a strong relationship with his daughter despite a contentious custody suit, allegations by Newdow that he had been "date raped" by Banning the night their daughter was conceived (a claim called "incredibly disingenuous" by Judge James Mize), continued controversy over where the daughter would reside, and religious disagreements between Newdow and Banning.[8] An atheist, Newdow objected to the religious inculcation his daughter faced while listening to her classmates recite the Pledge each day and filed suit to remove the offending words. Clearly, he also objected to the views of his daughter's mother, who had become a born-again Christian.

Because Newdow was recognized by all involved as the daughter's father, the gender sanctions in this case turned upon what legal privileges accompanied his status as a father who lacked legal custody yet had a parental relationship with his daughter. Because Newdow claimed paternity, provided for the child, and had developed an attentive relationship with her, the Ninth Circuit Court ruled that he did have standing as a parent, which derived "entirely from his relationship with his daughter." This parental status gave him standing to "object to unconstitutional government action affecting his child,"[9] even if his beliefs contradicted those of the mother and sole legal guardian. However, the court did not grant him status as the child's "next friend," a person who appears in court on behalf of a minor but is not a party to the lawsuit. A "next friend" is usually a parent or a close relative, and holding this status also rests on the existence of a close relationship between the adult and the child. Ironically, status as the girl's "next friend" would have given Newdow greater standing to challenge the constitutionality of the Pledge of Allegiance. Under California law, as a "next friend," his interests would be seen as coinciding with those of his daughter. As a father, however, Newdow's interests potentially conflicted with those of his daughter, a possibility that was underscored when the child's mother filed a claim counter to Newdow's.[10] In passing laws about a variety of topics, such as how the category of "next friend" is understood, legislative and judicial policymakers decide what privileges and responsibilities are granted to those who hold gender roles, in this case a father without legal custody, and therefore create gender.

As these cases demonstrate, when disputes over gender play out in family court, we often recognize them as being "about gender." We have a more difficult time seeing the contours of making gender when contested rules and regulations rely on implicit and unexamined assumptions about gender. We also have a difficult time seeing gender when the prima facie issue appears to be about something else entirely but cannot be resolved until elaborate questions of gender are answered. But a careful unpacking of these cases indicates that gender appears just as readily in the interstices of the laws and regulations used to implement them as it does in the high-profile, painful disputes involving child custody and the disintegration of families.

Much easier to see than these embedded and unspoken assumptions are basic patterns in attempts to shape gender. These broad patterns become part of the strictures that govern people's lives; they shape and restrict what people can and cannot do or be as gendered humans. When struggles over these broad patterns of gender erupt, much more public attention is directed toward them. Individuals, interest groups, and politicians alike know that they set the parameters for the narrower, focused quarrels of family disputes, and they fight passionately to establish the contours and precedents of policies that create gender.

Nowhere was this struggle more obvious than with the Equal Rights Amendment (ERA), which ultimately failed June 30, 1982. Trying to save women's roles as homemakers and helpmates, traditional ladies in red dresses and white gloves brought fresh-baked bread to state legislators. Women opposing the ERA fought to keep relationships between women and men the way they had been, with complementary, distinct, but important roles for each sex. Women should not be subject to the draft or exposed to the unseemly possibility of unisex toilets that would follow from equality. Men should be men—strong providers and protectors—and women should be women, nurturers and keepers of life's finer ways. Supporters of the ERA divided over tactics, with more conventional women using familiar womanly ways to cajole legislators, while more radical liberationists protested and pushed the very ideas of gender, in part through their tactics of being hard-edged women who spoke stridently and demanded equality in areas beyond what most Americans could fathom at the time. Yet even the conventional women backing the ERA were willing to support policies such as women being drafted because they believed that individuals, regardless of sex, should be treated the same. The supporters shared the goal of equal treatment with men, a standard of sameness for all individuals.

Another policy area in which broad patterns of gender are readily contested is women in the military. Although the jobs women could perform in the military were expanded greatly in 1994, women have been barred from smaller units assigned to a direct ground combat mission or from units that support combat troops 100 percent of the time. Nonetheless, the Iraq War effort has left the army tinkering with the Department of Defense rules, such that in practice women have been assigned to these smaller units that support direct ground combat, usually as mechanics. In May 2005, Representatives Duncan Hunter (R-CA) and John McHugh (R-NY) successfully inserted language into the 2006 Defense Authorization Act (H.R. 1815) that challenged this practice.[11] This amendment, formally about congressional oversight and civilian control of the military, reignited debate about women as warriors and the deleterious effect upon military men that follows from facing combat in mixed-sexed units. Proponents of the amendment expressed concern that there was "no reason to expose young women, many of them mothers, to direct ground combat" and that eliminating some exemptions on women's land combat "would be tantamount to suggesting that violence against women is alright."[12] Further, they argued, women lack sufficient physical strength for direct combat and cannot be trusted to carry a wounded comrade out of harm's way; thus their presence in a combat troop undermines the "psychological bonds essential for unit cohesion." Besides, they asserted, men will be turned off by the cultural changes needed to accommodate women in formerly all-male units. These policies hold in place ideas about gender, ideas that women—mothers—need protection from male violence and that only men are capable of such protection. The fact that military men are often fathers did not enter the discussion. Further, they acknowledge a cultural need to separate women from men if men are to be successful, presumably because women and men cannot bond together as warriors.

Governmental sanctioning of proper gender for men and women indisputably lay at the heart of the ERA and is readily apparent as women expand their roles in the military. How feminine must a woman be? What kind of man should a man be? What is proper masculinity? To make these policies was clearly to create gender. Less obvious was the fact that earlier the government consistently had set in place complementary roles of gender difference through a myriad of policies. It was only when those policies were challenged that the ways in which government created gender became obvious.

For example, questions about gender and gender relationships have been unraveled by the courts over issues including limitations on the length of women's workday (*Muller v. Oregon,* 209 U.S. 412, 1908), the prohibition on women bartending (*Goesaert v. Cleary,* 335 U.S. 464, 1948), the right of women with preschool-age children to work (*Phillips v. Martin Marietta,* 400 U.S. 542, 1971), the right of a mother to execute her son's will (*Reed v. Reed,* 404 U.S. 71, 1971), a woman's right to retain a job when pregnant (*Cleveland Board of Education v. LaFleur,* 414 U.S. 632, 1974), and limitations on a state's right to exclude women from jury trials (*Taylor v. Louisiana,* 419 U.S. 498, 1975). Each of these cases highlights a dispute over laws and policies put in place by Congress or a state legislature. In many of these cases, the gender relationships sanctioned by law were invisible or appeared neutral. But a closer inspection shows that the laws under question did indeed support a vision of complementary gender relationships. Regardless of the court's final opinion, it often takes a legal claim by aggrieved men and women to uncover the hidden sanctioning of gender in law and public policy.

- In 1972, Lt. Sharron A. Frontiero, a US Air Force physical therapist assigned to Maxwell Air Force Base Hospital in Alabama, was married to a full-time student and Vietnam veteran. Lt. Frontiero wanted to claim her husband, Joseph, as a dependent in order to receive an increased allotment for housing and to be furnished with medical and dental benefits. Federal law, however, limited Frontiero's claim because servicewomen were required to prove that their husbands were actually dependent, whereas servicemen could claim benefits for their wives solely on the basis of their marriage. Dependency was assumed for the wives but not for the husbands of military personnel. Because Joseph Frontiero received veteran's benefits, he could not prove dependence upon Sharron. The District Court in Alabama ruled against them and upheld the federal law because it was not based on a service member's sex, but on the nature of the marriage relationship in which Congress could presume dependency for women and independence for men. In overturning the lower decision, the Supreme Court recognized that Congress had indeed created a scheme based on sex and that this law discriminated against servicewomen.[13]

- Production processes at Johnson Controls took place in an area in which workers were exposed to high concentrations of lead. A progressive employer, it established policies beyond those required by the Occupational Safety and Health Administration (OSHA) to protect its workers' health. Over time, the policy evolved to protect fetuses from the dangers lead posed to them in utero. Johnson executives were particularly concerned about the effects of lead on fetal development because high levels of lead could harm a fetus before a woman knew she was pregnant and because lead lingers in the body for several months. Johnson Controls therefore established a policy that fertile women could not work in this unit. In April 1984, several employees at Johnson Controls filed a class action suit against the fetal protection policy, claiming sex discrimination. "Among the individual plaintiffs were petitioners Mary Craig, who had chosen to be sterilized in order to avoid losing her job, Elsie Nason, a 50-year-old divorcee, who had suffered a loss in compensation when she was transferred out of a job where she was exposed to lead, and Donald Penney, who had been denied a request for a leave of absence for the purpose of lowering his lead level because he intended to become a father." Many earlier cases proved unhelpful because in the past women were expected to procreate the race and not work in such dirty and dangerous jobs, whereas men were to provide for children, regardless of work's danger to their procreative health. Relying on gender equality laws to promote a change in such notions yet avoiding profound questions about what constitutes real choice, the court ruled: "The bias in Johnson Controls' policy is obvious. Fertile men, but not fertile women, are given a choice as to whether they wish to risk their reproductive health for a particular job."[14]

- In 1982 Ann Hopkins, a senior manager in an office of Price Waterhouse, was proposed for partnership. She had a very successful record of bringing in large contracts and had been praised for energetically getting projects done on time. However, consideration of partnership was delayed for a year. Despite an exceptional record of accomplishment and accolades for her professionalism, some partners saw her as suffering from interpersonal problems. She was called "macho" or in need of "charm school." Her tough-talking "masculine" mannerism included the use of profanity, which a partner deemed offensive "because it's a lady using foul language." Yet many men who were admitted as partners also lacked such interpersonal skills. In order to improve her chances for partnership, a supporter, Thomas Beyer, advised Hopkins to "walk more femininely, talk more femininely, dress more femininely, wear make-up, have her hair styled, and wear jewelry." In other words, she should perform masculine gender less and feminine gender more. Relying on government laws about what constitutes sex discrimination to decide this case, the court determined that such use of sex stereotyping resulted from a "cabined view of the proper behavior of women, and that Price Waterhouse had done nothing to disavow reliance on such comments."[15]

- Written in gender-neutral terms so that either a woman or a man could take leave to care for a family member, the Family and Medical Leave Act of 1993 was nonetheless largely designed to protect women's employment.[16] It recognized the fact that women now worked in paid employment but also that someone was still needed on occasion to tend to a family's care needs, including very young infants immediately after childbirth. In practice, women disproportionately use this law, despite the possibility that men can and will do care work. William Hibbs took time off to care for his ailing wife and sued his employer, the State of Nevada, when it refused to reinstate him after his leave. Chief Justice William Rehnquist defended the possibility that men can be caregivers, arguing that unless both men and women can take time off to care for their families, "mutually reinforcing stereotypes" will create a "self-fulfilling cycle of discrimination" in which women will always be the ones expected to stay home and so will be less attractive to employers.[17]

In these general patterns of gender, or gender paradigms, policies have required that legal gender options move away from fixed and complementary roles between women and men to a pattern in which treating individuals equally matters most. Women and men must be treated the same unless a very good reason exists not to do so. More recently, policymakers have been faced with radical challenges to the meaning of sex and gender. Most of these confront the very notion of what constitutes a woman or a man through policies that must be applied to lesbians and gays and, most particularly, transgendered people. These challenges are directed at laws relying on the assumption that there are only two types of humans, males and females who clearly fit one gender category or the other, physically and in the way they behave. These challenges also call into question the extent to which gender, the social construction of sex, aligns with sexed bodies.

In 1959, Bessie Lewis was born a girl. At an early age she believed that she had been born into the wrong body, a condition known as gender identity disorder, and she became preoccupied with ridding herself of the characteristics of the female sex. At age twenty-one, Bessie began taking testosterone and gained muscle mass, a lower voice, baldness, and other characteristics of males. He also began using the name Robert Sterling Simmons. In 1985, Sterling legally wed Jennifer Simmons. He had all his female internal organs surgically removed in 1991, and Jennifer underwent artificial insemination, bearing a child in 1992. Sterling signed an agreement accepting the child as his own, even though under Illinois law the husband in a legal marriage becomes the father of any child born to the couple. With the help of a doctor who swore procedures for a sex change had taken place, in 1994 Sterling had the sex on his birth certificate changed from female to male. By 1998, the tumultuous marriage ended in divorce, and Jennifer was awarded sole custody of the child on the grounds that the marriage had never been legal because Sterling's body had no penis. He had not undergone surgery to remove his breasts or external female genitalia and replace them with a small, reconstructed penis. Hence, Sterling was female, and because Illinois denies same-sex marriages, the marriage was not legal. Although he was granted visitation rights with the child, his signature claiming paternity on the insemination agreement also could not stand, and he was not considered the child's father.

Numerous policy questions are involved here, including what constitutes a sex change, parental rights in artificial insemination, the basis for declaring "sex" on a birth certificate, marriage licenses and same-sex marriage laws, and grounds for child visitation in a divorce (of a marriage that was voided).[18] At stake, of course, are larger questions about what constitutes female and male, what social significance is granted to those categories, and what situations and behaviors render gender irrelevant to how we organize ourselves as a community and care for those we love.

As policymakers wrestle with these questions, they review past policy decisions to see if changes are needed and address new policy dilemmas. They also determine who makes policy and which of the ideological beliefs they hold matter. That can be easily seen in the case of David Oakley, where the female justices in the Wisconsin court dissented from the court's all-male majority. One worried about state power and intrusion upon the private sphere if government required a "credit check" before adults could procreate. Another wrestled with the possibility that such laws would encourage abortions among the poor. The male and female justices—who otherwise predictably share perspectives along liberal and conservative lines—split along gender lines. The women believed procreation to be the highest human right, whereas the men focused upon the duties of a father, excoriating the conditions this father set for his children.

Whether the sex of the policymaker bears on policy decisions has been studied a great deal. Mostly, we have learned that a decision-maker's sex is less important than sharing a political party, liberal or conservative orientation, or some other strongly held belief or characteristic such as race or age. Yet as the following examples confirm, sometimes sex does matter in policymaking.

- In 1957, Gwendolyn Hoyt wanted to save her violence-filled marriage to her philandering husband. Without apparent premeditation, she hit him with a baseball bat when he refused to discuss their marital problems and then immediately called for help to stop the bleeding. An all-male jury convicted her of second-degree murder rather than manslaughter. In considering whether or not Hoyt had been tried by a jury of her peers, the US Supreme Court struck down a Florida law that excused women from jury duty because women, as a class, had "primary responsibility" for "household duties" and jury service "might place an unwarranted strain upon the social and domestic structure." It mattered that no women sat in judgment, and state legislatures could no longer exclude women from public life.
- During the 1991 Clarence Thomas hearings for appointment to the Supreme Court, the fact that an all-male Senate Judiciary Committee made light of accusations of sexual harassment by Anita Hill generated an unprecedented visit to the Senate by congresswomen from the House and galvanized professional women across the country, setting off the "Year of the Woman" in the 1992 election that brought more women to the US Senate.
- Less than two months after hitting the market in 1998, more than half of the prescriptions for Viagra, a medication to treat male

erectile dysfunction, were covered by insurance. Yet most state legislators across the country, about 75 percent of whom are male, had refused to require insurance to cover women's contraception. With Viagra as the catalyst, female state legislators and women's interest groups demanded birth control also be covered. By 2001, more than half the states had considered equity in coverage, and Senator Olympia Snowe (R-ME) led a bipartisan, House-Senate coalition of male and female members of Congress pushing for equity in prescription coverage of contraceptives.[19]

Although some effort has been made to consider whether or how sex matters in policymaking, less attention has been devoted to examining the intersection of gender and political ideology. However important ideology may be as a basis for policy decisions, only some academics, the highly attentive public, and the "political class" think much about it, in part because it is ephemeral, highly nuanced, and generally only indirectly related to the effects of policy upon people's lives. Moreover, although politically involved people are largely aware that liberal and conservative ideology plays a part in making policy, they are largely unaware that gender ideology also operates, even though agreement over gender can be the glue that holds alliances together.

As all these cases attest, struggles over many policies constitute ongoing battles over gender. In this book we take up the question of how gender is created when policy is made. We consider the ways in which ideas about gender both merge and do not merge with the familiar liberal-conservative governing ideology. We show that the liberal conservative ideology is not gender-neutral and that ideas about proper gender arrangements operate as a distinct ideology—gender ideology. We focus on the gender struggles in one policy area—namely, the political fight over the adoption and implementation of the Personal Responsibility and Work Opportunity Reconciliation Act (PRWORA). Commonly called welfare reform, this act replaced Aid to Families with Dependent Children (AFDC) with Temporary Assistance to Needy Families (TANF) and in doing so eliminated the entitlement to cash assistance for poor women and their children. It also gave states considerable discretion in fashioning their own welfare programs.

We concentrate on welfare policy here for two reasons. First, welfare is substantively important. AFDC and now TANF are major programs that shape the extent to which and the ways in which poor women, men, and children receive assistance from the government. What welfare programs we have, who receives benefits through them, what they have to do to receive those benefits, and how generous the assistance is have a direct effect on the lives of many people. Where these people live and their race also matter for the ways in which welfare policies are experienced by men, women, and children.

Second, it is in the realm of social welfare that so many gender battles are joined.[20] The state of the two-parent family; the proper upbringing of children; the entrance of women into the labor force; the desirable behavior of respectable men; the sexual behavior of virtuous citizens; and the responsibility of the state to punish, reward, and nurture its citizens all are controversial issues about gender that are connected to welfare policy. Because both the national and state governments willingly affix requirements of individual behavior to the receipt of public aid, political advocates of various gendered behaviors eagerly connect their causes to welfare policy. For example, those who lament the declining state of marriage in the United States may feel powerless to reach the general public and reverse what they see as regrettable trends in divorce and marriage rates, trends that manifest differently in urban black neighborhoods, rural poor communities, and white suburbs. Welfare policy provides a home for these worries; a way to experiment with policy designs that could gain political traction and spread to other policy areas; and a place to have grand discussions about our visions of the ways in which we organize and promote gender in ourselves, our families, and our communities.

In the larger literature on welfare policy, gender has long been acknowledged as central and has evolved from a gynocentric focus upon women to one that understands men have gender too and that gender varies by one's social location. Gender also is understood as a "given," a social phenomenon that goes beyond human bodies to practices, institutions, and the like.[21] Without this scholarship, the analytic framework offered here would not be possible. A substantial debt is also owed to comparative studies of European systems, in which scholars systematically examine the gendering of states and their policies.[22] However, this fine feminist political scholarship seldom is placed in conversation with conventional political science approaches to political ideology. For example, Joanne Goodwin documents the importance of gender in welfare policy by considering the effects of public assistance on women in the early decades of the twentieth century.[23] In this approach, gender is synonymous with women, and the gendering of men and masculinity is largely ignored. Gwendolyn Mink provides outstanding analysis of racialized gender but focuses on the targets of policy—poor women of color—more than on the entire contest over gender.[24] In Theda Skocpol's analysis, the targets of policy determine its gendering: she describes gender in welfare policy by examining the maternalist policies toward women and children that succeeded the paternalist policies directed toward soldiers in the Civil War.[25] Although it might be accurate to call policies directed toward mothers maternalist, soldiers were not necessarily fathers, and therefore the policies are somewhat mislabeled as paternalist. Her approach also shows the tendency to conflate parental and gender roles and the inclination to paint with too broad a brush by associating the whole of the feminale with maternal and the whole of the masculine with paternal (see Box 1.1).

In a blatant example of this conflation, Lawrence Mead has named welfare reform approaches since the 1980s "new paternalism."[26] He and other authors who employ the term *paternalism* for a "directive or supervisory approach" to social policy do not seem to think of paternalism as gendered; rather, they see it as "understandable" and "already widely used to characterize directive programs."[27] Mead claims that maternalism or parentalism could be substituted equally well because as many women as men have been involved in developing and applying these policies. Mead apparently genders his concepts according to who creates and controls the policy, although he uncritically assumes that women, men, mothers, fathers, and parents are interchangeable. Further, he assumes the term *paternal* best connotes the universal. In this case, men and masculinity—the paternal—have no gender; they are the norm. Clearly, he operates from a masculinist starting point. His unreflective declaration of the universality of paternalism shows a successful ideology at work—masculinism.

■ The Organization of the Book

We begin our examination of creating gender through the making of policy by considering in Chapter 2 the general patterns of gender, or gender paradigms, that result from policymaking. We describe the gender patterns in dispute and explain how they connect to specific policies designed to reward desired gendered behavior and punish unwanted behavior. In Chapter 3, we probe the ideological belief systems of policymakers. In order to explicate the ways in which gender interacts with political ideology, we have created a framework that brings together conventional governing ideology with gender ideology, and we apply this framework to our case of welfare policy. In Chapter 4, we trace the unfolding of these paradigms in the history of welfare policy, showing how disputes played out over time and set up the current controversy over gender and welfare reform. In Chapter 5, we detail how welfare reform upended the normative standards for good mothering and "made masculine mothers" by vanquishing mother-work and declaring paid employment to be the proper gender role for mothers. In Chapter 6, we analyze the contested

Box 1.1 A Brief Definition of Terms: Feminale, Feminality, and Masculinism

We explore the utility of the term *feminale* at great length in Chapter 3. Here, suffice it to say that the term has several advantages over the conventional term *feminine*. Foremost among these advantages is precisely the fact the term carries no baggage associated with women's politics, unlike the term *feminine* or its ideological counterpart, *feminism*.

Culturally, the term *feminine* has connoted particular behaviors of dress designed to heighten distinctions from men; softness of body and voice; and ladylike behaviors such as occupying a small space, sacrificing or ceding to the needs of others, and the like. It also is often used to refer to certain "women's issues" or policies considered to be "soft," such as health, education, welfare, and reproductive policies. Depending upon one's point of view, the feminine can be something to avoid because it is deemed weak and substandard by some groups (e.g., men in the military or on sports teams, early second-wave feminists, butch lesbians, or liberals who seek universal sameness), something glorious that must be revalued vis-à-vis the patriarchy (e.g., cultural feminists), something in which to revel for reasons of sexuality (e.g., third-wave feminists, many heterosexual men), or a civilizing force and prized complement to masculinity in families and society (e.g., social conservatives).

Similarly, feminism carries cultural baggage, whether being mocked as femi-Nazi, worn as a badge of enlightenment, adopted in practice but not in name ("I'm not a feminist, but . . ."), or cast as "antifeminist." In the latter case, women who are "for" women, such as Concerned Women for America, but not in the manner espoused by feminists, have no positive label. (During the ERA ratification period, Phyllis Schlafly used the term "positive woman.") Discussing pro-woman policy positions is difficult without using this "anti" characterization, and using an "anti" to be for something is at best unclear. Furthermore, feminism already has an array of hyphenated types, such as liberal, socialist, black, and second and third wave. As a result, feminism conceptually is difficult to treat as a monolith, despite such common usage. In short, feminists often try to avoid, change, or revalue the feminine, whereas nonfeminist women seek distance from—and may disdain—feminism. We have no neutral term to discuss constructs associated with females. For analytic

Box 1.1 Con't.

reasons, a new term is exceedingly useful. Most important, we need a term that makes possible an analytic discussion of all women and ideologies associated with them.

In addition, feminality is a better concomitant for masculinity than femininity. Interestingly, Funk and Wagnalls *New International Dictionary of the English Language* (*Comprehensive Edition*, 1997) defines feminine as "belonging to or characteristic of womankind; having qualities as modesty, delicacy, tenderness, tact, etc., normally characteristic of women" (p. 465). The word *female* is mentioned only as a synonym. In contrast, *masculine* is defined as "having the distinguishing qualities of the male sex, or pertaining to males; specially suitable for men; manly: opposed to feminine" (p. 782). In other words, masculinity is tied directly to the biological construct for males, but femininity is tied to the cultural construct of woman, which is "an adult human female; the female part of the human race" (p. 1,446). Feminality, which is defined as "the quality of being female" (p. 465), actually equates more closely with masculinity. It links to the biological female directly, much as masculinity links to males. Gender theory developed by Judith Butler, Judith Lorber, and others has made clear just how "given" the notion of biological sex is and how we construct biology itself, the idea of biological females and males, and the more widely recognized social constructions of men and women.

Further, because we deal with ideology in this analysis, the ideological marker of "ism" is important. We therefore will use *masculinism,* which carries the "ism" marker, unlike *patriarchy,* and juxtapose it to a female-rooted alternative, *feminalism.* As discussed above, feminism captures only half of the ideological spectrum, so it cannot be used for an analysis of gender ideology across the left-right continuum. An alternative term, *femininism,* is possible, but is both difficult to distinguish from *feminism* when reading and a mouthful to say aloud.

Finally, and most relevant for the framework introduced in Chapter 3, if we are to theorize equality—between males and females, men and women, masculinity and feminality, masculinism and feminalism—we need concepts that enable us to imagine this equality (Ferguson 1993). The extant but uncommon term *feminality* or its root, *feminale,* affords this imaginative opportunity in ways *femininity* cannot.

roles of fathers and debates by looking at policy initiatives intended to penalize deadbeats and scofflaws while rewarding good guys and promise keepers. Chapters 7 and 8 demonstrate quantitatively that the ideological framework has empirical grounding. Chapter 7 uncovers the operation of gender ideology inside the Wisconsin state legislature, when it passed one of the most restrictive work rules in welfare reform (Wisconsin Works or W2) under Governor Tommy Thompson, who went on to head the Department of Health and Human Services and oversee the implementation of TANF in the George W. Bush administration. Chapter 8 turns to Congress to explore the relationship between the gender ideology of House and Senate welfare activists and the gender paradigms adopted in policymaking. These two chapters tie compound ideologies and gender paradigms together with quantitative analysis, offering a better tool for understanding the gender and policymaking connection. We conclude with a brief reflection upon how and why we should consistently attend to the creation of gender through policymaking.

▓ Notes

1. Nahal Toosi and Jessica McBride, "Ruling on Prolific Dad Divides His Family: Mothers, Kids Themselves Disagree on Barring Him from Procreating," *Milwaukee Journal Sentinel,* July 15, 2001, 1A. See also Kathleen Parker, "Court Ruling on Procreation Opens New Can of Worms," *Milwaukee Journal Sentinel,* July 15, 2001, 4J.

2. "Judge Tells Woman She Can't Have More Children," *Milwaukee Journal Sentinel,* August 31, 2001, 3B.

3. Ellen Goodman, "What Makes a Father?" *Milwaukee Journal Sentinel,* April 28, 2001, 11A.

4. Lillian Thomas, "Triplets' Surrogate Mom Fights to Keep Baby Boys," *Pittsburgh Post-Gazette,* April 13, 2004, http://www.post-gazette.com/pg/04104/300019.stm.

5. "Appeals Court Rules Egg Donor in Surrogate Case Has Parental Rights," *Associated Press,* September 9, 2005.

6. Dean E. Murphy and Carolyn Marshall, "Family Feuds Over Soldier's Remains," *New York Times,* October 12, 2005, 14.

7. Table no. 56, "Married Couples by Differences in Ages Between Husband and Wife: 1999," *US Census Bureau, Statistical Abstract of the United States: 2000,* 120th ed. (Washington, DC: Government Printing Office, 2000), 52. Department of Defense fact sheet supplementing SBP Brochure, http://www.armyg1.army.mil/RSO/survivor_benefit_plan/fact/finanalysis.doc.

8. Information on this case comes from Tony Mauro, "The Man Behind the Pledge Case," *Legal Times,* November 10, 2003, http://www.law.com/jsp/article.jsp?id=1067351005985, p. 1 of 30.

9. *Elk Grove Unified School District v. Newdow 2004, No. 02-1624.* Find-Law: Legal News and Commentary, http://caselaw.lp. findlaw.com/.

10. For a discussion of these complicated questions of standing and the different rulings by the courts, see the majority opinion in the US Supreme Court

case, *Elk Grove Unified School District v. Newdow,* decided June 14, 2004. Here the Supreme Court ruled that although Newdow was the father, he did not have standing to sue.

11. Center for Military Readiness, "HASC Moves to Codify Rules on Women in Combat," May 24, 2005, http://www.cmrlink.org/WomenInCombat .asp?docID=248.

12. Center for Military Readiness, "CMR Policy Analysis, Frequently Asked Questions, Hunter-McHugh H.R. 1815 Codification of DoD Regulations RE: Women in Land Combat," http://cmrlink.org/CMRNotes/Hunter-McHugh% 20FAQ%27s%20052305.pdf.

13. *Frontiero v. Richardson,* 411 U.S. 677 (1973).

14. *Automobile Workers v. Johnson Controls, Inc.,* 499 U.S. 187 (1991).

15. Lexis, Lawyers' Edition Headnotes, *Price Waterhouse v. Hopkins,* No. 87-1167, Supreme Court of the United States, 490 U.S. 228; 109 S. Ct. 1775; 104 L. Ed. 2d 268; 1989 U.S. LEXIS 2230; 57 U.S.L.W. 4469; 49 *Fair Empl. Prac. Cas.* (BNA) 954; 49 Empl. Prac. Dec. (CCH) P38, 936, October 31, 1988, Argued; May 1, 1989, Decided.

16. Joanna Grossman, "Why the Family and Medical Leave Act of 1993 Should Be Amended: The Act's Tenth Anniversary Should Prompt a Rethinking," October 7, 2003, http://writ.corporate.findlaw.com/grossman/20031007.html.

17. *Nevada Department of Human Resources et al. v. Hibbs et al.,* 2003.

18. *In re Marriage of Sterling Simmons and Jennifer Simmons.* Nos. 1-03-2284 and 1-03-2348 (Consolidated). Illinois, Third Division, February 16, 2005. Findlaw, http://caselaw.lp.findlaw.com/scripts/getcase.pl?court=il&vol=app/2005/1032284&invol=3.

19. As of 2005, slightly more than half the states (twenty-nine) had addressed this inequity, Congress had not yet adopted the legislation, and Senators Snowe and Harry Reid (D-NV) continued to introduce their bill. See "Snowe Continues Fight for Equity, Affordability in Coverage of Prescription Contraceptives," news release from the office of Senator Olympia Snowe, http://www.snowe.senate.gov/pressap/record.cfm?id=238743.

20. Welfare policy provides a recurring home for a host of concerns about gender. For a discussion of the way the US policy process results in an array of problems and solutions joining together in a particular policy arena, see Kingdon, *Agendas, Alternatives, and Public Policies.*

21. Gordon, *Women, the State, and Welfare.*

22. Hirschmann and Liebert, *Women and Welfare.*

23. Goodwin, *Gender and the Politics of Welfare Reform.*

24. Mink, *Welfare's End.* See also, for example, Neubeck and Cazenave, *Welfare Racism;* and Schram, Soss, and Fording, *Race and the Politics of Welfare Reform.*

25. Skocpol, *Protecting Soldiers and Mothers.*

26. Mead, *The New Paternalism.*

27. Ibid., 35, note 1.

2

On Creating Gender

NATIONAL AND STATE GOVERNMENTS USE POLICY—INCLUDING welfare policy—to legitimize and support some gender-based behaviors and gender relations and to undermine others.[1] When mothers of even young children are required to engage in paid employment in order to receive welfare, public policy does not regard direct care of children by mothers to be an important activity worthy of government support. When unmarried women are required to cooperate in state efforts to establish paternity, public policy makes biological fatherhood paramount. When state governments move aggressively to collect child support from nonresident fathers, public policy is being used to reinforce the male role of providing financially for offspring, even for men who have little to no involvement in other parenting activities. When women on welfare are exhorted to marry and maintain good relationships with men, public policy questions and contests their capacity to manage independent households.

Government is central to creating gender as we know it because it establishes the norms and normality of gender through policies such as welfare. And just as important, only rarely (e.g., the Equal Rights Amendment, women in combat) are the citizenry and policymakers explicit about the fact that definitions of proper gender constructs are at stake. Gender is so ordinary, so deeply ingrained, so much a part of individual identity and collective consciousness that seldom do we notice, or make explicit, that policies set legal parameters for gender. In the process, some gender possibilities are legitimized and promoted, but others are stigmatized and even rendered illegal.

In this book, we maintain that struggles over welfare policy constitute ongoing battles over gender. To understand what is at stake in these disputes, we must move beyond thinking of social welfare policy in the usual frame of generosity and instead think of welfare policy in terms of the appropriate gendered behaviors it seeks to construct. Although much is gained by studying social welfare policy through the lens of generosity— with liberal programs offering higher benefits to more people and conservative programs providing lower benefits to fewer people—such an approach misses important facets of public policy, primarily the ways in which policy seeks to shape human behavior. Because social welfare programs in general, and Temporary Assistance to Needy Families (TANF) in particular, reward some gender roles and penalize others, a program can be generous in certain ways and quite stingy in others. We classify social welfare policies according to the gendered behaviors they seek to promote and discourage and the gender constructs they create in the process.

To understand the politics of these policies, we must also move beyond the usual explanations of partisan politics, liberal and conservative ideology, and the vicissitudes of compromise.[2] As political actors debate public policies, we contend that they employ gender ideologies, the larger belief set about gender and power, even though gender remains largely unacknowledged by politicians as well as academic observers. Thus, we develop a framework for considering gender as it operates in a compound fashion with other political ideologies—and often across so-called party lines. Through an analysis of ideas and beliefs about gender, we can explain why certain policies—for example, work requirements for mothers and strengthened child support enforcement—garner considerable support from liberals as well as conservatives. We also explain why certain disputes over gender continue, despite consensus about work-oriented welfare reform and its seeming success. We seek to interpret consensus and disagreement to better explain the dominance of some policies, as opposed to the shifting popularity of others, at the national and state level.

Our central focus is on gender, but sound analysis must include race and class, important and related social constructs that surface during political debate. We are grateful to the many scholars who have pursued these topics.[3] Race and class are important because they help to shape perspectives on particular programs and others' views of persons who receive certain kinds of benefits. As we know from Gwendolyn Mink's analysis of racialized gender, poor women were portrayed as black and unmarried and therefore immoral and undeserving in political debates about welfare. During the congressional debate on welfare reform, hostile attacks maligned black women for not living up to the expected standard of good mothering and blamed black children for the social problems facing the United States. By teasing out the ways in which discourse concerning welfare encodes black inferiority and white superiority without ever arguing for such explicitly, Sanford F. Schram's work helps us to understand how these narratives endure and why they escape the condemnation leveled at direct, explicit references to black inferiority.

There can be no doubt that racial animosity undermined support for Aid to Families with Dependent Children (AFDC) and promoted calls for reform, including the oft-stated call to "end welfare as we know it." As we know from Robert C. Lieberman's major study of race and the US welfare state, AFDC was unable to expand and still develop political support, unlike some of the other programs also burdened with race-laden provisions that were adopted in the 1935 Social Security Act.[4] Racial animosity undermined support for AFDC and prompted a search for punitive policies to replace it. As we will see, though, "ending welfare as we know it" can be done in any number of ways. Behind social welfare policy, ideas about standards of good mothering and good fathering, good husbands and wives, and good men and women lay deeply buried. It is these expected standards, the political debates about these standards, and shifts in these standards that most intrigue us here. Ultimately, we believe that understanding these ideas will resolve questions about how policies such as welfare construct what men and women have to do in order to be granted standing as good citizens, or once such standing has been granted, what kinds of claims will and will not be recognized as worthy of government support.

■ Paradigms of Gendered Policy

Public policies try to change people's behavior. Every public policy, as written in law and regulation and as implemented in practice, is an attempt to use government powers to induce certain actions and discourage others. Embedded in public policies are normative judgments of what is right, just, proper, and good for males and females, men and women, mothers and fathers.[5] A desired gendered behavior, such as inducing mothers of young children to work, can be promoted through a number of different policies. In order to capture and highlight the gendered behaviors that welfare policies are supposed to advance and to avoid getting lost in a thicket of policy details, we classify social welfare policies according to gender paradigms and the ideas that they reflect.[6]

Gender paradigms are normative models about the way men and women *should* live their lives and the kinds of choices that should be encouraged and discouraged through public policy. They encapsulate the goals of public policy and articulate what "good" men and women, mothers and fathers, and husbands and wives should do. Although proponents of a particular policy might marshal empirical evidence about what men and women actually do in hopes of building support for a particular policy option, gender paradigms are not empirical descriptions. They are not designed to provide an accurate account of the way men and women live their lives. Rather, they focus on desired outcomes and the set of postulated causal connections about the ways in which particular policies are supposed to achieve those goals.[7]

We classify social welfare policies into three gender paradigms of complementarity, individuality, and egality.[8] Their attributes and guiding principles are laid out in Table 2.1. They can be distinguished by their assumptions about biological essentialism, the relationship between biological sex and gender, and the extent to which social roles are mutable and permeable. They also differ in the relative importance placed on social structures, the individual, and the family for society's well-being and the value imparted to feminale activity. Finally, they have different assumptions about the extent to which government can and should reinforce particular gendered roles.

Welfare reform constitutes a struggle about which gender paradigm will dominate, as much as it centers on the best way to save money or divide responsibilities between the federal and state governments. AFDC allowed women to make a claim for government support based on their standing as good mothers. TANF no longer allows such a claim and instead promotes the good worker as the model citizen. The adoption of TANF is not only the end of an entitlement for poor women and children but a shift in the gender paradigm that dominates public policy.

The Complementarity Paradigm

Policies intended to encourage and reinforce traditional gender roles of the caregiving mother and the breadwinning father are classified in the complementarity paradigm. In welfare policy, they include grants to the states to encourage marriage, attempts to penalize out-of-wedlock births, and rewards for parents who fulfill their gender roles well. The complementarity paradigm prevailed when Aid to Dependent Children (ADC) was adopted in 1935. Although it is no longer dominant, this paradigm remains strong. It has been reinvigorated with renewed emphasis on marriage and fathers' involvement as a primary solution to poverty and welfare receipt among women and children. Reauthorization proposals, offered from 2002 through 2005, especially promoted policy options consistent with the complementarity paradigm.

The complementarity paradigm derives from ideas and beliefs about natural differences between two distinct sexes. The model rests on the assumption that men and women have distinct roles in life and adhere to different, mutually beneficial practices. Gender difference is understood as natural and/or rational. Women, mothers, and the feminale should have

Table 2.1 Gender Paradigms, Principles, and Policy Orientation

Gender Paradigm	Guiding Gender Principles	Welfare Policy Orientation
Complementarity "Marry or cope"	Sexed bodies "recommend" gender roles Gender roles exist regardless of who fills them Sees advantage in gender dualism; takes pleasure in sex difference Promotes orthodoxy of roles and power relations Public is masculine; home is feminale	Marriage is desirable and rational Rewards good gendered parents Morality of choices determines support Expects private sector and household solutions Model being a good parent for children
Individuality Civic "Make work pay"	Individuals more similar than different Individual gender options within ordinary bounds Deal with gendered inequalities Masculine can learn from feminale Approach change from inside extant masculinist system	Invest in individual Public provides services (day care, training, transportation, wage) Success from support Nurture good citizens through work Model good adult conduct for children
Corporative "Pull yourself up"	Interchangeable humans with potential Gender roles are mere functions and choices Desires a gender-irrelevant world Blind to difference and structural constraints Inequalities arise from individual action and choice Free within extant masculinist system	Force self-improvement; failure is chosen Promotes private sector and individual solutions Individuals earn own sufficiency and self-respect Work makes good citizens Requires good adult conduct
Egality "Real chances for every *body*"	Uncouple gender roles from sexed bodies Move beyond gender orthodoxy Increase value of feminale Change boundaries of masculine Add more sex-gender options Construct new system	Attack and redistribute structural constraints (sex-segregated jobs, comparable pay, education, and training) Reproductive work "counted," fluid, and shared Scrutinize and attend to differences; differences assumed Care for all paramount

primary influence in the home sphere and handle certain types of tasks in a womanly way. Men, fathers, and the masculine should have primary influence in the public sphere and handle certain types of tasks in a manly manner. The policies are based on assumptions that men and women are naturally predisposed to prefer their respective roles and are better suited to perform those roles, yet also inclined to abandon them. Consequently, government policy needs to bolster traditional gender roles by rewarding those who adhere to them and rebuke those who deviate from them.

Although not all proponents of policies in this paradigm see biological differences to be determinative, nor do all believe God ordains differences, nonetheless they believe gender roles are clearly recommended by sexed bodies. As a result, the advantages of gender dualism accrue when men and women develop expertise needed for the realistic division of labor and roles. Both masculine and feminale roles are necessary and desirable. Their value is best realized when citizens practice orthodox gender roles in the context of heterosexual marriage and the accompanying power relations created by the interaction of a masculine public sphere and a feminale domain in the home. For some proponents, the heterosexual, two-parent complementary family is held to be the foundation of society; upright and moral parents raise their children by providing them both a devoted mother and a disciplined, hardworking father.[9]

The Individuality Paradigm

The goal of policies in the individuality paradigm is to ensure individual autonomy and freedom to choose one's own gender path. The policies aim to foster individuals able to survive on their own, individuals who are good citizens because they are self-sufficient, autonomous, and independent of the state. Welfare programs that promote work fit neatly into this paradigm because it is through paid work that individuals become citizens who contribute to the commonweal and good parents who are role models for their children.[10] Policies are not designed to compel women and men into particular gender roles by dint of biological attributes. Instead, policies give individuals the freedom to choose what works best for them and their families. Because autonomy is the goal, however, not all choices are equally desirable. Policies in the individuality paradigm guide individuals to make the right choice—to move toward autonomy—and do not reward them when they make the wrong choices. Based upon ideas derived from classic liberalism and tempered by classic republicanism, the individuality paradigm has atomistic man as the standard.[11] Thus, policies in the individuality paradigm focus on the individual (although they can extend to groups of individuals) rather than structures or institutions.

Individual choice then operates largely inside extant options. Hence, in this paradigm, gender often results from adopted ideas and standards that emerged from past traditions of public and private practices rooted in complementarity.

Policies in the individuality paradigm share the goal of moving individuals toward autonomy. Policies can differ, however, on the means of achieving this goal. We identified two different approaches toward autonomy, and we call them civic individuality and corporative individuality. Policies under the rubric of *civic individuality* use governmental means to bolster individuals in their quest for autonomy, trying to build upon their particular strengths and to overcome their weaknesses, irrespective of sexed bodies and gender prescriptions. With an emphasis on supporting individuals as they succeed in becoming good citizens, these policies emphasize work supports, investment in individuals, and minimizing barriers to work. For example, civic individuality includes policies that recognize problems with child care as a barrier to work and try to remove it by helping mothers purchase out-of-home care for their children. Because of the importance it places on autonomy, civic individuality would not resolve child care problems by allowing mothers to care directly for their children in lieu of paid employment. Instead, policies in civic individuality would attempt to "make work pay."

Because it holds women and men to be more alike than different, civic individuality emphasizes that individual similarities more than outweigh cognizance of individuals as fully gendered and sex-differentiated beings. This version of the paradigm nonetheless acknowledges gender because the desire to support individuals leads to some awareness of gendered inequalities, particularly in terms of available opportunities and imbalance in valuation. Yet because of its focus on individuals, civic individuality only marginally recognizes the extant system as deriving from the masculine.

Policies under *corporative individuality* also endorse individual liberties in gender choice. But rather than relying on government means to support individuals, policies in corporative individuality turn to demands, requirements, and penalties to induce autonomy. State power is used to force individuals to do what they would not otherwise do. Nongovernmental means are used to shape individuals, with the expectation that people will improve themselves through their participation in the market. For example, governments might try to induce private employers to hire welfare recipients and then mandate that recipients search for jobs in the private sector. In the tradition of Jean-Jacques Rousseau, who believed it was at times necessary to "force people to be free" in democracies, corporative individuality would force individuals to become "good citizens" through work in the private sector and would be reluctant to create jobs in the public sector. The familiar phrase, "Pull yourself up by your boot-straps," is the mantra of this approach.

Like civic individuality, the term *corporative individuality* also draws from the ideas of classic liberal and republican traditions. It is distinguished from its civic cousin by its steadfast claim to the interchangeability of humans. It assumes "universal humans" and consciously ignores both "natural" individual differences and the structural constraints each person confronts. To do otherwise would undermine an individual's capacity of self-definition. Inequalities are the consequence of individual effort and choice. This version of the individuality paradigm accepts the extant masculinist system uncritically, largely because it assumes a genuine universal standard is possible. Hence, the extant system is understood to favor not the masculine and men but rather meritorious individuals.

The Egality Paradigm

Welfare policies consistent with the egality paradigm include eliminating sex-segregated job structures, engendering new, fluid household forms, changing orientations toward reproductive work, and making care for all paramount. Because such proposals assume that persons are embedded in a set of relationships and a larger community, the egality paradigm derives more from democratic socialism than classic liberalism, and even more so from poststructuralism. Unlike the individuality paradigm, it focuses on larger structures and relationships rather than the individual, resulting in an acute awareness of structural inequalities and constraints embedded in economic systems, household labor, and reproductive work. The policy options are designed to level the playing field so that women and men face similar circumstances and opportunities; the goal is to offer real chances for every *body.*

Policies in the egality paradigm seek to disrupt gender assumptions and undo gender as we know it. The egality paradigm might be thought of as "a brave new way" because its guiding principles strive to move beyond the dualism of feminale and masculine. The egality paradigm wants social and political roles to flow from each person—each body—rather than from prescribed understandings of proper conduct for the "given" sexes. Women and men have interchangeable roles and obligations, and the gender categories themselves are called into question. It strives to value the feminale and to unhinge the masculine from its hegemonic aspects in order to move to an egalitarian conception of gender.[12] Informed by ideas from both postmodern and poststructural critiques of the sex-gender system, it further seeks to open options and construct a new way of being recognized as human, moving beyond current conceptions whose roots anchor deeply in biological reproduction. Politically, the egality paradigm has not been dominant, as it has been the weakest model historically. Yet it has persisted, and its ideas are used especially to identify shortcomings in policies resting in the other two paradigms.

We contend that the adoption and implementation of the 1996 Personal Responsibility and Work Opportunity Reconciliation Act (PRWORA) marks the ascendancy of policies in the individuality paradigm. Rooted in masculine ideas about autonomy and independence through paid work, the law requires mothers to become breadwinners and justifies that demand by asserting that children need an employed parent to be raised well. To fulfill the standard of good mothering, poor women are forced to perform the masculine practices of parenting, and they can no longer use the caregiving role of mother to make claims upon the state.[13] The feminale practices of parenting are devalued because they are considered to be imperceptible influences on children's upbringing. Thus, we argue, welfare reform produced the oxymoronic masculine mother as a normative standard of good mothering by *requiring* that welfare mothers undertake the practices of fatherhood and even further demeaning the feminale practices of motherhood. Our argument is not that the standard of masculine mothers emerged when women work, for women have always worked. Rather, our contention is that the masculine mother has been created as an ideal because paid employment is now considered to be the normative standard for good mothering. It is employment, and not the "work" of the feminale practices of nurturing and caregiving, that enable women to be deemed good mothers. The reform can be seen as a triumph of masculinist ideology, especially because masculinism and capitalism make a "happy marriage."

Pejorative stereotypes of the mothering done by black women were a crucial part of the political process that devalued the feminale.[14] Yet even for white women whose children were born while they were married, welfare reform means that dependency is no longer considered to be a positive attribute.[15] As implemented for a decade, PRWORA and accompanying state policies mean that care for one's own dependent children is no longer defined as "work" by the government, even for white women who once were part of the middle class. Mothering was long understood to be a crucial political activity for women, but no longer can women claim to contribute to the polity by raising and nurturing their children. The Personal Responsibility and Work Opportunity Reconciliation Act marks the death of republican motherhood as an independent source of citizenship for women.[16]

The individuality paradigm appears paramount in denying caregiving as work worthy of state support. Its ascendancy marks a profound shift in the ideas that create and legitimize prescriptions about proper maternal roles in families and reveals changes in broader normative assumptions about women and employment. Yet even though this profound shift has occurred, the struggle among gender paradigms and their ideas persist. The individuality paradigm continues to be challenged by complementarity, with reauthorization proposals advanced by the George W. Bush administration stressing an increased—and masculinist—emphasis on reinvigorating the two-parent family. Today's advocates who promote complementarity and propose policies designed to encourage the formation of two-parent families assume that the presence of a husband/father is critical for upholding the feminale. According to these views, women can be good mothers only in the structure of a two-parent family; feminale caregiving has little worth unless it is coupled with masculine fathering. A husband should not simply defer in the private sphere of caregiving but should take on masculine fatherly roles. As a result, these attempts to revive complementarity harken back in time, but not to one of a revered feminale private sphere. For even in a two-parent family in which the husband works and the wife does not, masculine fathering is essential for the well-being of all and feminale caregiving is valuable only when it occurs within private patriarchy. Therefore, although they uphold traditional gender roles, recent policy proposals rooted in complementarity leave little room to demand that the state recognize and reward feminale caregiving.[17]

Proponents of policies in the egality paradigm struggle to find a toehold in these debates. But they still manage to raise questions about the equitable treatment of paid work, trying to hold policies in the individuality paradigm to the promise that work will result in economic gains sufficient to produce both economic and psychological autonomy, and pointing out to enthusiasts of complementarity that many men do not earn enough money to support a family. They have been less vocal in defending the feminale, for two reasons. First, their desire is to undermine gender as tied to sexed bodies. This goal of undermining gender dualism makes defense of one-half of the dualism difficult. Second, and probably more important to legislative policy debates, a primary step in creating gender egality is to raise the value of the feminale. However, many who shape public discourse and common knowledge have interpreted increasing the worth of the feminale as a radical idea. Partly this reaction occurs because to increase the value of the feminale would change the dominant form of the masculine in ways that diminish its power. Politically, egalitarian precepts are much stronger when they are linked to policies in the individuality paradigm because of that paradigm's ready alignment with classic liberalism and masculine preferences, both of which fundamentally shape US government and politics.

With the rise of the individuality paradigm, the concept of the masculine mother emerged as a critical goal of welfare reform. Although few dispute this goal itself, many have pressed additional goals, primarily by advancing policies within the complementarity paradigm that stress marriage as an essential mechanism to preserve two gendered roles. This view helps explain why the outcry over another policy, same-sex marriage, is so strong. Others invoke the egality paradigm to question the possibility that policies consistent with the individuality paradigm will accomplish the acknowledged goals. Regardless of which paradigm dominates at a particular point in time, what is clear is that the construction of gender is at stake in welfare reform.

■ Gender and Political Ideology

The ascendance of the individuality paradigm and challenges from the complementarity paradigm are the product of political struggles. Gender paradigms do not arise from nature, they are not accidental, and they do not result from an ongoing march of history. They reflect ideological thinking and are the outcomes of competitions among different ideologies and the ideas that form them. The contest over these paradigms and their competing visions of proper gender prescriptions takes ideological form. The disputes center on the nature of males and females, the distribution of power and resources by gender, and the benefits for and constraints on adults, expressed in gendered ways; these are all decisions that conform to definitions of political ideology.[18]

When analyzing political ideology, it is customary to rely on the conventional continuum of liberals on the left and conservatives on the right.[19] We recognize this continuum as important because it captures essential ideas about government and the market relevant to political debates about social welfare policy. But this continuum alone does not adequately explain the political contests over welfare policy and, in particular, the apparent convergence of liberal feminists and conservatives. Even if one accepts the idea that welfare reform was adopted as a politically expedient bipartisan compromise, there is still the need to explain why and how compromise was achieved in some areas but not others.

Explanations derived from the conventional ideological continuum are inadequate for three reasons. First, since the 1988 Family Support Act was passed, liberals and conservatives have agreed that work should be the reform route for welfare, and both camps were willing to use state power in unexpected ways, given their traditional attitudes toward government.[20] Liberals were willing to use government power to enforce punitive sanctions against poor women and children. Conservatives championed government creation of jobs, federal government restrictions on states, and constraints on individual choice. Given considerable differences between liberals and conservatives on most other matters, including disputes about *proper* family form, and the intense controversy over many aspects of PRWORA, bipartisan support for work-oriented reform begged for further scrutiny. When liberals and conservatives agree, something other than conventional political ideology must be operating.[21]

Second, much analysis of welfare policy has been gender-blind, yet gender matters substantively when an entitlement program designed specifically to grant public assistance to women and their children is ended. Perhaps ironically, liberals especially have failed to notice or acknowledge the gendered dimensions of their proposals, whereas conservatives have been far more open about the fact that their goals include particular gender patterns for family labor.[22] Conservatives explicitly introduced gender ideology into the welfare debate by proclaiming the properness of private patriarchy and separate spheres in the preamble to PRWORA, which declares that marriage is the foundation of a successful society. They have taken this stance further in debates over reauthorization. Why they would acknowledge gender and liberals would ignore it warrants consideration. Gender is linked in some fashion to conventional ideologies, but in what way is not immediately apparent.

Third, as we will show throughout this book, women who differ in their conventional ideologies at times agree with each other, coalesce, and challenge their male counterparts, resulting in conflict with men who otherwise share many similar attitudes and beliefs about government. These gendered conflicts were important in shaping welfare policy, yet they are not readily accounted for by relying on the conventional liberal-conservative continuum. Such reliance tends to lead to the conclusion that women are more liberal than men, yet not all women are liberal nor all men conservative. Casual observation, as well as numerous studies, confirm that "women are no more of like mind than are men."[23] We want to account for differences among women and among men, understand the reasons for agreement among women and among men, and explore the conflicts between the two.

In order to understand fully the ways in which ideas and beliefs about gender shape political thought and policy contests, we seek to develop a more accurate, sophisticated, and complete understanding of what gender ideology is and how it works in tandem with conventional political ideologies important to governing. We see gender ideologies as political ideologies that are contested and disputed in government. Thus, we develop a framework of gender ideology, presented in Chapter 3, which presents gender ideology as compounding, but independent from, the conventional ideologies. Our analysis recognizes the complexities of ideas needed to interpret the creation of gender and the meaning of masculine mothers. Further, because our framework includes both the masculine and feminale sides of gender ideology, it moves past treatments of gender as synonymous with women *and* beyond critiques of patriarchy or masculinism that paint all men as powerful vis-à-vis all women. These prior treatments of gender ideology also implicitly diminish and exclude women as political participants with their own agency.[24] Finally, it also opens the door for better analysis of the interaction of race, class, and gender because it allows us to consider how specific ideological stances can vary depending on ideas about these social constructs.

The vividness of the contests over constructing gender in the process of welfare policy provides extensive evidence of the government's role in establishing, adjusting, and otherwise enforcing particular gender paradigms to the detriment and delegitimation of others. These policies illustrate with the boldness of acrylic paint what we often must search for in the delicacy of pastel chalk: *Gender politics is more than personal politics; it is central to laws and policies created in our governing institutions.* Laws ostensibly about something other than gender bring the full weight of legitimate authority to gender paradigms. They also produce the advantages and disadvantages of particular resource distributions that follow from formal decisions by Congress and other public officials. In other words, our ideational analysis of welfare reform demonstrates that gender politics is central to major legislation, rather than a peripheral issue of concern only to a few "identity politics" radicals on the margins or in a few policy areas.

▪ Notes

1. Consistent with Lorber in *Paradoxes of Gender,* we proceed with the knowledge that "procreative and parenting statuses are rooted in social policies, not biological differences," 284.

2. Like Hawkesworth, we contend "that racing-gendering is distinct from and ought not to be reduced to partisanship" ("Congressional Enactments of Race-Gender," 546).

3. For an outstanding analysis of "racialized gender," see Mink, *Welfare's End;* and Mink, *Whose Welfare?* For an intersectional analysis emphasizing race much as we emphasize gender, see Schram, Soss, and Fording, *Race and the Politics of Welfare Reform;* and Neubeck and Cazenave, *Welfare Racism.*

4. Lieberman, *Shifting the Color Line.*

5. Butler, *Bodies That Matter.*

6. Our classification goes beyond a simple notion of more or less government intervention in the redistribution of wealth because it includes ideas about how people use resources, who should have available resources, and for what purposes those resources can be used. Classifying public policies has long been an important part of the study of policy. For one of the most influential classifications, see Lowi, "Four Systems of Policy, Politics, and Choice." Unlike Lowi's early work, we are not trying to engage in a debate over whether policy drives

politics. Our use of paradigms here is more akin to Schon and Rein's use of the term *frame*. See Schon and Rein, *Frame Reflection.*

7. In *Gender and Power,* Connell employs the term *gender regime,* defined as "the state of play in gender relations in a given institution" (120), rather than gender paradigm. He does not name particular gender regimes, instead seeking to inventory elements in particular settings.

8. We struggled particularly with the term *egality.* The terms *equality* and *equity* have many meanings and connotations, and they are not used consistently. Equality can mean the same, or can refer to the distinction between equality of results versus equality of access to processes. Equity sometimes is used to talk about a result being proportionally the same, as in an "equitable arrangement" for minority groups in proportional representation. In policy, equity tends to connote different but equally valued, as with sex equity in athletics under Title IX. Hence, these terms already had recognized but not necessarily consistently used meanings. More important, however, we sought to move beyond both of these conceptualizations in order to insert ideas from feminist poststructural and queer theory into the policy discussion. Hence, we adopted an Anglicized spelling of the French term for equality, egality. It has the advantages of being recognizable as related to questions of equality, but it does not bog down in equal rights, which falls into the individuality paradigm. It also carries a tinge of revolutionary connotation, given egality's association with the French Revolution. Like our use of *feminality* for *feminine,* egality also frees the imagination to theorize more readily about a different kind of equality in which the sexed body becomes less important than human potential.

9. Blankenhorn, *Fatherless America;* and Popenoe, *Life Without Father.*

10. For extensive work on the relationship between work, or providing for one's family, and assessments of citizenship, see Kann, *On the Man Question;* Kann, *A Republic of Men;* and Wood, *The Radicalism of the American Revolution.* Kerber demonstrates the highly gendered and raced dimensions of work and citizenship that were sanctioned by law. See Kerber, *No Constitutional Right to Be Ladies.*

11. For an outstanding critique of the liberal thinkers John Locke, John Stuart Mill, and other prominent male theorists, see Di Stefano, *Configurations of Masculinity.*

12. Connell has analyzed hegemonic masculinity in *Masculinities* and in his earlier work, *Gender and Power.* Kathy Ferguson is especially insightful in Chapter 1 of *The Man Question* on the potential derived from merging postmodern and poststructural critiques for creating a new way.

13. For a discussion of different positions toward motherwork and women's labor by activists for women's rights and the poor, see Boris, "When Work Is Slavery."

14. Mink, *Welfare's End;* Mink, *Whose Welfare?*

15. Solinger, "Dependency and Choice," 8.

16. The term *republican motherhood* comes from Kerber, *Women of the Republic.* She concludes that the idea of republican motherhood gave women a valued role that contributed to the public good without disrupting the separate spheres doctrine. As will be examined in Chapters 4 and 5, it is not quite accurate to simply say PRWORA ended republican motherhood, in part because the idea applied only to a segment of white women of some means, although it had been widely used to apply to all women of the US postcolonial era. Further, policies promulgated by social conservatives to endorse mothers staying at home

with their children indicate some life left for this concept of civically virtuous women. For related ideas, see also Kann, *On the Man Question.*

17. For an example of such ideas, see Murray, "Keeping Priorities Straight on Welfare Reform"; Blankenhorn, *Fatherless America;* and Popenoe, *Life Without Father.*

18. Although the definitions of political ideology vary, Hoover provides a basic definition that includes the following: political ideologies make judgments about humans, their differences, and their problems and promise; based on those judgments, they make decisions about the distribution of power and resources; and, in a characteristic that distinguishes ideology from theory, they develop a plan for putting those decisions into action. Policy is a primary way to put decisions about different types of humans and the distribution of power and resources into action. See Hoover, *Ideology and Political Life.*

19. At least since the early 1960s, political scientists have debated the definition of ideology, how constrained the beliefs need to be to qualify as ideology, the extent to which scholars impose elite definitions upon the mass public and then declare the masses inadequate or nonideological, and the adequacy of particular methodologies used in the measurement of ideology. We are aware of these disputes, but our research focus lies elsewhere. We therefore define our use of ideology clearly. Because much of this analysis deals directly with legislatures and voting, we also must grapple with the single continuum so diligently applied to legislative voting and behavior.

20. For an extended analysis, see Gordon, *Women, the State, and Welfare.*

21. Recent major studies on elite and mass ideological orientations are summarized nicely in Teles, *Whose Welfare?*

22. Gordon, *Women, the State, and Welfare,* chap. 1, note 4.

23. Sapiro, *The Political Integration of Women.*

24. Carver has correctly captured the idea in his book, *Gender Is Not a Synonym for Women.* Too often critiques of patriarchy or masculinism portray men as omnipotent, thereby denying agency to all but certain women who possess knowledge based on (often one particular) feminist vision. Our framework addresses both sets of problems. See Duerst-Lahti and Norton, "Gender Ideologies in Welfare Reform."

3

Toward a Suitably Complex Framework of Analysis

SERVICE TO DISABLED SEAMEN, A NEED RECOGNIZED BY PRESI-
dent John Adams in 1798, formed the unlikely beginnings of the National
Institutes of Health (NIH). The federal government provided medical
care to soldiers through national marine hospitals, first opened in 1803,
and the nation's early surgeon generals had careers in the military. With
the establishment of the Laboratory of Hygiene in 1887, the National
Marine Hospital Service took up the task of fighting cholera. In 1902
Congress strengthened and expanded the responsibilities of the Hygienic
Laboratory, giving it an explicit focus on public health. These efforts
were renamed the Public Health Service in 1912. By 1930, its Hygienic
Laboratory had become the National Institute of Health. Shortly there-
after, Congress authorized an institute to study cancer, and the NIH
became a prominent unit within the Public Health Service. After World
War II, a series of institutes and centers for research on various diseases
were authorized, a pattern that has continued since. Today, with twenty-
seven different institutes and centers, the National Institutes of Health
is one of the world's foremost medical research centers and the federal
focal point for medical research in the United States.[1]

Perhaps not surprising given its historical roots with disabled seamen, marine hospitals, and army surgery, federal research agencies
began to include women in their clinical research trials only after the
National Institutes of Health Revitalization Act finally required it in
1993. Until then, very little federally sponsored health research used any
female subjects. Because women bear children, all of them—even post-
menopausal women—were deemed a liability risk. Their monthly hor-
monal changes also made them inconvenient subjects because such fluc-
tuation introduced unwanted variability into studies. "The result was the
'male norm' of research. Research subjects were predominately men

since most researchers thought men and women were biologically the same except for their reproductive organs."[2] Biological sex differences were believed to be unimportant, or more accurately, women's differences from the male norm were deemed unimportant.

As the women's movement matured and doors opened for female professionals, women made it clear to Congress during the 1980s that their health was compromised by the exclusion of women from medical studies. By 1989, Congress found itself with a record number of thirty-one congresswomen, and unlike their male counterparts, these members of Congress valued research on women. Working with women's interest groups and male congressional allies, they succeeded in defining the exclusion of women from medical research as a public problem and put the issue on the public policy agenda. Through the bipartisan Congressional Caucus for Women's Issues, they developed a legislative package to improve health care research for women, which later became part of the National Institutes of Health Revitalization Act of 1993. Although Representative Henry Waxman (D-WA) and Senator Edward Kennedy (D-MA) sponsored this bill, it was a coalition of Democratic and Republican women who made the act possible. All the female senators and all but two women representatives in the House voted to support the bill, whereas only two-thirds of the House men supported it.[3] These female legislators, regardless of party, sought equal research attention for women. They also worked with women's interest groups to secure additional funding for related research, so that federal funding for women's health rose from $174 million in 1991 to $2.3 billion by 1999.[4] And, in an attempt to assure resources were directed toward women's health, the 1993 legislation also created the Office of Women's Health Research, a unit that some would see as providing unequal or special treatment for women.

As with processes for most public policy, this legislation involved political ideologies. Any political ideology makes judgments about human nature and distributes political power and resources accordingly. Different ideologies make different assumptions about the human condition, and in doing so craft ideas about power and resources that favor particular persons or groups of persons. We are familiar with choices made by political ideologies common to governing: Marxism favors workers; liberalism favors individuals—primarily propertied and educated persons; and conservatism favors established families or groups with status, wealth, institutional authority, or other resources. Not incidentally, all these familiar ideologies were premised on the assumption that men—and not women—should hold public power, an assumption that is no longer acceptable even though we continue to use these ideologies in governing. Proponents of ideologies make important judgments about who *should* hold political power and receive its advantages.

Feminism, an ideology that crosses many of these conventional governing ideologies, introduced a standpoint and critique that made it possible to see that all the ideologies known as "political ideologies" favored men, much as critical race theorists and activists made it possible to see that political ideologies favored whites. In the case of the 1993 NIH legislation, it was clear that prior to women's insistence, men did not deem allocating resources to women's medical research important, whereas women did. Even though, in 1991, women held only 6 percent of congressional seats, these thirty-one women saw value in research on women and joined forces to place it on the agenda. When the bill passed in 1993, the number of women in Congress had grown to sixty, fifty-four in the House and six in the Senate. By winning seats in Congress, these women succeeded in changing the usual ideological judgment that only men should hold office and wield political power. Once in office, their policy actions showed how the "ordinary" practices of resource allocation were predicated upon assumptions that males should disproportionately receive public resources. This policy illustrates ideology in action, both conventional governing ideologies and gender ideologies.

Separated into five parts, this chapter considers gender ideologies and creates a complex framework that enables analysis of how they function in ordinary policymaking. Gender ideologies are far less recognized than the widely acknowledged US ideologies—liberalism and conservatism—we call conventional governing ideologies. However, rather than dismissing government as a masculinist "master's tool," unworthy of effort because it will never make adequate feminalist change, we take these conventional ideologies seriously.[5] We acknowledge that they are indeed important in political decisionmaking, for they capture distinctive positions about human potential; the distribution of power and resources; and ideas about the relationship among individuals, government, and the market. In the first part of this chapter, we delineate the parameters and characteristics of liberal and conservative ideologies.

These governing ideologies, however, do not provide an understanding of the way judgments about gender relate to political beliefs. Gender is one of many features, such as class, individual ability, and race, that underpin judgments about human nature and produce governing ideologies. Because these bases of judgment about human nature serve as the first rank, typical, or original judgment, they function at the parental or proto level and can rightfully be called protoideological. Although they have not traveled by that name, the idea of protoideologies should be familiar to most because feminist critiques of patriarchy have long made this claim. So have nonwhite races and those whose impoverishment made participation in US classic liberal, rugged individualism a disappointment, more than a dream or reality. Gender as protoideology is akin to Carole Pateman's notion of the sexual contract as the primary contract that made any political organization possible.[6]

We contend that gender ideology should be considered a protoideology in relationship to conventional governing ideologies.[7] Hence, in the second part of this chapter, we lay out the justifications for employing masculinist and feminalist distinctions in political thought. We use these differences to develop two *variants* of gender ideology we title masculinism and feminalism. These variants have meaning for all humans who present themselves to the world as either men or women, as well as to phenomena that are attributed with gender.[8] These variants enable us to understand why and how women and men who share certain political beliefs will disagree at times, or more specifically, why conservative women might side with liberal women and disagree with conservative men. They provide a basis for understanding why individuals traditionally united by conventional governing ideology can still be divided by gender ideology; or as was the case in welfare policy, why individuals can be united by gender ideology even when they are separated by conventional governing ideology.[9]

We are not arguing that gender is always the most important element, although it is the focus of this book. Nor do we argue that women and men always differ on issues of gender, or that women always align with other women and men with other men. Considerable political differences exist among women and among men. Women and men align along the entire left-right spectrum in US politics, and other factors, such as race and class, help shape where women and men align.[10] Gender ideology also includes belief systems about gender that join some women and men and separate them from other women and men. In the third part of the chapter, through the concept of *gender strands,* we turn to aspects of belief systems about gender that women and men share. We concentrate on ideas about the extent to which women and men differ and the relative importance of those purported differences. Answers to questions about the importance of difference lead to another set of issues concerning the mutability of differences; the desirability of heightening, maintaining, or minimizing them; and the willingness to use government to achieve these aims.

In our gender ideology framework, we present six strands that capture important distinctions in judgments about gender, as well as the relationship among gender, state power, and the market. From left to right, these gender strands include the *gender left, intersectors, similarism, gender universalism, gender traditionalism, and patriarchalism.* We argue that these strands represent common ideological positions about gender that appear in US politics. Because both state power and the market are implicated in these ideas about gender, we see a strong correspondence between these gender strands and the six positions of governing ideology.

Thus, in the fourth part of the chapter, we link or compound the gender ideologies and conventional governing ideologies with which they align to fully frame the complex relationship. This idea of compounded gender ideologies is hardly original because feminism has long grappled with "hyphenated feminism" strands, such as liberal feminism, socialist feminism, or lesbian feminism.[11] Here, we extend this thinking both to nonfeminist women and to men. Few labels exist for men, and few men identify with a gender ideological position. Nonetheless, men too adhere to gender ideologies. Although one suspects a correspondence between the left-right governing ideology, gender ideology, and the paradigms introduced in Chapter 2, we show in subsequent chapters how the paradigms become tools toward ideological ends, which often are deployed by policymakers in surprising and seemingly contradictory ways.

Although gender ideology interacts with governing ideology, we show in Chapter 7 that gender ideology operates independently from governing ideology as well. To incorporate that independent functioning, each strand has within it two *protoideological variants*. For example, the gender traditionalism strand contains the variants of traditional maternalism and traditional paternalism. After exploring the shared components of each strand, we examine the points of contention between its variants. We discuss the kinds of disputes that generate political conflicts between women and men whom one would expect to be united. That approach enables explanations of seemingly odd alliances. It can explain both differences between women and men in their orientation toward policies such as welfare and similarities between women and men who align with each other in conventional governing ideology.

Our approach addresses one other common shortcoming of empirical gender analysis. In the final section of this chapter, we consider the frequently heard conclusion that women are more liberal than men, and instead suggest that women are more feminalist than men. Women and men are both the same and different in their ideological orientations toward US politics. Said another way, we offer an approach based upon both/and thinking rather than the either/or conundrum so familiar to gender research.[12] We therefore move beyond thinking rooted in sex trait research that focuses on the extent to which males and females, or men and women, are the same or different. This model recognizes that both are evident.

◼ Governing Ideologies: What Is Usually Thought of as Political Ideology in the United States

Usually, empirical analysis of political ideology in the United States demonstrates that ideology fits neatly on a left-right continuum. With a few exceptions, most studies of ideology in legislatures or policymaking reduce political ideology to gradations of liberal and conservative; the data seldom capture more than that simple orientation if survey research and quantitative methods are used. Unfortunately, such approaches also suggest a static meaning of liberal and conservative and obscure important nuances pursued vigorously by normative theorists whose scholarship is unfettered by quantitative measures.

Statistical artifacts aside, members of the attentive public cannot help but be aware that social conservatives have come to be more important in US politics since the 1980s. Similarly, they realize that New Deal, or perhaps more accurately, Great Society, liberals were supplanted by Clintonesque "new Democrat" liberals who bear a remarkable resemblance to the "Rockefeller Republicans" of the 1970s.[13] In the early 2000s, left-leaning liberals have been attempting to refashion and reassert themselves as progressives. Quite simply, the meanings of liberal and conservative ideologies are dynamic; they change over time.

Further, those who follow US politics also know that terms like *social liberal* or *libertarian conservative* are helpful in delineating types of liberals and conservatives and the policies each endorses. Such labels have meaning. With this in mind, we developed a set of ideological variants that distinguish subtle yet important differences among US liberals and conservatives and clarify the meanings we give to these condensed labels before explaining the compound relationship between conventional ideology and gender ideology. Table 3.1 illustrates the permutations of the usual left-right continuum that operated around welfare reform. It names ideological variants in familiar and descriptive ways and captures nuances among ideological orientations held by legislators and other political elites. Characteristics of these governing ideologies are also listed, including orientations toward fiscal and social policies, individual liberty, and state power and the market.

Liberals

Since their heyday during the Great Society of the 1960s, liberals have lost ground. But in the United States, liberals still can be found in at least three distinguishable camps. *Social democrats* prefer policies akin to European state programs, *social liberals* favor policies that follow New Deal and Great Society traditions, and *new liberals* of the "new Democrat" ilk lean toward market-oriented policies. All liberals maintain a progressive future-looking perspective and a willingness to use the state to bolster their fundamental belief in individual promise under equal conditions.

Although few legislators in the United States would claim to be *democratic socialists* quite in the manner common to Europe, their emphasis

Table 3.1 Characteristics of Governing Ideologies

Ideological Type	Characteristics
Social democrat	Strong social program spending for many purposes. Social good outweighs individual freedom. Sees structural inequality. Strong state. Tight control of market. Redistribution.
Social liberalism	Contemporary New Deal. Willing to spend for social programs and redistribute resources. Redresses group differences to help individuals. Social justice as civil and political rights. Active use of state power. Regulates market vigorously.
New (neo) liberalism	Moderate spending on social programs, especially to help individuals achieve full potential as responsible citizens. Laws to redistribute and equalize opportunities. Social justice as access to economic opportunity. Supports individuals by providing freedom from discrimination and freedom to achieve fully. Regulates market excesses.
Libertarian conservatism	Laissez-faire. Some spending on social programs that help individuals meet social standards. Opens way for individuals to compete and be responsible adults. Supports private sector for individual and collective benefit. Limited state. Minimal regulation.
Traditional conservatism	Pragmatic, limited state provides minimal social safety net. Individuals rely on familial and communal private solutions. Bootstraps and hard work are key. State ensures stability and order through social institutions. Individual rises to level of merit inside capitalist market structure with minimal regulation.
Social (neo) conservatism	Spends to support economic infrastructure. Draws upon, reinsitutionalizes tradition. Uses state power to create moral society and control individuals. Social order dominates individual freedom. Market provides solutions.

on an active use of state power to create greater equality across all groups can be found in US politics. For example, many supporters of Ralph Nader for the 2000 presidential bid, as well as a variety of interest groups and grassroots organizations, fit into this category. The National Welfare Rights Organization, with its focus on welfare rights for poor women and children and its desire for more social spending, is the largest and best known among them. Policies espoused by some Democratic presidential 2004 candidates, such as Dennis Kucinich and Carol Moseley Braun, also mesh with this orientation.

Social liberals were once a majority in many legislatures, but Clinton new Democrats supplanted them. Their policies acknowledge larger structural or group-based impediments to individual well-being, although individuals remain their central focus. They think the state should be used actively for civil and political rights, and their suspicion of the market leads them toward considerable regulation and away from unfettered private sector solutions. Several early 2004 Democratic candidates, especially vice presidential candidate John Edwards, reinvigorated calls for such approaches to policies.

New liberals use government more to ensure freedom from unequal treatment by other individuals, the market, or governmental authorities than to promote freedom to pursue self-designed ends. They rely upon rights and protections. They advocate far less spending on social policy than their more social counterparts, and they have turned to policies that rely upon private sector implementation strategies. They were boosted by the organizational, electoral, and strategic success of the new Democrats and now hold a central position within the Democratic party.

Conservatives

At least three conservative camps can be distinguished in contemporary US politics in Table 3.1: libertarian, traditional, and social conservatives. *Libertarian conservatives* value individual freedoms and advocate some protections but want limited spending generally. They endorse a limited state for both the public domain and the household. With a strong focus on individual freedoms, libertarians are kin to their liberal neighbors, but they have greater faith in market solutions and seek more freedom from government. Like other conservatives, they believe in drawing upon proven traditions rather than inventing new social orders, although they may champion innovations within these boundaries. Senator Olympia Snowe (R-ME) and former representative Jack Kemp (R-NY) often espouse such positions.

Traditional conservatives, whose pragmatic focus rests on fiscal constraint, will spend to bolster market solutions and, in times of crisis, individuals through social institutions. They emphasize modest and pragmatic interventions for individual protections, drawing heavily on "common sense" and tradition for guidance. They delineate sharply between the public domain and private households and greatly value social stability for both. They prefer stare decisis and status quo state policy toward private households. Senators Orrin Hatch (R-UT) and Arlen Specter (R-PA) often hold these positions.

The foremost concern of *social conservatives* is a moral social order, and they willingly use state power to impose their vision of proper order. Also, they will vigorously use state policy to bolster capitalism, especially for those whose proven success warrants such advantage. In terms of individual protections and state spending, social conservatives readily use government to reinforce a rigid set of programs that preserve moral order. President George W. Bush and his supporters frequently promote such policies.

Overall, libertarians want to live and let live with a limited governmental program, traditionalists pragmatically act when necessity dictates with targeted and specific programs that build upon what has been known to work, and social conservatives actively seek to implement a new set of conservative programs with a strong emphasis on proper moral conduct enforced through state power. Despite a desire for less government, conservatives actively pursue changes that they think recapture the best of the past.

The familiarity of these ideologies in US governing and policymaking is hardly remarkable. Public opinion polling has long been able to document which segments of the public are most likely to align with these permutations of liberal and conservative ideology. For example, the security moms of the 2004 presidential election have the same demographic characteristics as the soccer moms of 2000. They are white, suburban, married, just right of center, and not particularly partisan. African Americans fall on the liberal end of the spectrum, with only about 10 percent identifying as conservative. They generally support policies that level the playing field and ensure civil rights but are less likely to support abortion rights or gay rights than their ideological profile would otherwise suggest. Latinos tend to be socially conservative on family matters but are fiscally liberal and support social programs, especially education and workers rights.

Liberal-conservative ideologies are generally understood to be *the* important ideologies in US policy and legislation. So central is the unidimensional ideological continuum to studies of congressional voting and policymaking that any approach to ideology for welfare reform must address it. These categories capture distinctive positions about human potential; the preferred distribution of power and resources; and ideas about the relationship among individuals, government, and the market. But they do not provide an understanding of the way judgments about gender structure relate to such political beliefs. Thus, they provide an awkward and incomplete basis for understanding welfare reform, particularly why certain ideas were powerful enough to gather support from across the ideological spectrum, whereas others were disputed or ignored.

■ Gender as Protoideology: Masculinism and Feminalism

As a protoideology, gender has two overarching variants, masculinism and feminalism. We assume that people make judgments about males and females, and the masculine and the feminale, and then use these assessments to fashion their ideas about preferred distributions of power. We further assume that the differences between the feminale and the masculine are large enough to create substantive and meaningful distinctions in political life. This supposition is similar to Michael Dawson's work on African American political ideologies, in which he claims different understandings of politics between African Americans and whites require a different vocabulary for black ideologies.[14] He identifies and details four types: black nationalism, black feminism, black Marxism, and black liberation. In the same manner, we identify and detail masculine and feminale variants for each strand of gender thought.

Our definitions of masculinism and feminalism are notable in two ways. First, we constructed each definition in reference to its own variant rather than focusing on the relations between them. As a result, our use of the term *masculinism* is far less charged than usual. For example, R. W. Connell defined masculinism as an ideology that dominates and exploits women. He speaks of hegemonic masculinism, delineating the ways it structures gender inequality and provides a "patriarchal dividend."[15] Similarly, Sylvia Walby defines the patriarchal system—a concept similar to a system based upon masculinism—as one that "exploits, dominates, and oppresses women."[16] We strive to treat masculinism in a way that recognizes its positive aspects, along with its empirically observable hegemonic advantages and dominant status.

Second, the framework intentionally and explicitly sets masculinism and feminalism in the same terms in order to position them as theoretically equal. Kathy Ferguson maintains that such pairings usefully begin to theorize in ways that lead to actual equality.[17] However, we recognize that masculinism, by all empirical accounts, has dominated the public sphere, the power of the state, and other social institutions. Although it is not yet a reality, we create the framework on the premise that members of legislatures begin from equal positional power and that feminalist ideology must first be conceived of as equal to masculinism if it is to ever gain that stature in institutions and structures of power. Therefore, in the framework we use analytic definitions more than normative ones.

Accordingly, masculinism is defined as an ideology that begins from and generally prefers that which is associated with males and the masculine in its judgments about human nature and the way power ought to be structured and resources distributed.[18] To prefer the masculine means to favor, adopt, choose, and embrace that which is associated with human males, to begin from assumptions consistent with masculinity as it is constructed in a given polity. Although masculinity has many dimensions and guises, not all ideas about masculinity are equal. In an ongoing struggle for what R. W. Connell calls hegemonic masculinity, certain ideas dominate and set the parameters for judging inside the masculine. This domination, in turn, helps to sustain masculinity's prevailing position inside the governing system.[19] It also privileges those who are willing and able to closely approximate these parameters, a capacity that tends to vary by sex, race, and class, among other aspects of human existence and experience.

In using the term *masculinism,* we employ the language of US feminist theorists who shifted terminology from patriarchy to masculinism in describing the political ideology that buttresses masculine power and resource advantage.[20] Political scientists and foundational philosophers understand that John Locke's liberalism defeated Sir Robert Filmer's patriarchal ideology. The term *patriarchy* derives from the term *pater,* or father. Because the system actually advantages all adult men, at least within their own sociological groups, and the system especially advantages adult men who fulfill the dominant ideals of masculinity well, it is erroneous to link the ideological orientation firmly to fathers. Patriarchy has many contemporary meanings and uses, but masculinism, with its "ism" suffix, unmistakably connotes a political ideology.

Accordingly also, feminalism is defined as an ideology that begins from and generally prefers that which is associated with females and the feminale in its judgments about human nature and the way power ought to be structured and resources distributed. To prefer the feminale means to favor, adopt, choose, and embrace that which is associated with human females, to begin from assumptions consistent with feminality as it is constructed in a given polity. As noted in Chapter 1, we use the term *feminale* rather than *feminine* for several reasons.[21] Primarily, feminale is derived from the word *female,* which denotes a biologically sexed body, but feminine is derived from the word *woman,* a social construct of human females. Further, masculinity derives from the word *male,* so feminale's reliance upon female brings the term into closer correspondence as a genuine concomitant to masculine and thereby facilitates the potential dislodging of difference from dominance. This term also avoids some of the connotative baggage associated with both feminine and feminist: many feminists have criticized the weakness feminine behavior foists upon women, and women of the right actively avoid associations with feminism. The terms *feminale* and *feminality* get us beyond these conceptual shortcomings.

Another prime advantage of the term *feminalism* is its capacity to capture the full range of political thinking among women. Particularly, it can account for women's thinking along the entire left-right spectrum without using the feminist and antifeminist divide. It therefore captures conservative women's political thought as well as liberal women's thought.[22] Women's political thinking has never had the luxury of holding a hegemonic position. Hence, feminalist thought has been formulated largely in response or reaction to masculinism. Yet our approach acknowledges female agency for independent thinking, even as it occurs within a system constructed and perpetuated by men, with masculine assumptions at its root. Importantly, it assumes that, at an ideological level, most women would not willingly cede *dominance* to men and masculinity over females and feminality.

Perhaps ultimately, the roots of gender difference derive from meanings accorded to biological capacities. Never mind that not all adults have children; that various classes, ethnicities, or cultures develop widely varied practices around human reproduction; or that over time enormous changes surround these issues. Ideas about differences rooted in biological reproduction easily become explanations for gender differences more generally, even when reproductive differences have little bearing upon immediate circumstances.[23] Living under circumstances in which assumptions about individuals follow from sexed bodies makes these differences meaningful. They shape interpersonal interaction in innumerable ways. Socialization prepares individuals for gender roles derived from temporary reproduction demands. Although expectations for gender differences vary across race, class, ethnicity, and the like, some form of gender differentiation always exists within groups, usually along caregiving and breadwinning roles. Because these and many other social and political structures reinforce expectations, constrain and limit individual freedoms, and legitimate and sanction gender performances and deviance, constructed gender difference as a social fact becomes "real."

These gendered experiences, in turn, result in different viewpoints about life. Using feminist standpoint theory, Karen Tamerius demonstrates that the gendered *content* of life experience produces a gendered *perspective* about "objective" experiences in the world.[24] Further, these experiences are gendered *mutually* so they become shared; females experience women's experiences, and males experience men's experiences. And finally, despite individual efforts and desires to break free, most women and men spend a fair portion of their lives—from the elementary playground to adult workplaces and socializing—in sex-exclusive groups. Such *association* creates some shared knowledge, provides potential ongoing support, and reinforces expectations about distinctions between women and men, even if women and men only experience these associations "serially."[25] That is, even though they differ by race, ethnicity, and class, women tend to share some perspective, knowledge, and experiences. The same is true for men. Dominant societal expectations also come into play, and the often white and masculinist orientation of "universal standards" remains invisible. Whether or not any particular individual desires or is able to "fit" both dominant and specific expectations, society projects such expectations upon individuals. Consequently for our purposes, some sex differences in orientation toward politics and policies are not surprising. Elsewhere, Georgia Duerst-Lahti has examined the ways in which these gender-attributed differences have come into existence and been deployed in politics.[26] Suffice it here to say that an extensive literature has mapped out many points upon which gender differences occur.

■ Gender Ideology

Masculinism and feminalism, as protoideologies, draw attention to ideas about gender that divide men and women, but gender ideology also must include political ideas that men and women share and that align them along a left-right spectrum. Perhaps the most salient judgment involves the extent to which biological sex and gender are linked. Ideological positions usually fall on a continuum from the belief that biology determines every aspect of gender to the belief that gender is a complete cultural construction that should not be related to sex at all. A closely related view concerns the scope of difference, from great to minimal. These beliefs lead to judgments about the extent to which biological differences between females and males matter.[27] The spectrum runs from the belief that sex differences are destiny—and should be—to the claim that the few sex differences found are far overshadowed by individual differences, so they should not be relevant at all. Beliefs about such questions also lead to positions regarding state power and gender, ranging from claims that public policy should maintain and reinforce sex differences to the position that government should break such differences down. Most important for our purposes, these beliefs come into play in the sexual politics of policy.

We group beliefs about these matters into six strands of gender ideology that fall along a left-right continuum and neatly correspond with governing ideology. Each strand represents sets of ideas predicated upon shared beliefs about humans and the state. They result from an alignment between belief systems about gender and belief systems about government. Because these views contain both similarities and differences between women and men, each strand also includes gender variants. These variants form around primary points of contention that can be characterized by a dominating friction between the feminalist and masculinist viewpoints. For example, as Table 3.2 shows, strands range from the *gender left,* aligned with social democrats on the liberal end of the spectrum, to *patriarchalists,* associated with new right conservatism on the conservative end of the scale. The gender left strand contains the variants of "social democratic feminism," which is juxtaposed to "enlightened left masculinism." Patriarchalism incorporates the variants of "new right feminalism"—an ideological position impossible to understand through the usual conceptualizations—and "new patriarchalism."

The interaction between gender ideology strands and governing ideology produces distinct public policy preferences on issues that construct gender. In the next section, we discuss how each strand commonly approaches the gender paradigms important in welfare policy. Not only does gender ideology produce policy preference, it also produces divergence within each strand, resulting in gendered tension between women and men who otherwise share views. These tensions produce distinct policy preferences concerning welfare.[28] We discuss these shared and divergent policy preferences, which are summarized in Table 3.3.[29] Along with the gender paradigms developed in Chapter 2, this ideological framework forms the basis for analysis in the rest of the book.

◼ Compounded Ideologies in Welfare Policy

Gender Left and Intersectors: Social Democrats and Social Liberals

Proponents of the gender left and intersectors ideologies understand gender as a system of oppression that ensnares both women and men. Both strands emphasize the economy's role in perpetuating gender inequalities and struggle over the place of gender in the larger economic battle at hand. Aligned with social democrats and social liberals, respectively, proponents of both advocate an active and redistributive state, especially for civil and political rights. Adherents believe jobs in a strong economy will provide opportunity but want state support for individuals in need. Members of groups who frequently face discrimination and who have limited access to the means of advancement often espouse these positions. Aware of the gendered economy, they seek the means to redistribute

Table 3.2 Compounded Ideology: Gender Strands and Variants, Shared Dimensions, and Sources of Variance

Gender Ideology Strands	Critical Dimensions: Shared	Primary Contention Points	Dominating Friction	Aligned Governing Ideology
Gender left: Social democratic feminism Enlightened left masculinism	Gender as structural system of oppression. Compassionate, active state. Pro-humanist, redistributive similarity.	Structural inequality. Economic bias against "counting" feminale work. Value on feminale by men.	Inadequate response by men. Masculinism remains unmoved.	Social democrats
Intersectors: Social-liberal feminism Liberal masculinism	Acknowledges differences in available opportunity. State resources and services are needed. State as enforcer of social contract.	Genuine opportunity. Second shift and comparable worth. Broadening masculinity.	Inadequate response by men. Masculinism only accommodates.	Social liberalism
Similarism: Liberal feminism Neo-fraternalism	Autonomous individual, equal as similarly situated. Freedom to achieve with selective help. Legal protections, public-private partnerships.	Account for "dissimilarly situated"; both same *and* different. Personal is political, but state may intrude on personal. "Rationality" of responses.	Too much to lose if current system is stretched too fast and far.	New liberalism
Gender universalism: Corporative feminalism New paternalism	Autonomous individual, *equal* is define as *the same*. Forced to be free, failure as personal. Equal opportunity, private solutions.	"Nature" of difference. Whether system is universal. Add more feminale, but secondary.	Feminale performance inadequate. Women don't measure up to standards.	Libertarian conservatism

(continues)

Table 3.2 Con't.

Gender Ideology Strands	Critical Dimensions: Shared	Primary Contention Points	Dominating Friction	Aligned Governing Ideology
Gender traditionalism: Traditional maternalism Traditional paternalism	Socially desirable complementarity, pragmatic. State-supported separate spheres, private solutions, sex-segregated, equal treatment in work settings. Gender as rooted in biology but open to socially derived contingencies.	Value and control. Equal power and control in spheres, and rewards for women's roles. Focus on feminale diminishes sole breadwinner advantages.	Reconciling public and private values and rewards.	Traditional conservatism
Patriarchalism: New right feminalism New patriarchalism	Difference divinely and biologically ordained. Strong state, masculine public power. Separate spheres, fixed gender complementarity.	Feminale power needs masculine respect. Masculine needs to lead—gently. Proper conduct must earn promised rewards. Private patriarchy or public order dissolves.	Danger in disorderly women and an equal feminale.	Social conservatism

family-wage opportunities to welfare mothers and often strive to improve poor men's earning possibilities too.[30]

Despite these similarities, clear distinctions are possible between these two gender strands, as Table 3.2 indicates. The primary distinctions center on their orientation toward the existing system and the degree of attention they give to structural impediments due to their alignments with conventional ideologies. The gender left and corresponding social democrats have a stronger emphasis on systemic impediments and a relative focus on groups rather than individuals. Consequently, they want much more fundamental change. The gender left understands the system as producing artificial sex/gender differences. Its ideal end would be humanist, perhaps the "new and improved post-enlightenment humanism" of interest to Judith Grant.[31] This humanism seeks a revolt against gender itself and strives for the full human potential in every *body,* which means that gender must be detached from particular bodies. The state has a role to

Table 3.3 Compounded Views of Welfare: Shared and Divergent Policy Preferences

Gender Ideology Strands	Shared Welfare Policy Preferences	Welfare Policy Divergence	Aligned Governing Ideology
Gender left: Social democratic feminism Enlightened left masculinism	Gendered structures make women an economic class. Intersections of group identities and memberships largely determine individual opportunities. Restructure system. Redistribute wealth and values, and transgender opportunities. Men can do care work. Economic reform key; more family wage jobs needed. State provides support to poor groups. Full services for all.	Strategic use of extant gender roles for masculine and feminale advantage. Relative emphasis on race and class in support from state. Unevenly gendered benefits given to policy targets. Lack of value placed upon feminale work.	Social democrats
Intersectors: Social-liberal feminism Liberal masculinism	Class and race shape gender for individuals. Gendered economy has links to home roles. Redistribute values and open gendered opportunities. Economic options key to reform; good jobs needed. State provides support to poor individuals. Full services for deserving individuals.	Intersecting circumstances shape gendered options. Amount of support needed for women versus men. Comparable value for feminale work. How much men seek systemic change.	Social liberalism
Similarism: Liberal feminism Neo-fraternalism	Similar individuals, but gender conditions noted. Aware of gendered economy but open opportunities guaranteed. Focus on equal treatment of individual. Gender should not determine rights as citizens. Good economic options key; create jobs if needed because work is key to autonomy. Public services for those who work.	Dissimilar benefits from employment. Gendered willingness to challenge system. Masculine blindness despite rhetoric and symbolic action. Desire and ability to separate personal and public life differs.	New liberalism

(continues)

Table 3.3 Con't.

Gender Ideology Strands	Shared Welfare Policy Preferences	Welfare Policy Divergence	Aligned Governing Ideology
Gender universalism: Corporative feminalism New paternalism	Universal individual assumed. Gender is irrelevant. Market responsibility; enforces desired behavior if needed. Equality defined as same treatment for all. Women compete with men on same terms; opportunities and individual effort are key. Some public services for compliance.	Need to integrate more feminality into "same." What defines universal and equal? Too few individual women measure up. State must enforce individual rights. Recognize when gender matters.	Libertarian conservatism
Gender traditionalism: Traditional maternalism Traditional paternalism	Traditional family stressed as rational and pragmatic. Family sacrifice and hard work are ordinary. Complementary gender roles good. Creative private solutions with short-term limited public support. Jobs to survive.	Equality in power and control, given unequal spheres. Rewards for care work. Value of intangible benefits of love and care. Private sphere cannot address all problems.	Traditional conservatism
Patriarchalism: New right feminalism New patriarchalism	Traditional family morally superior. Marriage is foundation of society. Moral behavior key to deserving limited state support. Private household solutions preferred. Separate gender spheres desirable. Male breadwinner or mothers make own way. Masculine head of household.	Feminale is powerful, but men must respect and enable when they lead. Proper feminale conduct must reap promised rewards, which men control. Circumstances may impede private patriarchy. Fear of disorderly women.	Social conservatism

play in this revolt, and adherents desire a compassionate state predicated upon "compassionate authority."[32] Strategically, the state might need to recognize gender differences now, especially the undervaluation of the feminale, but only as a stage needed to transform the structural inequalities that hold gender inequality in place. Internally, the challenge is to transform men and masculinity. The aim is to use the state to achieve some imaginable postgender possibility. The presence of the gender left inside governing institutions is quite limited in the United States, although some interest groups and individuals espouse social democratic positions, fighting for structural changes economically, racially, and in sex segregation.

In contrast, intersectors, and the aligned conventional ideology of social liberals, are much more common inside government. In US politics, they fall at the end of the mainstream spectrum. Intersectors, as well as social liberals, concentrate more on individuals than on systemic impediments. As their name implies, intersectors pay firm attention to the nexus or intersection of aspects of humanness that carry political significance for individuals, such as race, class, and gender. Intersectors often have life experiences that make it easy to recognize the many protoideological roots of conventional politics and understand the importance of interactive effects for political power.

The United States has relatively few practicing socialist feminists, although often black feminists are associated with this strand, and the National Organization for Women straddles gender left and intersector thought. Inside governing politics, the feminalist position might best be characterized as social-liberal feminism. It draws from the equality positions of 1970s liberal feminism but also strongly understands that women are not similarly situated to men and hence require protective legislation as well. Therefore, adherents advocate transforming politics as it has commonly been practiced, urging a compassionate state and acknowledging structural and economic impediments for individuals. They willingly introduce legislation on behalf of women and children and fight for provisions that disproportionately affect them.

Profeminist men are found in both strands. Many have close ties to labor or other social justice and rights-based politics, as well as the women's movement. The enlightened left masculinists, whom Kenneth Clatterbaugh calls radical profeminist men, believe the system must be addressed for liberation to occur.[33] Some want to transform masculinity itself and to do away with gender categories, and some part company with social democratic feminists over the extent to which the struggle should be directed toward women's concerns or kept on the "larger" struggle.[34] A larger number of men, though, have matured into "progressive liberals" who have not abandoned the ideals of the Great Society. Liberal masculinists focus on conditions for individual equality and want to ensure human similarity rather than sex difference. Certainly, many profeminist men who espouse equal rights, reproductive rights, and shared household duties fall into these categories. Inside campaign politics, such a male candidate often causes disputes if faced with a female opponent known to be a feminist because his policy positions are largely consistent with corresponding feminalist positions, even if his body is sexed masculine.

In terms of the gender disputes indicated in Table 3.2, for the gender left, the point of contention rests with the structures of oppression. For feminalism, reproductive work figures prominently: bearing and raising children; performing the ongoing tasks of "reproducing labor power"; and caring for house, spouse, and self. Borrowing from socialist feminism, this variant challenges prevailing perspectives on what does and does not count in economic calculations of worth, and it questions the low value placed upon feminale labors. Enlightened left masculinists acknowledge that the feminale needs greater recognition and value. Yet those with racial or ethnic identities may advocate for poor men, sometimes at the expense of women's autonomy. They struggle to cope with masculine privilege as they work with women to make change. The friction arises from a perceived inadequate response by men and the lack of change in overall gender power relations; the latter is unsurprising in that few men, especially men of power, hold this ideological position.

Intersectors seek opportunity for all individuals and the equalizing of both personal and public politics. Social-liberal feminism seeks ways to bring comparable worth into workplace calculations and to accommodate private life demands in order to allow for public life success with limited costs to the former. Liberal masculinism takes a more incremental approach. Supporters acknowledge that the feminale is undervalued and that men should help out at home and in the workplace. However, they advocate equal pay more than comparable worth. Such masculinism faces the larger problem of broadening definitions of masculinity so that adherents can participate more in feminalist orientations without repercussions. The dominating friction in Table 3.2 again focuses on the inadequate response by men and the limited change in the masculinist public sphere.

Although both of these gender strands promote policies in the egality paradigm, certainly the individuality paradigm, especially its civic version, can be useful as a means to achieve egalitarian ends. The intersector strand and perhaps liberal masculinism most of all endorse policies in the individuality paradigm. In a debate dominated by more conservative views, adherents of these strands do not favor the complementarity paradigm. Nonetheless, some of their policy arguments may be consistent with it, particularly if they are arguing in favor of state support for poor people.

Gender Similarism: New Liberalism

The ideological strand of gender similarism stresses similarity yet acknowledges some differences between women and men and comfortably aligns with new liberalism. Arguably, this gender strand presents the most common gender orientation today, but between its masculinist and feminalist variants, it also offers widely divergent levels of gender awareness. Good classic liberals, adherents of this strand, emphasize the autonomous individual. Equal must be defined as closely to "the same" as possible if individuals are to be treated under the rules of equality. This sameness is necessitated by a state predicated upon a social contract, which itself depends upon rules to enforce the contract. To have rules is to limit the exceptions. Egalitarian impulses construct rules that ignore individual differences; otherwise, procedural guarantees of equality risk becoming hopelessly complicated. Women can be as free to achieve as men, although selective help—mainly legal protections to free them from discrimination—is available from government. Both men and women can gain from programs applied with careful sameness. For example, because only women can be pregnant, pregnancy leave for women was legally acceptable when it could be fitted into disability leave, a fringe benefit granted to both men and women. By logic then, if men became pregnant, they too would be eligible for pregnancy leave. Because men cannot become pregnant, however, any leave they might receive must be parental leave; hence, a fringe benefit is offered to both men and women.

Gender similarism, which aligns with new liberalism, willingly uses state power to improve each citizen, and thus supporters favor creating jobs if necessary. Both its variants, liberal feminism and neo-fraternalism, stress sameness over difference. Supporters want services to go to those who are employed because jobs can help produce the same basic conditions for individuals. Their efforts go toward providing equal opportunities to work, including employment in nontraditional gender fields, so women can be autonomous and achieve just as well as men. They also stress the rights of citizens and bristle at differential treatment, even as they acknowledge that public support may be needed to create the similar situations they so value.

No more mainstream version of feminism exists than liberal feminism, which has tirelessly pursued equal treatment.[35] Adherents believe individual women can compete successfully with men if the playing field is only leveled. Most adherents of this variant are well-educated professional women, most often white women. Liberal feminism has become mainstream precisely because it begins with the current masculinist system and works to reform it from within. In the process, it necessarily must accommodate—if not adopt—many extant assumptions established by masculinism. But the idea of feminalism requires that women who espouse liberal feminism be granted agency for thinking up this ideology and willfully adopting its tenets as their own. In other words, liberal feminism is not merely co-opted into liberal masculinism or neo-fraternalism. Indeed, this strand of feminale thought has given women access to credit, a right to keep their own name, an assumption of fitness for jury duty, medically based pregnancy leave, equal pay laws, and so on.

Ironically, the masculinist strand of neo-fraternalism seems among the least self-reflective of gender as ideology. Because proponents of this strand focus on equality as the same, usually supporting women in achieving that equality, they become blind to men's own gendering and masculinity's ideological dimension; their ideology is seen as universal. As Gordon S. Wood shows, the American Revolution was a series of changes from rigidly hierarchical patriarchy through patriarchal dependence and patronage to enlightened paternalism.[36] The latter opened the way for individual freedom and a new republican social order. Although Wood contends that this process made it possible for all kinds of individuals to be radically free, clearly this freedom remained predicated upon the (propertied) free white male of its onset and was a move from fathers to brothers. Because US politics never left paternalism as the model of the free citizen, the form of equality these new liberals seek today derives from paternalism.[37] The men who espouse this ideology have a difficult time seeing themselves as holding an ideology because their views have so long been the norm. The "normal" historical tradition of paternalism partly explains this blindness.

Adherents of this strand believe in using the state to help citizens reach their potential, to help produce good citizens. Of course, the state then also defines what human potential matters most and what type of good citizens deserve resource allocations. As indicated in Tables 3.2 and 3.3, the gender dispute within similarism centers on whether women and men are similarly situated so as to really be equal. Much of the social contract language surrounding welfare reform mirrors ideas used in gender equality legislation, ideas predicated upon an atomistic individual fashioned after propertied white males. These men vote to support women's equality so long as it matches masculine norms but seem less willing to support policies that would change women's social roles, one point of contention between masculine and feminale variants.[38] Most important, paternalism—whether neo-fraternalist, new, or otherwise—constitutes the most ordinary and dominant of masculine gender ideologies.[39] The new liberal variety of fraternalism supports its sisters but on its masculine terms.

From the feminalist perspective, the personal is clearly political, and the system must deal with the fact that women and men are both different and the same. It also must contend with the fact that women and men do not benefit the same from paid employment under extant gender arrangements. Therefore, approaches that assume different genders can be similarly situated themselves pose challenges, and negotiating both/and thinking in an either/or environment becomes a persistent need. In contrast, neo-fraternalism emphasizes the danger of politicizing the personal too much because the state might intrude in unwanted ways, such as the many social conservative policies regarding reproduction or homosexuality. Further, its admiration of the extant system leads to arguments for rational solutions within the confines of the system's ability to respond; hence, reforms fall within the bounds of ordinary thought. The friction reveals a pro-system bias more than either gender's ideological advantage, and it dwells upon what will be lost if the system is stretched too far too fast. The rub centers on judgments about the "too" in too far and too fast.

In terms of gender paradigms, civic individuality, with great help from its corporative cousin, is most important for this gender strand. However, such a policy approach largely ignores the masculinist underpinnings of the current system in its quest for the equal treatment of individuals. Certainly, the emphasis on equal rights lends support for moves toward the egality paradigm, but efforts toward role change receive less focus than equal treatment of individuals, undermining whatever arguments are made about egality and leaving considerable room for the individuality paradigm.

Gender Universalism: Libertarian Conservatism

Universalism is the gender strand accompanying libertarian conservativism. Corporative feminalism (sometimes called equality feminism) and new paternalism uphold the desirability of universal standards. Supporters believe in autonomous individuals with an "equal as the same" mentality; hence, they too draw upon extant norms derived from the traditions of masculinist liberalism. Freedom is their ultimate goal, and they are willing to "force people to be free," including letting them fail if necessary. The preponderance of adherents are white, and for most white Americans this ideological position is simply another option. Yet this strand can cross racial and class lines, even though individuals' relationship to the "bootstrap" American dream vary greatly. Immigrants from all races and ethnicities have prized this point of view, although not all can succeed with equal ease. Support for gender universalism from African Americans occurs, but when they espouse this variant, they often are seen as outside the norm in their communities.

With respect to welfare policy, supporters of universalism are willing to enforce behavior as needed because they are confident individuals can change their lives through effort. In spite of gendered opportunity structures, they believe everyone should be treated the same, and they may be willing to provide some services for those who comply in generating their own freedom. By and large, though, equality for individuals comes from equal opportunity found from opening up systems and letting the market determine fitness. This group trusts the market and demands individual effort. Solutions emerge from private enterprise, not the government.

"I'm not a feminist, but . . ." might best characterize the feminalist position inside the gender universalism strand. Supporters of corporative feminalism want to be free from discrimination, thereby having all opportunities open to them, but they also do not want governmental programs dictating too much. They have such faith in women's capacity that they are confident of success if only women are treated as individuals and are not artificially kept down. In the evolution of feminism, these feminalists would have supported Alice Paul's equal rights efforts, and they would have split away from those who moved too much toward protective legislation and special treatment for women, especially if the position was deemed too radical.[40]

Supporters of new paternalism, the masculinist variant of this strand, are even more certain than their neo-fraternalist brothers that a clear universal standard can be found. Their pull-yourself-up ideology ignores structural and individual differences entirely, a rub for some of their ideological sisters. The atomistic individual fashioned after propertied white males simply is the norm, so rationally one should pursue the norm to reap its rewards. Individual desire determines individual success. Because they see adults as interchangeable, many do not even attribute any gender connotations to the term *paternalism*.[41]

Gender universalism contests the nature of difference, especially the extent to which difference is acknowledged and accommodated in a belief set that values one universal standard, as Table 3.2 shows. Such feminalists know that women are able to deal with the masculine but want men to incorporate at least some of the feminale into a standard universal human. Women see the system as producing an uneven playing field, with men having an unfair advantage. They want women to be treated the same, which they know is not always the case.[42] For supporters of new paternalism, the system is believed to be universally fair already. Although adding feminale aspects might be fine, doing so remains a secondary enterprise. Friction surrounds the sense that women too often fail to perform adequately against the extant universal standards. Corporative feminalists would interpret this failure as evidence that the playing field is not yet level, whereas new paternalists would say women need to learn better the rules of the game.

Adherents of this ideological strand of thought turn most often to policies in the corporative version of the individuality paradigm, although they will also turn to civic individuality. They ignore, deny blindly, or relegate to a matter of private choice the complementarity paradigm, rather than reject it. The egality paradigm could prove useful for the atomistic individual at the heart of this gender strand because it represents freedom from the gender prescriptions tied to a sexed body, and freedom remains a primary value. However, because the egality paradigm would shake the system's foundation, its policies are infrequently employed.

Gender Traditionalism: Traditional Conservatism

Drawing from the governing ideology of traditional conservatives, gender traditionalism is most of all pragmatic. Its supporters therefore reason that nature recommends that women care for children and men enter the competition in the public domain dominated by other men. Gender complements are a socially desirable (*vive la difference*) as well as practical way to get through life. Nonetheless, family need, death, disability, and other bad luck sometimes dictate contingencies. In these instances, it is ordinary for women to work and men to take on more household duties, but such work remains gendered or is regendered to remain socially desirable. Adherents value the traditional nurturing functions of women and the manly conduct of men. Biology and reproductive capacity matter in important ways. Structures and functions coincide with sex difference, but not in a rigidly deterministic fashion, because choice is valued and should be privately made. A family wage for men and homemaking duties for women make sense, even if necessity dictates that the boundaries be permeable and women work. Therefore, the state can be used to support separate spheres for women and men, although each family always should attempt nongovernmental solutions; governmental solutions would impinge too much upon household privacy.

Supporters of gender traditionalism stress private solutions and see the nuclear and/or extended family as rational and pragmatic. Sacrifice for family is ordinary, so mothers, widows, or divorcées may need to be employed; fathers have many household responsibilities and may forgo career advancements to stay near children, and so on.[43] These adherents of traditional maternalism and traditional paternalism believe that mothers and fathers offer distinct worldviews and strengths. As traditional conservatives, they believe solutions should come from nongovernmental sources, so they endorse only very limited public support. For parents to be upstanding role models for children, they must hold jobs, although a mother could have a "job" at home with the family. Even though this *Leave It to Beaver* family orientation is often held up as the stereotypical norm for white and Latino families, families of all races and ethnicities struggle to meet its precepts.[44]

Traditional maternalism supports legislation that protects women from the harshest aspects of the world of work and enables them to fulfill their feminale duties. This variant represents what came to be known as "social feminism," the protective track of women's activism between the world wars, a track that tactically stood in opposition to equal rights proponents whose initiatives, maternalists believed, would harm most women. Groups like Concerned Women for America now take such positions, although they part with their early sisters on the desirability of mothers working outside the home.[45] Inside feminism today, a tension still surrounds the need for women's protections and a revaluing of the feminine, which has been promoted by cultural and maternal feminists such as Sara Ruddick and Ann Ferguson.[46]

Traditional paternalism prefers limited state power and stands upon tradition within the household, advocating limited state intervention in private affairs. Although this stance clearly benefits men in the power of private patriarchy, traditional men may actually commit a greater portion of themselves to household responsibilities than their more liberal brothers.[47] One part of this commitment is recognizing a partnership with wives, which in turn creates a broader appreciation than might be immediately apparent. For men, governing is one option for their social role, although sometimes women must step up to this task too, especially for politics close to home such as school boards. In this strand of thought, it is considered normal for men to rule, whether seen as traditional paternalism, a brotherhood, or viriarchy—rule by adult men.[48] Although wise traditionalists value women and the feminale greatly, little stops men from being household tyrants, if they choose. Adherents of this strand see something realistic about a traditional paternal and maternal stance toward gender ideology.[49]

As Tables 3.2 and 3.3 detail, because gender traditionalism adopts the "natural attitude" about the biological basis for gender perspectives, internal contests surround the value given to the feminale and masculine roles, along with the amount of control inherent in each.[50] Maternalists would insist upon equal power for women, derived from their valuable home responsibilities. Yet they continually confront few material or public rewards for maternal duties, despite rhetoric in praise of them. Even when they work, often in feminale jobs, their rewards seldom match their effort or perceived worth. Paternalism recognizes the competitive advantages that accrue to households in which "two-person single careers" flourish and therefore believes in the advantage of breadwinning. Such adherents may also be willing to add some feminale into their orientations, but they know that too much will diminish the masculine advantage and hence the paternal capacity. The friction rubs at the need to reconcile the values of and rewards given to the distinct spheres.

Policies in the complementarity paradigm are most important for adherents of gender traditionalism because they best match their view of the ideal world, but they also support and justify policies in the individuality paradigm, especially those with corporative elements. Their interest in having every family strive for nongovernmental solutions to their problems leads them to make arguments consistent with this paradigm. Their pragmatism, and their realization that life sometimes requires flexibility in gender roles, introduces at times a touch of the egality paradigm to their thinking about public policy.

Patriarchalism: Social Conservatism

Unlike their pragmatic cousins in the conservative camp, this gender ideology stands firm on gender difference because it is God-ordained and biologically determined. This strand depends more upon fundamental religion than race or class. For patriarchalism, separate spheres indeed exist, although women can enter politics to fight for God and motherhood because it is proper for women to care about such matters. Women must submit to the thoughtful dominance of private patriarchy, regardless of their public power.[51] Men are ordinarily understood to control public power, and women manage the household. Adherents of this strand see connections between household arrangements and the public domain. Much like the classic patriarchy of Sir Robert Filmer, men do rule, and they should rule, because God has made them in his image. Women who participate in governance may do so only if they are single and childless (i.e., still morally fit), widowed, or have the permission of their husband, usually in accord with the 20-20-20 rule offered by Phyllis Schlafly. The rule says that a woman should spend the first twenty years educating herself and preparing for life, the second twenty years raising her children, and the last twenty years of productivity doing whatever she chooses.[52] A strong state supports the proper moral conduct that underpins this strand of gender ideology. Gender roles for the good of order take precedence over the autonomy of individuals. Those unwilling to fit into conventions need to pay the price for their deviance, and the state can be an instrument to inspire compliance.

Patriarchalism touts the traditional family and marriage as the foundation of a sound society. Private patriarchal families, with a male head and female who attends to home, are deemed superior, both morally and practically. Such new right feminalists and new patriarchs believe proper moral conduct is critical to attaining status as deserving of the limited state support that is offered. Even though new right feminalists worry

about children, if welfare mothers refuse the support of male breadwinners, especially through marriage, then advantages of private patriarchy
should not go to them. To succeed, such mothers must undertake both
gender roles, and patriarchalism's advocates are skeptical of any woman's
ability to do that well, given the fixed gender differences between men
and women.

A considerable body of writing by new right women emphasizes the
positive value of the feminine/feminale. These women delineate the
power women possess through the giving of life, the nurturing of children
and all others, the sexual control of men, and their moral superiority.
Often through churches, they promote women's public power through
feminine tactics and sheer numbers (e.g., Beverly La Haye's Concerned
Women of America). Most believe women should not step outside traditional feminine roles because these roles contribute so much to women
and to the world. Nonetheless, the state should support women who fulfill these traditional roles and duties, even more than it now does. So great
is women's contribution to civilization, especially through the proper raising of children and the taming of men, that the state has an interest in
ensuring traditional families can thrive so that mothers can raise good
future citizens. It is a position akin to the "republican motherhood" of the
founding period, in which women needed to be liberally educated in order
to produce the good individuals needed by the republic.[53]

New patriarchalism advocates strict adherence to gender separation
and the necessity of one person making the ultimate decisions in a
household. As in John Locke's reasoning, a single head of household is
needed to avoid contention and to maximize the family's efforts through
singular purpose. Moral order is important, and moral men have the
responsibility—and burden—to set the terms for all others. Men therefore should control public power, but they must do so in ways that
enhance society. Society is more important than individuals: traditional
social institutions must be strengthened and individual excesses curbed.
As a result, individual freedom must be subordinated to traditional
mores and ways. Private patriarchal families are seen as the bedrock of
a just and moral polity. Not surprisingly, a conservative interpretation of
the complementarity paradigm figures most prominently in their positions on public policy, although adherents will turn to corporative individuality when individuals (i.e., single mothers) refuse the advantages
that flow to those who create patriarchal families.

Gender disputes among patriarchalism center on questions about
control and rewards of respect and properness, as both tables indicate.
Particularly important is the amount of respect the feminale can achieve.
Women believe the feminale is powerful, but the separate spheres and
role arrangements mean that men and the masculine must endorse this

respect because men bear the responsibility to lead. Further, new right feminalism demands that proper feminale conduct must reap promised rewards. Again, because of public power discrepancies, the feminale depends upon the masculine to ensure these rewards, even though it has some means to bring such masculine response about. From the new patriarchalist perspective, the masculine must dominate in order to lead, but it should do so gently. Private patriarchy is the bedrock of a sound public weal, and without such households, the larger polity cannot sustain itself properly. The friction dominates in the masculine direction, with disorderly women being the greatest rub. Further, feminale equality must be very narrowly prescribed if new patriarchalism is to succeed.

■ An Advantageous Clarification: Women and Feminalist Do Not Equal Liberal

As the above framework shows, we should not expect complete agreement from women and men, even if they share many views, particularly on subjects not closely tied to gender. The differences regarding policy that result from the gender variants detailed in Table 3.3 are rooted in gendered ideology and not in liberalism, as is often claimed. Women are not best understood as more liberal than men; instead, Americans often conflate concern about women with liberalism. Although such concern occasionally joins women across ideological strands, the ends sought for a shared concern usually differ, depending upon governing ideology. The use of protoideological variants helps make sense of these differences, despite the shared views. This approach then draws attention to a persistent claim of popular and scholarly political analysis that women in Congress and state legislatures tend to be "more liberal" than their male counterparts. However, some aspects of the framework require more explanation.

First, this approach may seem to smack of inappropriate pairings of the feminale and the masculine. The feminale position in each strand may seem to be more liberal than the masculine counterpart. Instead, we contend that, consistent with most empirical research on gender and policy, women and men agree on many left-right ideological positions, even if they hold somewhat different orientations about many policies. A major advantage of this approach is that it enables a sorting out of gender ideological dimensions from other governing orientations. Said another way, this approach improves the ability to explain differences between legislators who otherwise seem ideologically alike. Some of these differences are rooted in gender, with feminalist "deviations" from masculinist assumptions and preferences usually drawing the greatest attention. Feminalist preferences should not be conflated with liberal positions, much as positions derived from race should not, and this approach provides a method for distinguishing between gender and conventional governing ideology.

Second, we conjecture that an uneven distribution of women and men exists across the spectrum. This gendered distribution of proponents likely results in further conflation of the feminale with liberal. If, on average, as most polling and voting data confirm, more men fall further to the right on the conventional governing ideology continuum and more women fall further to the left, the tendency to assume that feminale equates with liberal may persist. However, such equation masks the greater variation among women and among men than between them. Nonetheless, feminale and masculine ideological positions are not exactly the same, even between women and men who share similar views on most issues. The notion that feminalist ideological orientations are more "liberal" than masculinist ones emerges because of ideological orientations and extant power distributions, which have heretofore favored men.[54] As the dominant of the system, masculinist assumptions become the norm. If masculinism ensures that men are stronger, and if liberalism has been defined as an ideology that uses the state to bolster all members of society rather than just the dominant, then feminale is readily confused with liberal.

But the feminale should not be conflated with liberal. To begin from, and to generally prefer, that which benefits the feminale currently means pushing an agenda to allocate more resources—fiscal and legal—to benefit women directly. Doing so is feminale—preferring that which has been associated with females—not necessarily liberal. For example, conservative women often raise concerns about families and children, good government, citizen involvement, women in business, reproductive policy, and so on. Nonetheless, the ends they want can differ dramatically from policies on the same topics advocated by social-liberal women, as Tables 3.2 and 3.3 detail. Reproductive policy, especially abortion, offers a familiar example.

Feminist scholars have undertaken considerable critique and rereading of foundational political theory.[55] They, and hence feminalism, have carefully delineated the gendered, patriarchal, or masculinist nature of the theories and their ideological implementations as governing systems. In contrast, only a small handful of male scholars, and hence only a few who contribute to masculinism, notice the masculine preference embedded in conventional theories or ideologies; instead, masculine preference is normal. This pattern is not uncommon. As innumerable feminist critiques of conventional ideology have detailed, men have set the conventions of the ideologies. As R. W. Connell concludes, "Politics-as-usual is men's politics."[56] To challenge such usual politics should be understood as feminalist if matters affecting women are at stake. To advance policies that advantage men should be understood as masculinist. At times liberal and conservative may correlate with feminale and masculine, respectively, but scholars err when they overly attribute causality to the liberal-conservative continuum and ignore gender. Most important, they miss the ways policy creates gender.

To summarize, the framework employed in this book is based upon systematic theorizing of gender ideology as it pertains to an empirical analysis of welfare policy. It treats gender as a protoideology that operates independently from conventional governing ideologies and underpins them. It establishes two theoretically coequal variants of gender, masculinism and feminalism, each of which begins from, and generally prefers, that which is associated with masculinity and feminality, respectively. It shows how these variants compound with conventional governing ideologies on the left-right continuum, thereby enabling explanation and interpretation of both similarities and differences. Coupled with the gender paradigms introduced in the previous chapter, this framework helps us to systematically approach the conflicts of sexual politics involving ideas about gender and demonstrate how gender is created and legitimized in one potent area of policy, welfare.

▪ Notes

1. US Department of Health and Human Services, National Institutes of Health, "Frequently Asked Questions," http://www.womenshealthresearch.org/background.htm.
2. Society for Women's Health Research, "Background Information," http://www.womenshealthresearch.org/background.htm.
3. The two women who voted against the measure in the House—Barbara Vucanovich (NV) and Ileana Ros-Lehtinen (FL)—were Republicans.
4. Society for Women's Health Research, "Background Information," http://www.womenshealthresearch.org/background.htm.
5. A term and argument made famous by Lorde, *Sister Outsider,* 112.
6. Pateman, *The Sexual Contract.*
7. Georgia Duerst-Lahti especially thanks Kenneth Hoover for the suggestion of protoideology, which improves upon the term *metaideology* used in *Gender Power, Leadership, and Governance.*
8. Although more than two genders exist and are possible and the transgender movement is beginning to be recognized, so far these other options have limited meaning in legislatures, except perhaps with sex change laws. We also run the risk of "essentializing" gender from sex; however, our focus is on gendered performances adopted by individuals, or their projection of their gendered selves, rather than some measure of their biological sex. The framework can be ever more complex; for example, see Buker, *Talking Feminist Politics.*
9. Hawkesworth makes a similar point in "Congressional Enactments of Race-Gender," in which she foregrounds the active processes of racing and gendering in policy.

10. Women and men probably are not equally distributed along the continuum. Men disproportionately favor the right and women the left, a condition that has become evident in US elections with their routine gender gaps. The distribution could be established through further research.

11. As Freeman aptly notes, hyphenated feminisms were adopted "to identify oneself in relationship to both feminists and non-feminists." The need to show allegiance to the basic propositions of the adjoining conventional political ideologies has always been strong because feminist thinkers inevitably drew upon these existing ideologies as they assessed political concerns both theoretically and practically. Freeman, "From Seeds to Harvest," 406.

12. See Duerst-Lahti and Kelly, *Gender Power, Leadership, and Governance,* chap. 2, for an extended explanation of both/and versus either/or analysis.

13. For a discussion of the reasons behind these shifts, see Brown, *States of Injury,* 10.

14. Dawson, *Black Visions.*

15. Connell, *Masculinities,* 81–85.

16. Connell, *Gender and Power;* Walby, taken from *Gender Transformations,* 5, in reference to her earlier work, *Theorizing Patriarchy.*

17. Ferguson, *The Man Question,* 27.

18. Much like feminism, the contemporary men's movement has recognized the intersection of other elements of identity and masculinity; see for example, Connell, *Masculinities,* and Kimmel, *The Politics of Manhood.* As ideology, it is necessary to recognize the extent to which these other elements help to constitute gender and to determine the relative power and privilege of any particular mode of masculinity. For example, in *Manliness and Civilization,* Bederman traces the ways race has been used to construct the dominant masculinity in the United States. For a discussion about the way in which differences among men are crucial for creating masculinities, see Brod and Kaufman, *Theorizing Masculinities.* The dominance of heterosexuality could not be maintained without the denigration of homosexual men; see Hearn, *Men in the Public Eye.* These protoideological aspects require the same type of analysis as do feminalist intersections and will not be undertaken here. Group differences are very much implicated in power and are important, however.

19. For a discussion of the concept of masculinity, various views of masculinity over time, and dominant beliefs within masculinity, see Connell, *Gender and Power;* Connell, *Masculinities;* and Kimmel, *Manhood in America.*

20. For a fuller explanation of this shift and the functioning of masculinism as a governing ideology, see Duerst-Lahti, "Knowing Congress as a Gendered Institution."

21. See Chapter 1, Box 1.1 for more details.

22. Because we are dealing with ideologies important to legislation, we work within the constraints of the usual liberal-conservative spectrum here. The spectrum extends further, even if only on the left-right continuum, and could incorporate challenges to it such as those from black feminism or gay men.

23. Hawkesworth, "Confounding Gender," 649–685.

24. Hartsock, *Money, Sex, and Power;* see also *Women and Politics,* 1997, vol. 18, no. 3, for a special issue dedicated to the topic.

25. Tamerius, "Sex, Gender, and Leadership," 96–98. See also Young, *Intersecting Voices,* 12–36.

26. Duerst-Lahti, "Knowing Congress;" and Duerst-Lahti, "Governing Institutions, Ideology, and Gender."

27. Such judgments hinge upon whether only one biological category of males and one of females exists, rather than the five discernible sex categories now recognized by biologists. The growing awareness of intersexed humans, estimated at 1 in 1,000, who increasingly seek political recognition will push this question into the public consciousness. It was not visible in welfare reform, however. On the "givenness" of biology, see Butler, *Gender Trouble*. On the five sexes, see Lorber, "Believing Is Seeing."

28. Earlier and somewhat altered versions of the figures used in this chapter have appeared in Duerst-Lahti, "Knowing Congress"; and Duerst-Lahti, "Governing Institutions, Ideology, and Gender."

29. One overarching observation about Tables 3.2 and 3.3 is found in the apparent oddity of "hyphenating" masculinist categories. For example, our approach categorizes many strands under feminalism as they are commonly labeled, such as Marxist feminism, liberal feminism, and so on. Yet, the dominance of men and masculinist protoideology has made Marxism, socialism, liberalism, and the like ordinary and therefore not in need of the hyphenated compound. These conventional ideologies clearly fall within masculinist protoideology, and we have located them accordingly. The "unnatural" sound of such strands as liberal masculinism underscores the success of masculinism generally as a protoideology.

Strands of thought not widespread in US policymaking have been excluded from both Tables 3.2 and 3.3, although many of these perspectives have been important as part of scholarly analysis of gender in US politics. Radical and cultural feminism and men's rights and mytho-poetic masculinism were not included because they are not part of conventional politics. Marxist and socialist feminism and their masculinist counterparts were not included because the dominance of the capitalist economic system coupled with entrenched assumptions about individuals found in classic liberalism make these perspectives largely irrelevant in US policymaking. Students of gender theory will notice that not all variations of feminist thought, such as black feminist thought and lesbian thought, are included. Duerst-Lahti has included more of these strands of thought in "Governing Institutions, Ideology, and Gender."

30. The economy also is raced and classed, although it is less clear that white people, for example, are aware of the racing or that those with higher socioeconomic potential understand how class shapes economic possibilities.

31. Grant, *Fundamental Feminism*, 184.

32. Jones, *Compassionate Authority.*

33. Clatterbaugh, *Contemporary Perspectives on Masculinity,* identifies six major perspectives regarding men and masculinity in North American society. They are conservative, profeminist, men's rights, spiritual, socialist, and group-specific. His sociological orientation does not align fully with our political one, although his work has been enormously important in devising the masculinist categorization.

34. Writing about the gendered split in the National Welfare Rights Organization, Boris concludes, "Maternalism distinguished women welfare activists from the men of their own movement, who sought universal entitlements rather than rights based on motherhood and the labor of mothering." Boris, "When Work Is Slavery," 50.

35. For an extended treatment of liberal feminism's pursuits, see Mezey, *Elusive Equality.*

36. Wood, *The Radicalism of the American Revolution.*

37. For a discussion of fathers and fraternity, see Kann, *On the Man Question*. Kann uses the term *patriarchy* in the sense academic feminism employs it.

38. Norton, "Uncovering the Unidimensionality of Gender Voting in Congress," 65–85.

39. Sartorius, *Paternalism*.

40. Good research has been done on women's activism "between the wars," after suffrage and before the second wave of feminism ensued. Much of it analyzes the dispute between social feminists who sought protections for women in the workplace and to fulfill women's care roles, and equality feminists who moved hard for political rights and "equal treatment." See Offen, "Defining Feminism." Gayle Graham Yates named the latter corporative feminists in her analysis of the reemerging women's movement, *What Women Want*. We take our label from her and note the empirical correspondence between this position and the views of many prominent women who work in the corporate world.

41. For example, see Mead, *New Paternalism*. Mead explains that he uses the term *paternalism* to denote social welfare programs that supervise individuals, but that he could just as easily have used *maternalism* or *parentalism*.

42. This clearly is the position taken by Demi Moore's character in the movie *GI Jane*, a point noted also by Kimmel in "Saving the Males."

43. Hochschild finds that spouses in "traditional" marriages spend more time on household tasks than men in "equality" marriages. See Hochschild, *The Second Shift*.

44. Stacey, *In the Name of the Family*.

45. Based upon interviews by Jusztina Traum, in Duerst-Lahti, "Conservative Women's."

46. Ruddick, *Maternal Thinking;* Ferguson, *Blood at the Root;* Crittenden, *The Price of Motherhood*.

47. Hochschild, *The Second Shift*.

48. Pateman writes extensively on the brotherhood or fraternity—"a sleight of hand"—as change from patriarchy, in *The Sexual Contract*. See also Waters, "Patriarchy and Viriarchy;" Hearn, *Men in the Public Eye*.

49. Minogue, *Conservative Realism*.

50. Hawkesworth, "Confounding Gender," 3.

51. Clatterbaugh, *Contemporary Perspectives on Masculinity;* Sartorius, *Paternalism*; Gilder, *Sexual Suicide*.

52. According to interviews with staff members of Eagle Forum, conducted by Jusztina Traum, May and June 2000.

53. Kerber, *Women of the Republic;* and Wood, *Radicalism of the American Revolution,* especially p. 357. Considerable recent writing reminds us that not all women of the founding era could undertake the republican motherhood role, but rather only white women married to propertied men, or "family men." See Kann, *A Republic of Men;* and Newman, *White Women's Rights*.

54. It also may be a by-product of a preponderance of liberal Democrats among women elected to state and federal office, which in simple analysis masks differences among women. This factor, coupled with Republican elected women who have on average been more moderate than the mode of their male counterparts, also contributes to this pattern.

55. See, for example, the works of Wendy Brown, Christine Di Stefano, Zilla Eisenstein, Kathy Ferguson, and Carole Pateman.

56. Connell, *Masculinities,* 204.

4

Unfolding Gender Paradigms: A History of Sexual Politics in Welfare Policy

WHEN THE FEDERAL GOVERNMENT BEGAN TO GIVE PUBLIC ASSIS-
tance to poor single mothers and their children in 1935, Aid to Dependent Children (ADC) was endorsed by Democrats and Republicans alike.
Without controversy, Congress agreed to provide federal funding for state
grants to children who lacked a breadwinner due to death, desertion, or
disability so they could be cared for by their mother in their own home.
"In its own home the child becomes the beneficiary of the tender love, the
gentle solicitude, and the gracious care of its own mother," explained
Representative William Sirovich (D-NY) during the House floor debate,
for she was the "queen and angel of the home." "Since God could not be
everywhere, he created mothers to take His place."[1]

Sixty-one years later, the Personal Responsibility and Work Opportunity Reconciliation Act (PRWORA) ended ADC, replacing it with a
program whose different name—Temporary Assistance for Needy Families (TANF)—was not merely symbolic. Welfare was not supposed to be
a "way of life." Children no longer needed the direct care of their mothers; rather, they needed a working parent, someone who could "draw a
paycheck, not a welfare check," and thus join the "world of work that
gives structure, meaning, and dignity to most of our lives."[2] Welfare
could only be temporary help through a short-term crisis, after which
women, like men, should work to support themselves and their children.

Through public policy, legislators, executives, and judges authori-
tatively allocate resources and values.[3] They legitimize some values and
support them with resources and, in the process, ignore, undermine, and
even penalize others. Thus, the replacement of ADC with TANF was
more than a shift in political beliefs about state power, the market, and
poverty. It also indicated a significant shift in the gender roles supported
by government, for no longer can women make a claim for public support

simply on their role as mothers of children. Now they must work, or marry a man who works, and thus prove themselves to be meritorious citizens through their ability to be self-sufficient and independent of government assistance.

Using the gender paradigms central to our analysis, this chapter presents the historical development of welfare policy that led to the demise of ADC and the adoption of the 1996 reform. Through public policy debates over what government should do, why it should act, and how it can best accomplish its goals, problems are framed in different ways at different times, and solutions are altered, refined, and replaced to fit these frames.[4] Following the history of these debates about welfare, we trace political fights about gender paradigms over time, demonstrating how various ideas about normative gender roles were challenged and how these contests led to competing understandings of social problems and desired government solutions.

The Personal Responsibility and Work Opportunity Reconciliation Act breaks completely from the standard set initially by ADC. ADC was rooted in complementarity, the gender paradigm of a female caregiver and male breadwinner. Fully conflating biological sex with cultural gender constructions, this program assumed that only males could perform the masculine breadwinning role and only females could perform the feminale caregiving role. Early challenges to this model centered on whether never-married mothers and black mothers could claim the feminale status of female caregiver and receive aid on that basis.[5] In the late 1960s, after efforts to deny aid to these groups had been repelled, the individuality paradigm began to emerge, and policymakers started to emphasize work. Yet a belief in the importance of mothers staying home to raise their children persisted, and initially, policies consistent with the individuality paradigm were unable to oust those rooted in complementarity.

Not until the 1980s and the Democrats' acceptance of work requirements under the Family Support Act did the individuality paradigm eclipse complementarity. Numerous quarrels erupted about the best approach to take within the individuality paradigm, however, and the Personal Responsibility and Work Opportunity Reconciliation Act resulted from a concerted effort to push policies toward the corporative version of the paradigm. Although no longer the dominant model used to guide welfare policy, the complementarity paradigm continued to influence policy through renewed efforts to invigorate marriage as a solution to poverty. The egality paradigm, never a dominant model throughout this period, even though opportunities arose for policies to shift toward egality, receded even more as the individuality paradigm rose in importance.

■ Complementarity and the Deserving Caregiver in ADC

Adopted in 1935 as part of the Social Security Act, Aid to Dependent Children was one of three public assistance programs jointly run by the states and the federal government. Federal law set broad rules of eligibility, required states to operate programs throughout the entire state, and provided matching funds to state grants for destitute children in homes without a breadwinner. Within the boundaries of federal law, states could decide how high monthly grants would be, the income levels used to determine eligibility, and what other behaviors could be required of recipients. Thus, states could decide how generous their grants would be, and average monthly grants varied widely across the states throughout the history of the program. States also could structure their program in a manner that made it easier for poor women and their children to receive assistance, or they could adopt various rules and procedures that thwarted women and their children from obtaining aid. This discretion granted to the states eased the adoption of the program in 1935. Legislators knew that states had the leeway to fashion programs according to their own needs and desires.[6]

ADC was grounded on complementarity, an unsurprising finding given the strong tradition of separate spheres for women and men.[7] ADC rested on the normative value of a male breadwinner and a female caregiver. Men were expected to work, and women were expected to care for children, husbands, and other family members. These were ideal types used to guide expectations of what men and women should do and to establish criteria for assessing how well they lived up to the standards of good citizenship. Men and women who complied with these norms could be rewarded, whereas those who did not meet their terms could be castigated as inadequate and penalized for their failures. But those who failed could also be presented as potential good citizens who could overcome their inadequacies if given proper support from government and society. As ideal types, however, the male breadwinner and female caregiver had to be maintained, not weakened. The worry was that any effort to help struggling men and women would undermine the high standards of the complementarity paradigm.

The need to maintain the standards for breadwinning led Congress to adopt programs that rewarded men who met this role successfully but did not assist those who struggled to earn through paid labor. Old-age insurance (what today we commonly call Social Security) and unemployment compensation were designed to protect working men from the vagaries of the market. These programs offered income support to those who had demonstrated their success as breadwinners, but only at times when men were seen as vulnerable to circumstances in the market beyond their control.[8] Any other assistance, such as assistance to supplement the wages of men, would supposedly reduce the work ethic and jeopardize men's breadwinning role, a role intimately connected to dominant ideas of proper masculinity. Consequently, two-parent families were not eligible for ADC unless the father was disabled and therefore physically or mentally incapable of fulfilling the breadwinner role. Whether men's role in the family extended beyond breadwinning was not relevant for income transfer programs. Men were expected to support their families; to do so, most had to work. What else men did with their families in the household was a private matter.

This lack of concern with men's involvement in the work of the household did not mean that home activities were ignored. Rather, housework and child care were the responsibilities of women, and paid employment by women supposedly interfered with their ability to perform these tasks. At the time, policymakers believed that employed mothers led to juvenile delinquency or the breakup of the home.[9] Good mothers were expected to stay home and care for their children.[10] When mothers engaged in paid work, they either had to leave their children unsupervised—thus the fall to juvenile delinquency—or consign them to public homes. In the absence of a male breadwinner, public assistance would provide "regular payments to mothers to take care of their children" in order to keep the family together.[11] Indeed, women receiving ADC were not expected to work, and until 1967 the regulations provided no economic gain for doing so. ADC was adopted to maintain the role of the female caregiver, to enable mothers in single-parent families to leave the labor market and care for their children in their own home. In announcing their support of ADC, legislators proclaimed their desire to provide for "the security of motherhood and of childhood."[12]

Prior to the adoption of ADC, states had treated grants to mother-only families as a reward for the worthy mother and her children, rather than aid to prevent destitution, and this notion carried over to the implementation of the federal program.[13] An important aspect of the complementarity behind ADC was an idealized vision of a good mother, one who was worthy of public aid and whose children would benefit from the salutary upbringing she would provide. In this vision, the good mother was understood to be a widow, specifically a white widow. A widow was considered deserving because she was not held responsible for her and her children's destitution (no one argued that she had contributed to the death of her husband) and because the public could be assured that the father was not shirking his breadwinner obligations. Moreover, through marriage a widow had sustained a connection to a male worker and had children (and presumably sex) only within a marriage.[14] A widow was moral, chaste, and, as demonstrated by her connection to a male bread-winner, hardworking. Because her children would benefit from her care, they were worthy of public support. Marriage granted her and her children legitimacy.

It was this deserving widow that legislators referred to when they professed their support for ADC in 1935. They did not discuss the extension of ADC to other types of families, even though the federal law they passed clearly allowed other women and their children to be eligible for ADC. The law specified that children were eligible for assistance if they lacked a breadwinner due to death, disability, or absence from the home. Never-married, separated, and divorced women and their children met one of these criteria. But legislators did not discuss the implications of granting assistance to these women and children. Questions about whether ADC weakened the family by using the state to replace the male provider emerged later.

Contrary to the expectation that ADC would "wither away" once widows and dependents were included in Social Security, the program grew in the 1940s and 1950s.[15] Congress increased federal matching funds, states raised their monthly grants, and more women and children who were eligible for aid began to receive it.[16] Yet many of these women did not fit the normative vision of the female caregiver embedded in the ideas of complementarity that structured ADC. Because widows were now eligible for Social Security benefits, fewer recipients were widows, and more were never-married mothers and black mothers.[17] These women had not married or sustained a marriage, so they lacked the legitimacy provided by a legal connection to a man. Those who were not white were expected to work; any claims they might make to the feminale ideal of caregiving touted for white women was interpreted as laziness. Their morality, chastity, and industriousness were doubted. The value of their children was also questioned, as was their ability to mother children in a way that would yield meritorious citizens.

Constrained by federal law, states could not directly deny aid to unwed mothers and black mothers and their children, even though many saw marital status and race as simple, straightforward indicators of worthiness. They relied instead on a variety of policies that regulated maternal behavior, including employable mother rules, substitute father rules, and suitable home rules. These rules were ostensibly about the behaviors constituting good mothering, but they were implemented in a manner that enabled states to deny aid to women they thought were not worthy, mainly never-married and black women. These rules were not aimed only at black women—northern states with low black populations also adopted them in order to target white women who had children out of wedlock—

but they were used most aggressively by southern states against black women. Because black women were more likely than white women to never have married, any targeting of "illegitimacy" would disproportionately affect black women and their children.[18]

In this attempt to preserve ADC for the deserving, one approach was to simply deny the feminale role of caregiver to black women, excluding them from the ideal of the good mother who needed to be home with her children. Instead, black mothers were expected to work. Southern states in particular presumed that black women were employable and therefore not eligible for assistance, as long as jobs were available. Louisiana adopted the first "employable mother" rule in 1942, denying aid to families with children aged seven and older as long as there was work in the fields. Georgia followed in 1952, prohibiting aid to women with children three and older, and even forbidding county welfare agencies from supplementing with aid the wages earned by women in the fields.[19] When workers were needed, aid was rejected on the grounds that black women were employable, even if they were responsible for the care and upbringing of children. Such an approach maintained a system of low wages for agricultural workers and domestic servants because women had no alternative but to work at those jobs. Employable mother rules were overturned in 1968, when a federal court struck down Georgia's regulations on the grounds that they discriminated against black women and children.[20]

Second, as unwed mothers began to receive aid, the belief that ADC allowed women to form families without male heads led states to start questioning just what constituted "absence" of a male breadwinner. Some states decided that the presence of a "substitute father" meant that children were not "deprived of parental support" and thus were not eligible for ADC. Any man could be labeled a substitute father by a welfare agency, no matter what his relationship to the children or how tenuous his association with the mother. It was not unusual for a welfare agency to hold that a man with no legal obligation to provide financially for the children was a substitute parent and then declare the family ineligible for assistance. In one case a family was denied aid when a man was seen entering but not leaving an apartment building, even though the agency did not know which apartment the man had entered. Agencies also concluded there was a substitute parent when they found residue of a man but no such man himself. One family was kicked off ADC when investigators found a man's shirt, even though the mother and son said it belonged to the son.[21] The attempts to find such men, or even traces of them, were as sly as the conclusions themselves and involved highly intrusive investigative techniques, including midnight raids of dwellings in the hopes of catching a man unawares or finding some physical evidence of a man.[22] Substitute father rules were curtailed in 1968 when the Supreme Court ruled that only men who were legally responsible for the children (generally the biological or adoptive father) could be considered a possible source of parental support when determining if a family was eligible for ADC.

Finally, in order to ensure that women were maintaining the virtuous homes expected of a female caregiver, many states adopted suitable home rules to supervise the domestic life of recipients. These rules vaguely demanded that women maintain suitable homes in order to receive aid and were justified on the grounds of protecting child well-being. Their advantage as an administrative device was their ambiguity, which gave states sufficient discretion to deny aid to any woman deemed unworthy because of marital status or race. Under these rules, illegitimacy indicated immorality, irrespective of the woman's actual daily care of her children. For example, Georgia listed "repeated births of children born out-of-wedlock" as grounds for unsuitability.[23] Asserting that "flagrant and continued violation of the moral and social standards of the community usually result in emotional and sometimes actual physical damage to the child," Mississippi included "failure to provide legal marriage" and "casual relations and the birth of an illegitimate child."[24] States used these grounds to summarily dismiss families from the welfare rolls yet offered no other services or assistance to protect the children whose well-being was allegedly jeopardized because they lived in these unsuitable homes.

These actions by the states garnered little national attention until 1960, when Louisiana adopted a suitable home rule specifying that illegitimacy alone indicated that the home was not fit. Applying its new rule retroactively, Louisiana withdrew ADC from approximately 6,000 families with more than 23,000 children, 95 percent of them black.[25] Charitable organizations were overwhelmed, and local emergency funds were exhausted in efforts to provide food, clothing, and shelter for these families. Louisiana's actions received national and international attention as the British press picked up the story, and British residents donated funds to private charities in Louisiana. In the city Newcastle-on-Tyne, women on the city council began a campaign to bring the children to England, proclaiming they would care for them if others refused.[26]

Controversies over the receipt of public aid by black and never-married women moved to northern states a year after these actions by Louisiana, with a proposal in 1961 to cut ADC drastically in Newburgh, New York. Joseph Mitchell, a newly hired city manager, thought the city's riverfront district was deteriorating because of relief, and specifically relief to newcomers who were black and lazy. Mitchell first ordered a "muster" of 300 welfare recipients, requiring people to come down for a lineup at the police station in hopes of "weeding out the chiselers."[27] No chiselers were uncovered, but Mitchell thought the exercise was still useful. "If nothing else, it scared the daylights out of them," he said.[28]

Mitchell was not content with simply scaring people through an abuse of police power. He followed up the muster by a proposal that "challenged the right of social parasites to breed illegitimate children at the taxpayer's expense, . . . challenged the right of moral chiselers and loafers to squat on the relief rolls forever, . . . and challenged the right of citizens to migrate for the purpose of becoming or continuing as public charges."[29] Mitchell advised the city to grant aid only three months a year, cut off from assistance unmarried mothers who had a child out of wedlock, require able-bodied men to work forty hours per week at the city's building maintenance department, and dispense only one week of relief to any newcomers who moved to Newburgh without a specific job offer. Mitchell's proposal went far beyond the genteel use of suitable home provisions by professional social workers, and in the brouhaha that followed, the New York State Board of Social Welfare refused to allow Newburgh to implement most elements of the plan.[30]

As both the Louisiana and Newburgh controversies received national attention, the battle over which families could receive aid moved from quiet clashes between states and the federal Bureau of Public Assistance to a noisy and more public debate in Congress about deservingness. The opportunity for this fracas was prompted by President John F. Kennedy's initiative to make changes in the public assistance programs.[31] While the Kennedy administration, too, was anxious about growing welfare rolls, its initial concern in 1961 was with unemployment due to recession, and it proposed to expand ADC temporarily to cover two-parent families in which the breadwinner was unemployed, a proposal with clear egalitarian potential.[32] The following year, when the administration proposed permanent changes in the program, the recession had abated, and its attention focused more on preventing poverty and rehabilitating the poor through social services.[33] Resting on the assumption that the number of people receiving welfare should be reduced, this emphasis on prevention and rehabilitation provided a perfect foil for a discussion of deservingness, illegitimacy, and the morality of mothers.

In question was the states' prerogative to deny aid to never-married mothers and children born out of wedlock. Legislators favoring such a position stated explicitly what had only been alluded to in 1935—children born out of wedlock had no value because their mother had not submitted to marriage with their father. These children were "mistakes" that should not be supported with public funds. Barry Goldwater (R-AZ), already a contender for the Republican nomination for president in 1964, thought the Newburgh reforms were "refreshing as the clear air of Arizona." "I don't like to see my taxes paid for children born out of wedlock," he declared.[34] In the 1961 House floor debate on temporary amendments to ADC, Representative Harold Gross (R-IA) asked the chairman of the

Ways and Means Committee (which reported the bill to the floor) if the bill included aid "for those people who have been hatching out illegitimate children." Gross wanted aid to be limited to "one mistake and you are out; instead, in some cases of 8 or 10 so-called mistakes."[35]

In this perspective, these children lacked value because their mothers were immoral and could not provide a proper upbringing. Granting aid to never-married mothers and their children challenged the norms of complementarity because it extended public support to women who did not conform to the idealized feminale role of caregiver who gained morality and legitimacy through an attachment to a male breadwinner. Legislators who supported the states' actions could see no justification for such public aid. When women had children out of wedlock, they had committed a sin. Because they were immoral, they could not be good mothers. If not good mothers, they were presumed to raise their children in unsanitary, neglectful, and immoral conditions, so it was perfectly reasonable to use suitable home rules to deny them public aid.[36]

Those who opposed the states and supported granting assistance to never-married women and their children tended to defend the children more than their mothers. The children were innocent and helpless, and the sins of their mothers should not be visited upon them. These supporters pointed out that states justified suitable home rules on the grounds of child protection but then did not intervene when families were kicked off ADC because they did not meet suitable home rules. States claimed that the home life did not provide a proper upbringing for the children, but then they did not remove the children from the home or arrange for any remedial services to correct the problems. Supporters argued that using suitable home rules to deny these children public assistance was hypocritical.

Legislators supporting aid to never-married mothers did not defend them so much as perceive them as redeemable. They recognized that these mothers challenged complementarity by having children outside of marriage, and certainly this transgression raised concerns about their ability to be good mothers. Yet in a break from the dominant interpretation of complementarity, they also believed that good mothers did not come about only when children were born in the confines of a legal marriage. Certainly the complementarity paradigm assumed that women were good mothers by definition if they were married. However, these legislators were also arguing that women could be taught to be good mothers by social workers who could figure out their problems and then offer appropriate services. Introducing the bill to amend ADC to the House of Representatives, Representative Wilber Mills (D-AR), the chair of the Ways and Means Committee, pointed out that the bill funded state efforts to "give extensive counseling services to the recipients to encourage more acceptable behavior."[37] Every mother had the potential to be worthy. The power of the state need not be limited only to punishing those who were not deserving; rather, it could be marshaled to transform them into worthy caregivers. This liberal interpretation of the complementarity paradigm uncoupled good female caregiving from male breadwinning in marriage.

As the paradigmatic struggle continued, this faith in redemption did not eliminate a belief in both penance and punishment for women who did not reform. Although the amendments passed by Congress in 1962 restricted states' use of suitable home rules as a device to deny aid to unwed mothers and their children, the provisions still rested on the assumptions that unwed mothers had to be monitored carefully and that states would have to intervene in many such families. The amendments required that when a state cut aid to a family on the grounds that a suitable home was not maintained, the state had to take action to remove the children from the home. Legislators did not include this requirement with the belief that such actions would seldom be taken. Rather, they were afraid that states would not invoke suitable home rules and remove children from their mothers' homes often enough. To encourage them to take these actions, Congress adopted federal matching funds for the foster care of children previously receiving ADC. They provided additional funding for a program with professional social workers, effective casework, and extensive social services that could provide "special services and safeguards to children in families of unmarried parents, in families where the father has deserted, or in homes in danger of becoming morally or physically unsuitable."[38]

In the 1961 and 1962 amendments, provisions concerning men were justified by a relatively charitable view of their motives, yet were still centered on upholding the male breadwinner role. Arguing in favor of extending ADC to two-parent families when the breadwinner was unemployed, President Kennedy and the legislators backing him asserted that men wanted to be with their families, but when they were jobless they deserted so their families would be eligible for public assistance.[39] Men were not shiftless good-for-nothings who shirked their responsibilities; rather, they were benevolent fathers who left out of love and the hope of doing what was best for their families. Their unemployment was due to structural economic factors, not their own lack of effort.[40] Consequently, extending aid to these families would buttress rather than undermine the breadwinning role because fathers would stay with their families and then resume working when jobs were available.

Congress met President Kennedy's request and adopted AFDC-UP (ADC was renamed Aid to Families with Dependent Children, and UP stood for "unemployed parent"). Yet as the states responded to this change in federal law, concern about granting aid to two-parent families was sufficiently strong that various policies constrained the expansion of AFDC-UP. First, federal law allowed states to choose to adopt AFDC-UP, and at any given time about half the states did not offer this program. Second, strict rules were adopted concerning the number of hours men could work and still have families eligible for aid. Men had to accept jobs if offered them; refusing a job would result in the denial of aid. These restrictions meant that few two-parent families were eligible for aid, and throughout the lifetime of AFDC, only a small percentage of recipients lived in two-parent families.

The agreement to extend aid to two-parent families could have moved public assistance toward egality, even though such a gender paradigm had not yet made its way into the common imagination. It held the potential to break down the rigid distinction between breadwinning and caregiving and the association of these roles with males and females, respectively. But this move toward egality did not occur. Policymakers continued to focus on whether public assistance would reinforce or undermine male breadwinning. In an example of conflating sex with gender, only females were believed capable of being feminale and giving care, and only males were thought able to be masculine and do breadwinning. The complementarity paradigm held firm, and other gender options remained dormant during the early 1960s.

■ The Male Breadwinner: Egality, Complementarity, and the War on Poverty

Only two years after Congress passed legislation intended to redeem the poor through social services, national attention again focused on poverty with President Lyndon B. Johnson's declared War on Poverty. AFDC was peripheral to these initiatives; thus policymakers avoided the political disputes that seemed to inevitably follow any discussion of this program. Moreover, their theories about the causes of poverty and the policies needed to fight a war against it centered on male employment and access to education and training that was supposed to result in equal opportunity. Race was a more central and explicit political issue than gender, both in the design and implementation of the war's central battle plan, the Economic Opportunity Act of 1964, as policymakers were preoccupied with questions of how to incorporate black men into American prosperity.[41]

Yet gender paradigms lurked in the War on Poverty. They were fundamental to the emphasis on eliminating poverty through male employment. The War on Poverty was supposed to enable men to acquire more stable and higher-paying jobs by providing access to education and training.

Never specified completely nor examined thoroughly was the assumption that this focus on male employment would reduce poverty among women and children. But certainly the approach of the War on Poverty presupposed that men who had good jobs would marry and support their wives and children. The War on Poverty promoted complementarity, not only by continuing the earlier emphasis on women's conformance to the ideal of the female caregiver, but also by advancing policies intended to invigorate the male breadwinner.

Although policymakers did not often discuss their assumptions about desirable gender roles in the preferred family structure, one explicit account is commonly called the Moynihan report, written by Daniel Patrick Moynihan, at the time an assistant secretary of labor.[42] The report relied on an explicit yet unquestioned use of the male breadwinner and female caregiver roles as a solution to poverty. Legitimately concerned about high rates of black poverty, Moynihan was afraid that the policies developed by the Johnson administration lacked sufficient emphasis on creating and maintaining two-parent families. In the report, he strove to highlight that "at the heart of the deterioration of the fabric of the Negro society is the deterioration of the Negro family."[43] Noting higher rates of illegitimacy and father absence in black families than in white ones, Moynihan argued that the black community had been forced into a matriarchal structure that was a tangle of pathology. Although he recognized external forces responsible for these mother-centered families, he asserted that this tangle of pathology was "the principal source of most of the aberrant, inadequate, or anti-social behavior" that would "perpetuate the cycle of poverty and deprivation" among the Negro community.[44] Thus, he viewed mother-centered families as problematic not just because they lacked a breadwinner who could support the family financially, but also because they strayed from commonly accepted gender roles, which then led to deviant behavior by their children.

Although Moynihan was correct in arguing that War on Poverty programs did not focus explicitly on creating two-parent families, they certainly presumed that marriage and not employment was the route out of poverty for women. This assumption was evident in the Job Corps, a major training program in the War on Poverty. Initially, administration officials made it clear that they wanted this program targeted at men, and they thought centers for women would only deplete available funding for men's training sites. At the insistence of Representative Edith Green (D-OR), Congress specified that one-third of the trainees be female. Yet this statutory requirement did not translate into a program designed to reduce women's poverty through their employment. The training offered to women centered on low-wage jobs, not the skills needed for higher-paying, blue-collar work. Moreover, for women job training was secondary to "intensive training in home and family life and the development of values, attitudes, and skills that [would] contribute to stable family relationships and a good childrearing environment."[45] Young women needed education to "develop insights into interpersonal relationships; opportunities to learn how to plan and prepare nutritious meals; skills in child care and guidance; and the effective management of money in the home."[46] Women were trained to obtain and sustain a marital relationship, run a home, nurture a family, and break the cycle of poverty by passing on middle-class values to their children. Men were trained for employment.

The design of antipoverty programs was influenced by the expectation that women would be caregivers in the structure of a two-parent family, as well as by the belief that poor women needed to be taught to be good caregivers. Members of the Job Corps Task Force asserted that young women who grew up in poor, fatherless families had a "distorted 'image of the husband-wife relationship'" and could be taught how to interact properly with men through various coeducational activities such as dances, skating parties, and picnics.[47] In essence, they had to be taught to want a marriage, to desire the "undistorted" complementarity paradigm. Head Start also incorporated the notion that women had to be taught how to be good mothers. A child development program for preschoolers, Head Start was not day care; rather, it was generally only a half-day program, and it required parental involvement. Mothers, for they were the parent who usually participated, were taught how to budget, cook, and discipline their children in an appropriate manner, and this instruction in the art of caregiving was deemed necessary for the eventual success of their children.

■ The Individuality Paradigm Emerges: The 1960s and the Work Incentive Program

Despite continued reliance on complementarity in the War on Poverty, the male breadwinner–female caregiver model was vulnerable to challenge as a normative guide to social policy. Social workers were supposed to have gotten families off the rolls by offering them services, and the War on Poverty was supposed to have prevented the need for public aid in the first place. Yet caseloads continued to increase, as more and more families began to receive the aid for which they were eligible. To various legislators, the policies grounded in the complementarity paradigm appeared remarkably unsuccessful.

Although these policies had not necessarily resulted in outcomes the legislators desired, what to do remained perplexing. Some of their proposals held fast to the complementarity paradigm but emphasized an explicit return to the deserving caregiver of the 1930s. Others represented fledgling elements of the individuality paradigm, with an emphasis on work as a route toward independence and autonomy. In 1967 Congress adopted a work-training program for women receiving AFDC, the first of many subsequent policies that would diminish the feminale portions of complementarity. Although rhetoric about the need for this program was based on corporative individuality, many aspects of the program design as well as its implementation were aligned with civic individuality. However, the program was never implemented fully, and at the end of the 1960s, welfare policies were still consistent with the complementarity paradigm.

The opportunity for these changes arose because the Johnson administration proposed a series of revisions in the Social Security Act. The majority of its proposals focused on reducing poverty among the elderly, yet the president also recommended requiring states to increase their public assistance payments and offering federal funds to encourage them to provide voluntary job training programs. Congress, however, rebuffed this attempt to force states to be more generous with their welfare programs and instead, because of anger, frustration, and racial hostility, searched for policies that would move families off the welfare rolls.

One policy, a freeze on federal aid for children born out of wedlock, was consistent with the complementarity paradigm's emphasis on the deserving caregiver but turned away from the idea that never-married mothers could be rehabilitated through social services. The freeze stressed the idea that never-married mothers were not—and could not become—deserving. Racial animosity was critical here, for it was used to present never-married mothers as black and therefore undeserving. For example, Senator Russell Long ranted about "broodmares," derogatorily referring to black women who had protested at a congressional hearing.[48] Representative Paul Fino (R-NY) complained about giving aid to "the so-called poor who hop out of Cadillacs to loot and pillage" and to the "teenage punks who drive up to poverty offices in purple convertibles."[49] Granting aid to never-married mothers and their children and then trying to reform them did not work; rather, they should be denied aid. A technically easy way to do so was to refuse additional federal funds for aid to these families. Congress adopted this freeze in 1967, but it was never implemented. After states protested, it was first postponed and then repealed in 1969.[50]

A second policy approach started to break from complementarity and instead align with the individuality paradigm because it emphasized work rather than marital status as a mechanism to bestow worthiness. In 1967 Congress also adopted the Work Incentive Program (its acronym was WIN, not WIP), with the professed goal of moving each individual into the labor force in order to become self-sufficient. States were supposed to ensure that each adult in the family would receive employment counseling, testing, and job training. Congress expected WIN to be mandatory, but Congress also specified that states would refer each adult to WIN where it was "appropriate," and in reality this meant that states regularly exempted women with children from WIN requirements.[51] As implemented by the states, then, WIN was mostly voluntary, relied more on incentives than requirements to work, and targeted men more than women. Once the contours of the program became evident, Congress did little to change it.[52] Because women with children under six and wives in a family where the man was registered for WIN continued to be exempt from the requirements, as many as 75 percent of women receiving AFDC were excused from participating in WIN. Moreover, funding was insufficient to cover the participation of all who were required to participate.

WIN rested on the presumed need to require welfare recipients to work. Its mandatory requirements and sanctions were consistent with corporative individuality's emphasis on forcing people to be free. According to this view, single mothers needed to work to be worthy; they needed to do something useful, and even low-wage, unskilled work was useful. Defending himself in a televised broadcast, Senator Long explained that "we don't intend to help those who refuse to help themselves," and women receiving welfare "could be picking up litter in front of their homes" rather than protesting against Congress.[53] To rationalize the conclusion that women receiving welfare were not worthy if they did not labor, members of Congress frequently relied on rhetoric disparaging the mothering done by women on welfare. For example, Representative Martha Griffiths (D-MI) presented hypothetical cases in which the mothers, because of their age, marital status, and intelligence, apparently had no value as caregivers: "Do you really feel that it is a good idea for a woman with a 400-word vocabulary to remain at home with 13 illegitimate children, or to have a little 14-year-old girl saddled with an illegitimate child never to have the opportunity to be trained, never to have the opportunity to get out of that house, and never have day care for that child?" "How silly," she concluded.[54] Such women needed training and work, and their children needed to be cared for by others. Through racial prejudice and stereotypes, poor mothers were portrayed as black, and they did not fit the ideal of a good mother. Their maternal caregiving was not valued and did not justify their receipt of public assistance.

Despite this racial animosity, the punitive policies passed by Congress did not survive. Rather, the major policy change that endured this period of change and lasted until the 1980s was one that rested on incentives and choice rather than requirements and force. As part of WIN, Congress adopted a measure to entice women into the workforce through economic incentives. Concordant with civic individuality and the possibility of making work pay for caregiving mothers, this work incentive provision, officially known as an earnings disregard, was commonly called the "thirty plus one-third" rule. When ADC was adopted in 1935, if women engaged in paid labor, their grants were reduced by the amount they earned. Because women who earned $1 through work lost $1 in their grant, they had no economic reason to work unless they could earn more than the grant itself.[55] The thirty plus one-third rule was designed to counteract this work disincentive by allowing women who earned money through employment to retain a portion of their grant and thus combine work and welfare. In addition, expenses incurred because of work, such as transportation costs, could be deducted from income when determining the size of the grant a family would receive. With these changes, women on welfare could increase their income by working. If adequate employment were available, the incentives offered a chance for women to take charge of their own lives rather than being subject to the stern hand of welfare intrusion and sanctions.

The principle behind the thirty plus one-third rule is important for two key reasons. First, consistent with the belief in the separate spheres of the male breadwinner and the female caregiver, public assistance programs were grounded on the idea that there should be a clear-cut distinction between those who were expected to work (and they would receive no aid), and those who were not expected to work (they could receive aid). The thirty plus one-third rule was based on the contrary notion that work and welfare could be combined and that paid work did not always yield enough earnings to climb out of poverty. Second, and more important, the use of a work incentive rather than a requirement allowed women to decide for themselves when they should work and how much they should work. The principle implied they could make these decisions based on what was best for them and their families, rather than being forced to comply with what others—husbands, fathers, or the government—deemed to be their best option. For the first time, women receiving welfare were assumed to possess adult autonomy.

This emphasis on work as a route to autonomy corresponded with ideas fomenting in the nascent women's movement. Through the Kennedy Commission on the Status of Women, the two branches of the women's movement tenuously reunited. The "conservative" social feminism branch that collaborated with the Women's Bureau in the Department of Labor pursued good working conditions for women and services for mothers to care for their children. It came together with the "liberal" Alice Paul equality branch that focused on equal rights. Both recognized that women could gain autonomy through work. Both also knew that Betty Friedan's book, *The Feminine Mystique,* was helping to shake white mothers into questioning why they were supposed to be happy with being at home and articulating the concept of sexism, "the problem that had no name." In times of highly sex-segregated job structures with legitimized pay differentials based on sex, no way for a woman to get credit on her own, difficult divorce laws, few contraceptives, and little protection for women and children from domestic violence, any means to grant women more autonomy was welcomed. For unmarried women, especially unmarried women with children, or mothers in a dysfunctional marriage, work offered freedom from private patriarchy and a public sphere system that made independence for women difficult. One of the few means to gain autonomy was work.

The budding women's movement forced the government to start paying more attention to women, and the mostly well-connected white women of state commissions on women that came together under presidential auspices fostered a national agenda that supported both women's work and more governmental services.[56] With calls by some women that careers should be encouraged and opened, it was not difficult for members of Congress to exhort poor women to work and to criticize those who did not. Still, these ideas were new. The majority of married women with children did not work outside the home.[57]

Despite the chaos of frequent policy changes, the array of different kinds of policy solutions, and the numerous opposing forces and political conflict, welfare policies were still consistent with the complementarity paradigm by the end of the 1960s. Public assistance for able-bodied men was still abhorred. The AFDC-UP program did not operate in about half the states and had restrictive rules that kept the program small. Legislators were starting to discuss requiring paid employment by women, yet the policies as implemented emphasized transforming them into consummate mothers and wives. Public aid to women still rested on the fulfillment of the caregiver role. What had changed was that black and never-married mothers could now receive aid under this rubric. The National Welfare Rights Organization organized and mobilized poor women, and they demanded benefits that they were legally entitled to receive. A number of Supreme Court cases eliminated practices such as the substitute father rule and residence requirements that had prevented poor families from receiving aid for which they were eligible. Families who had long been eligible for aid began to receive it. However, political support for extending deserving status to never-married and black women was weak, leaving open the possibilities for further challenges to the complementarity paradigm.

■ A Guaranteed Annual Income and the Potential for Egality

Somewhat surprisingly, President Richard M. Nixon introduced a proposal for a guaranteed annual income for parents and children in 1969.

The Family Assistance Plan (FAP) would have replaced AFDC with a federal program providing a minimum grant to single-parent and two-parent families. FAP did not extend benefits to childless adults; if poor, they were to fall back on the meager general assistance programs run entirely by the states. Despite this exclusion, FAP would have been a considerable expansion of public assistance because it offered aid to two-parent families, including families with a working father, as well as a federal minimum grant. Because FAP challenged assumptions about the male breadwinner role embedded in the complementarity paradigm, it was consistent with some tenets of the egality paradigm. Yet FAP was only grudgingly egalitarian. Its low benefits and work requirements were supposed to appease conservatives, but they instead undermined its promotion of egality. FAP was defeated when conservative Republicans, who were unhappy with the extension of aid to able-bodied men, joined with liberal Democrats, who were disconcerted by the low benefits and work requirements they felt would undermine female caregiving, to oppose the proposal.

In explaining the need for FAP, Nixon declared that welfare was a "quagmire" with rising costs, increasing caseloads, unjustifiable disparities in state benefits, and perverse incentives that discouraged both marriage and work. FAP, he argued, could provide for the poor and still facilitate marriage and employment. The minimum grant to all families with children would mean that poor men would not have to desert their families so they could get aid. The work incentive would make employment worthwhile for the majority of recipients, who would work voluntarily. For those few who could work but did not want to, the work requirement would ensure that they would not be able to shirk their responsibility to be productive members of society.[58]

By including two-parent families with children in public assistance, FAP would have granted aid to fathers who were unemployed, as well as to fathers who worked but had low wages. It continued the possibilities inherent in the thirty plus one-third rule that mothers could choose to work. It also, hypothetically at least, would have allowed fathers to stay with children and mothers to be employed. Consistent with egality, it directly challenged the underpinnings of masculinity's idealized male breadwinner—that any form of aid would reduce the work ethic, threaten the breadwinner role itself, and then damage the two-parent family.

Conservative critics who embraced the complementarity paradigm argued that the plan was destined to result in these dire consequences. Granting aid would destroy rather than maintain two-parent families, they argued, and they delighted in coming up with convoluted scenarios in which families expended considerable initiative and energy to maximize their welfare benefits but not their household income because adults did not want to work. These critics argued that the poor would have numerous children but not support them, they would form multiple households in order to get multiple welfare benefits, they would make laborious calculations about various schemes to increase their aid, but they would not use the work incentive of FAP to combine work and welfare. Even if men wanted to work, conservatives claimed, welfare would undermine their work ethic and breadwinner role because it would diminish their initiative and the respect they garnered from their children. Moreover, this subversion of the work ethic would spill over to other men who were not collecting any aid and threaten the wage system of the nation. Much rested upon their views of complementarity and what was needed to maintain it.

Liberals were not entirely pleased with Nixon's proposal either, despite the fact it had egalitarian potential. They championed the work incentives but disliked the work requirements Nixon had included to appease conservatives. In their perspective, men were not lazy, conniving, or selfish but benevolent figures who left their families so that they would be eligible for AFDC. FAP would allow them to stay with their families, and a work incentive would enable them to combine work and welfare in order to increase their household income. Thus, they argued that work incentives would sustain two-parent families rather than damage them. In addition, they denounced work requirements, arguing that they could not meet the complementarity paradigm's aim of promoting male breadwinning. Work requirements, they claimed, would upset the breadwinner role, because they could force men to take lousy jobs with low wages. To guard against such a result, liberals supported provisions to ensure that adults were not compelled to work without labor protection, such as stipulations that jobs pay at least the minimum wage.[59]

Somewhat different fault lines erupted in debates over women's caregiving responsibilities and employment obligations. Even though most mothers were exempt from the work requirement in Nixon's proposal, it incited criticism from liberals who relied on arguments from the egality and complementarity paradigms and conservatives who used arguments of corporative individuality. The plan excused from the work requirement mothers with preschool children and mothers in two-parent families in which the father worked. If child care were not available, women with older children could not be directed to participate in the work program, and Nixon's proposal offered little money for child care. These arrangements satisfied neither conservatives nor liberals. Conservative critics, relying on corporative individuality, grumbled that the requirement was feeble and that government needed to exert more power to force people to work, including mothers. Senator Long, for example, complained that he would not be able to find anyone to iron his shirts.

They also derided the complementarity paradigm's emphasis on maternal care of children. Further assaulting the feminale role of caregiving, Representative Joel Broyhill (R-VA) declared that it did "not require a genius to take care of a child" by referring to a study that retarded children raised by retarded women ended up as productive workers.[60] These derogatory remarks, as well as references to low-wage, low-skill work, incensed liberal advocates for the poor, who delivered both egality and complementarity responses. Representatives of the National Welfare Rights Organization advanced egality. They announced that poor people wanted well-paying jobs and had no intention of doing anybody else's laundry and cleaning, including Senator Long's.[61] Liberal critics wanted to exempt all mothers of dependent children from any work requirement, and they invoked the desirability of maternal care to justify this position. For example, Representative William F. Ryan (R-NY) argued that the work requirement for mothers of school-age children was "philosophically objectionable." "No mother should be required to substitute day care custodians for her care and love," he asserted.[62] Not completely comfortable with the complementarity paradigm even as they invoked the need for maternal care, liberals did not want to return to the days when paid employment was discouraged; rather, they preferred to rely on incentives so that those who wanted to work would find it worth their while economically, but no mother would be coerced into paid employment. Their approach bolstered the egality paradigm by promoting fluidity in caregiving and breadwinning roles and a chance for each adult to choose the best option.[63]

Supporters of Nixon's proposal were in the awkward position of arguing that FAP was an adequate compromise, an arrangement that promoted the best tenets of the egality, complementarity, and individuality paradigms. The annual benefits were low, but they provided a national floor under benefits for poor parents that was missing entirely from AFDC, and although benefits were higher than public assistance benefits in only eight states, these were southern states with a history of low benefits. All women could work, but women with young children would be able to devote time to their care, and women with older children could be expected to work. The work incentives would facilitate employment among those who wanted to maximize their income, and the work requirements would serve as a backup plan to catch any laggards. The Senate refused to pass FAP, however, and the attempt to put together a middle position failed. Congress did, though, manage to adopt a similar program called Supplemental Security Income (SSI) for the elderly and disabled poor.

In the late 1970s, the debate over President Jimmy Carter's minimum income proposal was a wearier one, but it was otherwise little different and similarly blended elements of the egality, complementarity, and individuality paradigms. Carter emphasized the same goals as Nixon when he introduced his proposal, with the addition of job creation so that adults could fulfill their work requirements. Through a complicated system of work requirements and different benefit levels, Carter hoped to alleviate the concerns about indolence that plagued FAP.[64] Women's work requirements depended upon the age of their youngest child, but men were expected to work, irrespective of their children's ages.[65] Despite Carter's efforts to come up with a compromise to resolve the dispute over work incentives and work requirements, his proposal did not even receive a complete consideration by Congress.

With the defeat of both Nixon's and Carter's guaranteed annual income proposals and the adoption of SSI, AFDC was separated from the other public assistance programs it had been joined with in 1935. Provisions of SSI resulted in aid to the poor elderly and disabled that was more generous and more stable over time than the aid provided to poor families with children. Although most states had more generous benefits than those proposed in Nixon's FAP, that generosity was not maintained over time. From 1972 to 1991, real benefits under AFDC declined by 41 percent.[66]

The debates in the 1970s defeated both presidents' proposals, but they did not resolve controversies about male breadwinner and female caregiver roles. The structure of AFDC was still consistent with ideas about complementary gender roles that had dominated during its inception, even though there was much less consensus about the value of those ideas. States could extend aid to families with a male breadwinner, but because of state policy choices, AFDC-UP remained a small program, and certainly men were never considered seriously as caregivers. In principle, Congress had endorsed work requirements for single mothers receiving AFDC, but in practice the requirements were not stringent, the WIN program was poorly funded, and only a small percentage of women ever enrolled in it.[67] The work incentive provided through the thirty plus one-third rule began to break down the dichotomy between welfare and work, but Congress hesitated to continue in this direction, with many legislators loath to grant public assistance to adults able to work, particularly men, and others uncertain that incentives would be sufficient to induce work. Even though the complementarity paradigm was cracking considerably, no alternative had garnered enough political support to replace it.

■ From Citizen Mother to Citizen Worker: The 1980s Onward

With the resurgence of conservatism in the 1980s, social policy debates were framed even more than in earlier years around the problem of dependency. No longer an unfortunate consequence of public assistance or a "natural" condition for wives in marriage, dependency was defined as the central problem to be ameliorated. The complementarity paradigm was crucial to this analysis, not because it guided the desired policy solutions, but because it provided a framework for conservatives to argue that welfare was the cause of the problem. Reinvigorating their attacks on welfare, conservatives argued that AFDC caused poverty because it seduced women into having children out of wedlock, enticed fathers to forgo marriage and abandon their children, and corrupted the work ethic of all who received it.[68] AFDC was complementarity gone wrong—it facilitated female caregiving outside the structure of marriage and debilitated male breadwinning.

In this perspective, gendered clichés of women who had children in order to get cash assistance and men too irresponsible to work and marry were reinforced by racial stereotypes. The poor were portrayed as urban blacks caught in a ghetto culture sustained, if not created, by welfare.[69] Despite empirical evidence to the contrary, conservatives weakened public support for social programs serving low-income Americans by portraying them as programs that benefited undeserving, reckless blacks at a high cost to white taxpayers.[70] Although race shaped this critique of welfare, conservatives did not apply it only to blacks. They argued that people made rational choices using an economic calculus, and whites and blacks would respond to the choices offered by AFDC in the same manner. Indeed, they held up family life among poor, urban blacks as a harbinger of things to come in the white community if changes were not made soon.[71]

Although ideas of complementarity were important in framing the problem as one of welfare causing poverty, in the early 1980s the complementarity paradigm was not central to policy solutions. For solutions, conservatives instead turned to the paradigm of individuality. Its emphasis on autonomy and self-sufficiency was a compelling counterpoint to dependency and provided a firm ground from which liberal ideas about government social programs could be repelled. It allowed conservatives to claim that they had accommodated their ideas to the tenets of the modern women's movement and the increased number of mothers in the labor market. As a result of the women's movement and changing economic conditions, it was now common for mothers to work, even married white women with small children.[72] If these women worked, conservatives argued, so could poor women. Women on welfare did not *need* government support to be caregivers. They could be their own breadwinners and hence were not deemed by the Reagan administration to be the "truly needy," defined by two White House aides as "unfortunate persons who, through no fault of their own, have nothing but public funds to turn to."[73] The Reagan administration was not willing to grant deserving status to unmarried mothers, especially because doing so would at least tacitly endorse female caregiving outside the confines of marriage. Women in mother-only families were considered responsible for their own poverty—they had not married, they had a child out of wedlock, or they had not sustained a marriage—and they should be expected to work, to do their own breadwinning. *They could be masculine mothers.*

By paring recipients down to the "truly needy," the administration suggested a variety of policies intended to straighten out what it perceived as shortcomings in the safety net.[74] In 1981 Congress approved the administration's proposal to eliminate AFDC for the working poor. The thirty and one-third rule, adopted in 1967, was limited to the first four months of employment—after that time, $1 was deducted from the grant for every $1 earned through employment—and a ceiling was placed on work-related expenses that could be deducted from income when determining the level of a grant.[75] With this change, the administration returned to a clear-cut distinction between welfare and work. Families in which an adult worked were supposed to be independent and not use cash assistance to supplement their earnings.

Even though the Reagan administration promoted the use of incentives to encourage work and savings in other policy areas, it backed regulations to require work among welfare recipients. Consistent with corporative individuality, the Reagan administration wanted to order states to operate workfare programs that required adults receiving welfare to work off their grants in public service jobs. Congress rejected this mandatory approach, however, and instead encouraged states to experiment with job programs, allowing but not requiring them to implement workfare, work supplementation, and demonstration programs under WIN that emphasized education and training. States put together an array of programs incorporating elements of both civic and corporative individuality. Some states had modest workfare programs—by 1983, twenty-two states had community work experience programs, yet only six states operated them statewide.[76] Others adopted more ambitious work programs with an emphasis on education, training, and support services, such as child care and transportation.

In some respects, what the Reagan administration wanted to do was nothing new. Arguing that the poor were indolent and should be made to work was not an innovation in conservative thought, and principles of corporative individuality had long been applied to men. But several things were different in the way the Reagan administration addressed work. First, it disregarded the feminale caregiving role almost entirely. It was predisposed to expect mothers to work, even mothers with children too young to go to school. Second, it emphasized the idea that the purpose of work was to fulfill an obligation the recipient had to society rather than to increase family income. Women became good citizens through the public sphere activity of work rather than their private activities in the home. Third, it was a conservative administration prepared to exercise government authority to put people to work, not just to expect them to find whatever work the private sector had to offer. This willingness put the government in the position of creating jobs, an exercise of governmental power not usually supported by conservatives.

Although liberals disdained corporative individuality's workfare, their opposition did not displace the critique of welfare based on the complementarity paradigm. Liberals brandished empirical evidence rebutting the assertion that welfare caused poverty, and they argued that they had better ideas than conservatives about ways to help the poor, including income maintenance more firmly rooted in the egality paradigm. Yet they embraced the value of reducing welfare receipt by facilitating work. Their arguments accepted the notion that welfare receipt was equivalent to dependency and that dependency was undesirable. For example, even Senator Ted Kennedy (D-MA), often held up by conservatives as the epitome of liberalism, declared, "the premise is simple. It is better that families have money from work than from welfare."[77] *They too accepted that breadwinning was more valuable than caregiving.* This stance allowed conservatives to maintain the upper hand in controlling the terms of the debate; any proposal to increase benefits or expand welfare eligibility was portrayed as creating dependency.

The Reagan administration never introduced a comprehensive welfare reform proposal—in his 1987 State of the Union address, Ronald Reagan simply called for more state-based demonstration projects[78]—but Democratic committee chairs in the House and the Senate insisted on tackling welfare reform in the 100th Congress. Because of Democratic persistence in negotiations and their willingness to sacrifice egality tenets in order to gain a bipartisan consensus, the Family Support Act combined civic and corporative individuality to create a policy that was supposed to transform AFDC from an income maintenance program with a work element to a jobs program with an income maintenance component. Passed in 1988 with overwhelming support in Congress, the Family Support Act was hailed by Democrats and Republicans alike as the most significant welfare reform since AFDC's inception in 1935. In fact, President Reagan characterized it as "real reform" that would "lead to lasting emancipation from welfare dependency."[79]

Egality was important in early discussions about welfare reform as various people and organizations called for increasing benefits and expanding coverage to include two-parent families. The policy statement issued by the National Governors' Association endorsed a system of income supports to ensure that all families, "including poor two-parent families in which someone work[ed] full time, had incomes as high as the minimum living standard."[80] Moynihan urged a system that would use government assistance to bring families up to a minimum income if child support from noncustodial parents and earnings by custodial parents were not sufficient.[81] Representative Harold Ford (D-TN), then chair of the House Ways and Means Subcommittee whose bill served as the foundation for House action, included in his bill provisions requiring states to increase their benefits until they reached at least 15 percent of each state's median income and to extend benefits to two-parent families in which the primary breadwinner was unemployed.

These calls for benefit expansion were consistent with the egality paradigm blended with complementarity. All the proposals allowed either parent to be breadwinner and tacitly acknowledged the necessity of parental caregiving by focusing on only one working adult. But rhetorically, they were justified primarily by civic individuality, and politically it was very easy to dismiss them. The benefit expansions were grounded in the concept of a social contract between the poor and the government specifying that if the poor engaged in a socially useful activity—that is, paid employment—government would then have an obligation to them, one that could be fulfilled by income maintenance to supplement their earnings so that family income reached a minimum standard. Such an approach would have been a novel change, upsetting the long-held notion that a breadwinner should be economically self-sufficient and receive no public assistance. Yet because only paid employment and not any other activities, such as parental caregiving, would fulfill a citizen's responsibilities, these overtures were not entirely egalitarian; *they recognized only the traditionally masculine activity of work as socially productive behavior that yielded meritorious citizens worthy of government support.*

When discussing such proposals, it was easy for opponents of benefit expansion to ignore egality—after all, masculinity had set the standards for good citizenship, and most egalitarian tenets fell outside dominant masculine expectations. The overtures quickly disappeared, as critics simply resorted to the idea that any public assistance jeopardized breadwinning and created dependency.[82] With the denigration of feminale caregiving, only breadwinning mattered normatively. Conservative animosity toward assistance for two-parent families was so strong and their preference for workfare so ingrained that they insisted on federal control and abandoned their conventional governing ideology of granting autonomy and discretion to states. In fact, at one point in the negotiations, when Democrats considered the possibility of eliminating the requirement that states carry AFDC-UP in order to avoid a mandatory workfare program, the Reagan administration threatened a veto because the bill would not include a workfare obligation. The Reagan administration found itself in the ironic position of insisting on a provision it did not like in order to get mandatory statewide workfare. Eventually, Democrats accepted the workfare provision, and the Family Support Act required primary breadwinners in two-parent families, generally thought to be men, to work for at least sixteen hours a week in exchange for receiving public assistance. Mandatory workfare applied to family men became acceptable; masculine mothers would soon follow.

With the eventual collapse of egality, the final provisions of the Family Support Act were fully grounded in civic and corporative individuality. The concept of a social contract was still used to justify the reform, as the idea that the poor had an obligation to strive for self-sufficiency and "to assume the primary financial responsibility for their children" was endorsed by Democrats and Republicans alike.[83] But the government's duties were not nearly so extensive as recommended in earlier proposals. The social contract lying behind the Family Support Act called for government to offer services that helped people find and keep jobs, not income support to supplement their earnings and raise their income above a minimum level. The primary goal was not reducing poverty but reducing dependency by moving welfare recipients off the rolls and into paid employment.

To achieve this aim, the act required states to establish work, education, and training programs, called the Job Opportunities and Basic Skills Training Program (JOBS). In these programs, states had to include various educational activities, such as remedial education and high school equivalency exams; a number of job preparation activities, including job readiness, job development, skills training, and job placement; and support services, namely, child care and transportation.[84] Once a person left the rolls for paid employment, states also had to provide child care assistance and health coverage through Medicaid for up to one year in order to facilitate the transition to work. This emphasis on education, training, and job preparation rested on the belief that women receiving welfare needed to improve their human capital to get jobs that increased their family income. But it also acknowledged that upward mobility would not come immediately and thus recognized the need to supplement these earnings, albeit for only a short while, by assisting with child care and health care expenses.

Conservatives were not satisfied with this approach because they believed it did not place sufficient emphasis on work. They maintained that welfare recipients would use these programs to avoid actually going to work, instead enrolling in endless education and training programs without ever acquiring a job, and that it was through working that poor women would acquire the habits they needed to keep a job and get off the rolls. In order to appease them, the Family Support Act also required states to incorporate two out of four work activities in their programs. The possibilities were job search; on-the-job training; work supplementation, in which employers received the welfare recipient's grant and used it to subsidize her earnings; and community work experience, commonly called workfare, in which a recipient worked off her grant at the minimum wage.[85] These components were intended to move adults more quickly into the workforce and relied on work experience to increase earnings rather than education and training.

Although conservatives and liberals clashed over what kind of activities the states needed to develop in order to get women off the rolls and into paid employment, they did not disagree over the objective. Work was the goal, and work was defined as paid employment.[86] Moynihan explained that he wanted to transform AFDC into a "program that will bring a generation of young American women back into the mainstream of American life. And they are out of it now."[87] Mothering was not work; rather, it was an obstacle to entering the American mainstream that could be removed through work and support services such as child care. Moreover, women wanted to work, they argued. Women who did not wish to engage in paid employment were not mothers who believed it was more important to spend more direct time with their children. Rather, they were insecure about their ability to compete in the labor market or confused about the gains they could achieve through work and thus unable to make respectable choices about paid employment. Ironically, because this approach turned activities done by mothers into paid employment, it commodified caregiving. Caregiving shifted from mothers taking care of their children in their home to jobs done by people in exchange for wages.

Because work came to be considered the only desirable option a woman receiving welfare should select, it was not difficult for members of Congress to agree on work requirements rather than work incentives to induce participation in the JOBS program. There was little discussion about relying only on work incentives, and Democrats certainly did not insist on work incentives as an alternative to requirements. Work incentives were appropriate when there was more than one socially desirable option and individuals were granted the authority to select the alternative that was best for them and their families. As long as work was designated the only desirable outcome, there was little reason to grant individuals choice. The paradigm of individuality might recognize individual autonomy and choice, but individuals whose autonomy was undermined by their receipt of public assistance could not be trusted with choice. Women receiving welfare again lost the autonomy to choose.

The Family Support Act made a significant change in participation requirements because it included women whose children were too young to go to school, long considered the primary group of children who most needed maternal care. It included mothers with preschool-age children and allowed states to require mothers with toddlers to enroll in work programs. Despite this important shift, though, the Family Support Act still included several caveats on participation requirements for mothers of young children, limitations that recognized at least some of the demands of caring for children.[88] This approach granted some value to feminale caregiving, but it was an approach adopted out of fiscal pragmatism—child care for infants and toddlers is especially expensive—more than respect for mothering.

Although earlier work requirements had not been extended to mothers whose children were not old enough to attend school, there was relatively little debate about when mothers should be expected to work. Opposition to including mothers with preschool-age children was minimal, and what discussion there was focused on whether the age should be lowered. House Republicans wanted the minimum age to be six months, and a compromise bill sponsored by conservative Democrats had a minimum age of two. A potential challenge to this consensus occurred when the House Education and Labor Committee, which along with the Ways and Means and Commerce Committees reported out the bill, included a provision that states had to provide child care for youngsters up to the age of fifteen in order for mothers to be required to participate in JOBS. Although this condition was grounded in a defense of maternal caregiving, it received little serious debate and was quickly shot down. The paradigm of individuality that underlay the social contract expected women receiving welfare to fulfill their parental responsibilities for their children by engaging in paid employment. The masculine breadwinner role superseded the maternal caregiving role.

The notion of parental responsibility was also extended to noncustodial parents, who were understood to have a financial obligation to their children as well as to taxpayers in those instances when children received public assistance. Thus, the act contained several provisions that tightened child support enforcement, including automatic withholding of child support from the noncustodial parent's paycheck and greater efforts to establish paternity for children born out of wedlock. Increased diligence in child support enforcement was remarkably consensual. In fact, Senator Moynihan referred to child support enforcement as "the little engine that could" because it pulled along the other elements of the Family Support Act.[89] Men had long been understood as breadwinners who should provide financially for their children; expecting noncustodial fathers to fulfill this obligation challenged few of the gender precepts held by legislators, and the provisions were supported by liberals and conservatives and

Democrats and Republicans. In essence, complementarity remained for men, even though it was significantly diluted for women.

Given the widespread bipartisan support for the Family Support Act and proclamations about the significance of its changes, it might appear surprising that only a few years after its adoption, politicians began agitating for reform of welfare. In his 1992 State of the Union address, President George H. W. Bush, who had said little about welfare in previous years, called on state governments to experiment with policies that would require certain behaviors of recipients in exchange for aid.[90] Vice President Dan Quayle and Representative Newt Gingrich (R-GA) lambasted the "failed welfare state," identifying it as the major cause of a host of social problems. Nor was this agitation common only to Republicans—Bill Clinton, running for the Democratic nomination in 1992, found a catchy phrase that captured public anxiety about social problems and promised to solve them in some, albeit unspecified, way when he vowed to "end welfare as we know it."

Support for the Family Support Act was wide, but not deep, and the consensus between proponents of civic and corporative individuality fell apart quickly. After early enthusiasm, the act quickly encountered implementation problems during the recession of the early 1990s.[91] Caseloads increased as the recession hit, putting even more burdens on the states. The promise of the Family Support Act, that welfare dependency would be reduced as recipients found jobs and got off the rolls, went unfulfilled.

Of course, politicians could have defended rather than attacked the Family Support Act, explaining that its approach would take time, not only because the act itself expected states to implement the JOBS program incrementally, but also because it relied on providing education and training to welfare recipients so they could obtain better jobs. Moreover, a healthy economy that produced these good jobs mattered, too. Using investments in human capital to enable women to acquire better-paying jobs is a lengthy process, and legislators could have argued that during a recession this process would slow down considerably. A few took this position; for example, Senator Moynihan introduced legislation calling for full funding of the JOBS program. But it was much more enticing to attack the combination of civic and corporative individuality that had bolstered the act. Criticisms came primarily from two directions. First, proponents of corporative individuality argued that the act leaned too far toward civic individuality because it offered too many opportunities without demanding reciprocal obligations. Second, a group of Republicans turned to the complementarity paradigm, not just to critique welfare, as they had done in the early 1980s, but also to seek ways to bolster marriage and deter out-of-wedlock births as a primary solution to poverty.

■ Personal Responsibility and Masculine Mothers

The collapse of the merger of the civic and corporative versions of the individuality paradigm that had buttressed the Family Support Act meant that a new amalgam had to be constructed in order to adopt any welfare reform. Although the individuality and the complementarity paradigms were the more likely candidates for anchoring some kind of reform, the egality paradigm had not disappeared entirely and still could serve as a basis for criticism of other plans. Behind the apparent partisan clash between Democrats and Republicans was considerable divisiveness within each party, as advocates quarreled over various interpretations of the paradigms and the best policies to advance them.

President Bill Clinton started the bidding with a plan that had stronger corporative individuality aspects than previous Democratic proposals because it required those receiving welfare for more than two years to work, at jobs created by the government if they could not find jobs in the private sector. Yet Clinton still retained an emphasis on civic individuality by proposing policies that would make work pay and including support services such as child care, an increase in the earned income tax credit, an increase in the minimum wage, and of course, national health insurance.[92] With its tough corporative measures joined to civic individuality, this proposal drew support from the gender-ideological strands of intersectors, similarism, and universalism. In other words, policymakers who approved of the autonomous individual but saw a need for selective state intervention informed the paradigmatic approach supported by the administration.

Despite the two-year time limit, Republicans were not impressed, and they complained that the plan did not have sufficiently strict work requirements; exempted too many people, including mothers with children under age one; and cost more rather than less money. Senate Minority Leader Bob Dole (R-KA) retorted that the plan would only mean "the end of welfare reform as we know it";[93] Senator Duncan "Lauch" Faircloth (R-NC) and Representative James Talent (R-MO) countered with a bill dubbed the "Real Welfare Reform Act of 1994."[94] By the fall of 1994, the Republicans had put together their own welfare reform proposal, and it became a central element in the Contract with America. Vowing to "reduce illegitimacy, require work, and save taxpayers money," this proposal was a compromise between the corporative individuality and the complementarity paradigms.[95] It included the same two-year work requirement that was the centerpiece of Clinton's proposal, but followed it with a five-year lifetime limit on benefits, not a guaranteed government job.

The elements of this proposal consistent with the corporative individuality paradigm appealed to proponents of universalist and perhaps traditionalist thought. To appeal to patriarchalist ideology, the Republican proposal also focused on family formation, including provisions that would have required states to deny aid to unwed teen mothers, reduce the aid provided to children for whom paternity was not established, and adopt family caps—a policy that refused aid to children born to women already receiving welfare. These proposals were important substantively, for unlike the corporative individuality paradigm, they directly targeted the formation of mother-only families and questioned the ability of women to raise children without a husband. The proposals were also important politically, for by advancing a conservative version of complementarity, they kept alive an approach that could split apart support that might coalesce around the individuality paradigm. Corporative individuality did not have to merge with civic individuality in order to provide a basis for welfare reform; rather, the complementarity paradigm could join with corporativism, yielding a potentially powerful set of policy proposals.

The subsequent political battle was contentious, intense, and long, and just about every aspect of the Republican proposal was disputed. But the idea that women/mothers should work was not contested, and when President Clinton signed the bill into law on August 22, 1996, the central elements of the initial Republican proposal served as the framework for the law. Work requirements, a five-year lifetime limit on the receipt of aid, and the end of the entitlement status for public assistance are the crucial elements of the PRWORA. These provisions ensure that welfare can only be temporary assistance, that work and not caregiving are the activities recognized as meritorious by public assistance, and that no woman is entitled to demand aid for her and her children based on her status as a mother. In short, these provisions create masculine mothers.

◾ Conclusion

Throughout the lifetime of AFDC, the complementarity paradigm was a powerful set of ideas that guided welfare policy. Despite considerable dissatisfaction with granting aid to never-married and black mothers, women continued to receive public assistance because they were mothers who cared for children, until the passage of PRWORA in 1996. Elements of the individuality paradigm began to appear as early as the mid-1960s, but it was not until the 1980s and, more specifically, the adoption of the Family Support Act in 1988, that the individuality paradigm rivaled complementarity as the framework for welfare policy. With its emergence, more emphasis was placed on expecting women to work and granting them aid on the condition that they took on the breadwinning role.

With the adoption of the Family Support Act, the individuality paradigm became an influential set of ideas in welfare policy, but disputes about gender paradigms were not resolved, and debate over welfare did not end. The union of the civic and corporative versions of the individuality paradigm was unstable and could not sustain sufficient political support through the implementation of the Family Support Act. Questions remained about which version of the individuality paradigm should prevail and how adherents of the various strands of gender ideology would unite and divide. Bill Clinton's pledge to end welfare as we know it invited proponents of gender universalism to work with adherents of intersector and similarist thought to fashion a plan steeped in the individuality paradigm. But the Republican takeover of Congress in 1994 gave an institutional voice to patriarchalist rhetoric and opened the door for a major confrontation over gender paradigms and welfare policy. That confrontation played out in adoption of the Personal Responsibility and Work Opportunity Reconciliation Act.

▦ Notes

1. Representative William Sirovich, 74th Cong., 1st sess., *Congressional Record* 79 (April 16, 1935): 5786.
2. "Clinton Says Welfare Bill Is 'Real Step Forward,'" transcript of President Clinton's July 31 news conference announcing that he would sign the welfare reform bill. Reprinted in *Congressional Quarterly Almanac 1996* (Washington, DC: CQ Press, 1996), D17–D19.
3. Easton, *A Systems Analysis of Political Life;* and Lasswell, *Politics.*
4. For a more general discussion of how issues come to be defined as social problems, solutions are generated, and proposals find a place on the political agenda, see Stone, *Policy Paradox;* and Schon and Rein, *Frame Reflection.*
5. Because gender paradigms and ideologies are social and cultural constructions, it is possible to define some human females as not fitting feminine or feminale qualities, despite the fact they are biological females. Considerable writing by women of color, especially African American women, take up this theme, much as Sojourner Truth did in her speech, "Ain't I a Woman?" We deal with this subject more in the next chapter.
6. When Congress adopted the Social Security Act, the public assistance titles, which included Aid to the Blind and Old Age Assistance as well as ADC, were not controversial. The public assistance programs preserved the federal-state relationship and allowed considerable state responsibility and discretion. Thus, although members of Congress declared their support for ADC, they did not debate it in depth. The majority of the floor debate in both the House and the Senate centered on two very controversial programs in the act—old-age insurance and unemployment insurance. For a discussion of the history of the Social Security Act, including the design and adoption of ADC, see Lieberman, *Shifting the Color Line;* and Mettler, *Dividing Citizens.*
7. Jean Bethke Elshtain first introduced a critique of this position in *Public Man, Private Woman.*
8. Like ADC, when these programs were first adopted, they were not generous in their provision of benefits, and they were also "race-laden." For a discussion of

program design, institutional arrangements, and changes over time, see Lieberman, *Shifting the Color Line.*

9. Kessler-Harris, *Out to Work,* 254–255.

10. As we discuss below, this way of defining "good mothers" clearly was aimed at white women and has had lasting implications for women of color who, when ADC was initially adopted, were expected to work in most states. See Roberts, "Welfare's Ban on Poor Motherhood."

11. Representative Stephen Young (D-OH), 74th Cong., 1st sess., *Congressional Record* 79 (April 13, 1935): 5594.

12. Representative Arthur Greenwood (D-IN), 74th Cong., 1st sess., *Congressional Record* 79 (April 11, 1935): 5455–5456.

13. For a history of the precedents and early years of ADC, see Gordon, *Pitied But Not Entitled;* Skocpol, *Protecting Soldiers and Mothers;* Mink, *The Wages of Motherhood;* Abramovitz, *Regulating the Lives of Women;* and Frankel and Dye, *Gender, Class, Race, and Reform in the Progressive Era.*

14. The widow's connection to a male breadwinner in establishing her claim to public support was indeed important as it justified the subsequent inclusion of widows in Social Security and determined the amount of assistance they received. Under Social Security, widows' benefits were determined by their husbands' earnings, and women who had been married to more successful breadwinners received higher benefits. Finally, because white women were more likely to be widows and because Social Security covered few black workers, granting aid to widows facilitated the denial of aid to black women, both under ADC and through Social Security. For a discussion of the extension of Social Security to widows, see Kessler-Harris, "Designing Women and Old Fools," 87–106.

15. During the 1940s and 1950s, the federal agencies responsible for ADC pushed for the expansion of the program and for more objective standards of eligibility. Both the Bureau of Public Assistance and the Social Security Board viewed ADC as a program to reduce destitution rather than to reward the worthy. Thus, in the eyes of the federal administrators, family structure and birth status of children were irrelevant in determining eligibility. In 1943 the Social Security Board recommended to Congress that it provide aid to all children, irrespective of their family status or the employment of their parents. Federal Security Agency, Social Security Board, "A Basic Minimum Program of Social Security," Excerpts from the Eighth Annual Report of the Social Security Board for the Fiscal Year 1942/43, reprinted in *Social Security Bulletin,* January 1944 (Washington, DC), 3–12.

16. A summary of the changes in federal funding adopted in several legislative enactments can be found in *Congress and the Nation, 1945–1964* (Washington, DC: Congressional Quarterly Service 1965), 1280–1283. When ADC was first adopted, federal funding for a family was based on the number of children in the family, not the total number of persons in the family. In historical research this exclusion is often noted but not explained. Patterson emphasizes hurry and "simple negligence" (Patterson, *America's Struggle Against Poverty,* 70). In the 1940s and 1950s Congress moved to make federal funding for ADC more generous, and as part of these changes added funding for the adult caretaker in 1950 with little discussion.

17. Patterson, *America's Struggle Against Poverty,* 78–96. For a discussion of the ways in which race shaped the structure of ADC and extension of aid to African Americans, see Lieberman, *Shifting the Color Line.*

18. The term *illegitimacy* for children born out of wedlock highlights the capacity of governments to authorize and legitimize some values over others.

Critical for gender, women who were mothers but were not subject to a man through the private patriarchy of marriage were not supported. Said another way, only women who agreed to marry, and hence lose many aspects of legal personhood, could legitimately be mothers.

19. Piven and Cloward, *Regulating the Poor,* 134–135.

20. Ibid., 308; Davis, *Brutal Need,* 62.

21. Bell, *Aid to Dependent Children,* 76–90.

22. Abramovitz, *Regulating the Lives of Women.*

23. Bell, *Aid to Dependent Children,* 94.

24. Ibid.

25. Bell, *Aid to Dependent Children,* 137–138; for a review of the Louisiana state law and the federal government's response, see Bell, "Source Materials," 203–214.

26. "Suffer Little Children," *Nation,* September 24, 1960, 171.

27. Mayor William Ryan quoting Mitchell, as quoted in William B. Rollins and Bernard Lefkowitz, "Welfare à la Newburgh," *Nation,* September 16, 1961, 159.

28. Joseph Mitchell, quoted in William B. Rollins and Bernard Lefkowitz, "Welfare à la Newburgh," *Nation,* September 16, 1961, 159.

29. Joseph Mitchell, "The Revolt in Newburgh," speech delivered before the Economic Club of Detroit, Michigan, November 20, 1961, reprinted in *Vital Speeches of the Day,* January 15, 1962, 214–220.

30. Newburgh was allowed to require that able-bodied men receiving assistance work. In the weeks after the plan was announced, only one such man was discovered, described as a "one-eyed apprentice steelworker who was laid off some months ago, was later a patient in a mental hospital, then lost out on a job because he had to care for his five children while his wife was hospitalized with pneumonia." This man was white and born and raised in Newburgh. Steiner, *Social Insecurity,* 110–112.

31. See the *Congressional Quarterly Almanac,* 1962, 212–218 for an account of the administration's proposals and congressional responses and 883–885 for the text of President Kennedy's message, transmitted to Congress on February 1.

32. "Letter to the President of the Senate and to the Speaker of the House Transmitting Bills Extending Unemployment Benefits and Providing Aid to Needy Children," February 6, 1961, reprinted in *Public Papers of the Presidents of the United States, 1961* (Washington, DC: U.S. Government Printing Office), 56–57.

33. "Special Message to the Congress on Public Welfare Programs," February 1, 1962, reprinted in *Public Papers of the Presidents of the United States, 1962* (Washington, DC: US Government Printing Office), 98–103.

34. Quoted in "New York: The Welfare City," *Time,* July 28, 1961, 17.

35. Representative Harold Gross, 87th Cong., 1st sess., *Congressional Record* 107 (March 10, 1961): 3768.

36. Representative Thomas Curtis (R-MO), 87th Cong., 2nd sess., *Congressional Record* 107 (March 15, 1962): 4271.

37. Representative Wilber Mills, 87th Cong., 2nd sess., *Congressional Record* 107 (March 15, 1962): 4268.

38. "Special Message to the Congress on Public Welfare Programs," February 1, 1962, reprinted in the *Public Papers of the Presidents of the United States 1962* (Washington, DC: US Government Printing Office), 98.

39. "Program for Economic Recovery and Growth," presidential message sent to Congress on February 2, 1961, reprinted in *Congressional Quarterly Almanac,* 1961, 863.

40. For an example of such an argument, see the comments by Senator Hubert Humphrey (D-MN), 87th Cong., 1st sess., *Congressional Record* 107 (August 29, 1961): 17348–17349.

41. Piven and Cloward, *Regulating the Poor;* Davies, *From Opportunity to Entitlement.*

42. Moynihan, "The Negro Family: The Case for National Action," 39–124.

43. Ibid., 51.

44. Ibid., 76.

45. Job Corps Task Force, quoted in Quadagno and Fobes, "The Welfare State and the Cultural Reproduction of Gender," 176.

46. Guidelines for Program Development, quoted in Ibid., 180.

47. Ibid., 180.

48. Senator Russell Long (D-LA), Testimony before the Senate Committee on Finance, *Social Security Amendments of 1967,* 90th Cong., 1st sess., September 20, 1967, 1647.

49. Representative Paul Fino, 90th Cong., 1st sess., *Congressional Record* 113 (August 17, 1967): 23085.

50. Patterson, *America's Struggle Against Poverty,* 174.

51. When debating WIN, the Senate, but not the House, included exemptions for mothers with children. Even Senator Long, who made many offensive remarks about women receiving welfare, accepted such an exemption without question. See the exchange among Senators Kennedy, Curtis, and Long in 90th Cong., 1st sess., *Congressional Record* (November 21, 1967): 33531. The final bill gave discretion to the states. The requirements under WIN were to register for work and to accept a job if one was offered, not to actually work. WIN was never fully funded, and the number of volunteers for the training program always exceeded the available slots. Handler, *Poverty of Welfare Reform,* 58–60.

52. Moynihan claims that Congress never expected the freeze or the strong work requirement to be implemented. See Moynihan, *The Politics of a Guaranteed Income.* In 1971 Congress adopted the Talmadge amendment, setting priorities for participation in WIN. The revision gave precedence first to unemployed fathers and second to women who volunteered, and then delineated precisely the other groups who had to register for the program.

53. Senator Russell Long, 90th Cong., 1st sess., *Congressional Record* 113 (August 17, 1967): 23085.

54. Representative Martha Griffiths, 90th Cong., 1st sess., *Congressional Record* 113 (August 17, 1967): 23081.

55. The health of the economy figures as an important subtext in welfare policy. During the Depression and the initiation of ADC, one goal was to move women out of the workforce so that men could hold the scarce jobs. More recent economic trends have shaped policy at several junctures, including 1996, when labor was needed by a strong economy.

56. Duerst-Lahti, "The Government's Role in Building the Women's Movement."

57. In 1967, the labor force participation rate for married women with children under six was 26.5 percent. Breakdowns by race were not available. The labor force participation rate for mothers, regardless of their marital status, was also not available. See Department of Labor, *Manpower Report of the President, 1970* (Washington, DC: Government Printing Office, 1970), 248.

58. Patterson, *America's Struggle Against Poverty,* 192. The minimum grant was $500 per adult and $300 per child. The work incentive allowed the first $60 earned per month and one-half of subsequent earnings to be disregarded in determining benefits. Nixon provided fairly detailed explanations for FAP in an

August 11 welfare reform message to Congress and an August 8 speech on public welfare. They are reprinted in *Congressional Quarterly Almanac,* 1969, 69–78.

59. Burke and Burke, *Nixon's Good Deed,* 143.

60. Representative Joel Broyhill, 91st Cong., 2nd sess., *Congressional Record* 116 (April 15, 1970): 11890.

61. Burke and Burke, *Nixon's Good Deed,* 162.

62. Representative William Ryan, 91st Cong., 2nd sess., *Congressional Record* 116 (April 16, 1970): 12048.

63. Liberal critics were also annoyed with the low benefits provided under Nixon's proposal and the limited coverage. Benefits were $1,600 for a family of four, at the time lower than the aid offered through AFDC in all but eight states. Childless adults were not included, and, unwittingly playing into conservative ideas that the poor made bad decisions in order to collect welfare, several liberals argued that poor adults would have children just to be eligible for assistance. Extending aid to the childless would prevent these births and make people better off in the long run, they argued. Taken altogether, liberals felt the low benefits, the restricted coverage, and the work requirements constituted a stingy program for the poor.

64. For a complete description of the Carter administration's proposal and the politics that led to its defeat, see Califano, *Governing America,* 320–367.

65. Women with children under seven were not expected to work and would receive higher minimum benefits. Women with children over fourteen were expected to work and would receive lower minimum benefits. But if they worked they would be able to retain a portion of their grant, so their total family income would be higher than the minimum benefits of women with young children. Women with children between seven and fourteen years of age were in an awkward position. They were expected to work, but only part-time while their children were in school.

66. Through SSI, aid to the poor elderly and disabled was nationalized, with federal minimum benefits indexed to inflation and work incentives provided through earnings disregards. AFDC remained jointly run by the state and federal governments, with widespread disparities in benefits across the states, no minimum benefit, and benefits that were not indexed to inflation. Although food stamps were indexed to inflation, the combination of food stamps and AFDC still declined significantly in real terms from the mid-1970s to the early 1990s. For a discussion of federal transfer programs and poverty, see Danziger and Weinberg, "The Historical Record," 18–50.

67. Patterson, *America's Struggle Against Poverty,* 201.

68. Gilder, *Wealth and Poverty;* Auletta, *The Underclass.*

69. Kaus, *The End of Equality.* For a more extensive discussion of racism and AFDC, see Neubeck and Cazenave, *Welfare Racism.*

70. Noble, *Welfare as We Knew It,* 111–115; Edsall and Edsall, *Chain Reaction.* For an excellent empirical study of durations and patterns of poverty and welfare receipt, see Duncan, *Years of Poverty, Years of Plenty.*

71. Murray, "Have the Poor Been 'Losing Ground'?" 427–445.

72. The labor force participation rate for married women with children under six topped 50 percent in 1984. For married white women with children under six, it went over 50 percent in 1985. Table 624, "Married, Separated, and Divorced Women—Labor Force Status, by Presence and Age of Children: 1960 to 1987"; and Table 625, "Labor Force Participation Rates for Wives, Husband Present, by Age of Own Youngest Child: 1975 to 1987"; *Statistical Abstract of*

the United States, 1988 (Washington, DC: US Department of Commerce, Bureau of the Census, 108th edition), p. 374.

73. Carlson and Hopkins, "Whose Responsibility Is Social Responsibility?" 10.

74. One central proposal, to grant states complete control over AFDC and food stamps in exchange for the federal government's assumption of Medicaid, was rebuffed by the states. Meyer, "Budget Cuts in the Reagan Administration," 78.

75. The ceiling was $160 per month per child for child care and $75 per month for other work expenses. Because of these changes in the thirty plus one-third rule, about 400,000 families were no longer eligible for benefits under AFDC. Meyer, "Budget Cuts in the Reagan Administration," 55, 86.

76. Mead, *Beyond Entitlement*, 126.

77. *Congressional Quarterly Almanac*, 1987, 557.

78. Reprinted in the *Congressional Quarterly Weekly Report*, January 31, 1987, 202.

79. *Congressional Quarterly Almanac*, 1988, 349.

80. Julie Rovner, "Governors Jump-Start Welfare Reform Drive," *Congressional Quarterly Weekly Report*, February 28, 1987, 377.

81. Julie Rovner, "Congress Takes Ball and Runs After State of the Union Punt," *Congressional Quarterly Weekly Report*, January 31, 1987, 208.

82. The National Governors' Association never pushed for expanded benefits; rather, it dubbed them part of a long-term strategy and postponed any benefit increases until they could be financed by savings incurred through work and training programs. Moynihan's proposal included a requirement that all states offer AFDC-UP but no benefit increases. He defended this choice by arguing that it was not politically feasible to expect benefit increases to pass Congress. In order to get approval from a sufficient number of Democrats on the House Ways and Means Committee, the required benefit increase in Ford's bill was eliminated and replaced with an incentive in which states would get additional federal government funding if they increased their benefits, but the Senate bill included no such incentive. States were offered a "higher federal matching rate of up to 25 percent for each dollar of additional benefits." Julie Rovner, "Panel OKs Welfare Plan on Party-Line Vote," *Congressional Quarterly Weekly Report*, June 13, 1987, 1266.

83. Senator Daniel Patrick Moynihan (D-NY), quoted in Julie Rovner, "Congress Takes Ball and Runs After State of the Union Punt," *Congressional Quarterly Weekly Report*, January 31, 1987, 208. For a discussion of the concept of the social contract used in these debates, see Julie Rovner, "Daniel Patrick Moynihan: Making Welfare Work," *Congressional Quarterly Weekly Report*, March 21, 1987, 503.

84. Knowing that states were likely to "cream," or focus their job programs on the welfare recipients they expected to leave the rolls quickly and thus needed less assistance with employment, states were also required to target their programs at those persons who were more likely to receive welfare for a long time, namely, young adults without a high school diploma or work experience, families in which the youngest child was within two years of being ineligible for assistance, and families that had received assistance for more than thirty-six months in the preceding five years. Julie Rovner, "Congress Approves Overhaul of Welfare System," *Congressional Quarterly Weekly Report*, October 8, 1988, 2825–2831.

85. *Congressional Quarterly Almanac*, 1988, 353.

86. This apparent consensus over the desirability of work for mothers did not extend beyond welfare, however. At this time, a child care bill was running into considerable opposition because of the belief that it would encourage mothers to work outside the home, a direct challenge to complementarity.

87. Julie Rovner, "Senate Finance Endorses Modified Welfare Bill," *Congressional Quarterly Weekly Report,* April 23, 1988, 1068.

88. In single-parent families, women whose youngest child was six had to participate full-time in the JOBS program. Women whose youngest child was between the ages of three and six had to participate at least twenty hours per week, and states could reduce this age to one year if they had sufficient resources to provide child care. Teen mothers and mothers in two-parent families faced somewhat different participation requirements. Teen mothers who had not graduated from high school or received a general equivalency diploma were required to participate full-time in educational activities or part-time in other JOBS activities if they were not making sufficient progress in education or if education was deemed inappropriate for them. In two-parent families receiving benefits under AFDC-UP, the primary breadwinner had to participate in workfare, and states could require the second parent to participate in the JOBS program if child care were available.

89. Julie Rovner, "Child-Support Provisions Are the 'Engine' Pulling Controversial Welfare-Reform Bill," *Congressional Quarterly Weekly Report,* June 18, 1988, 1649.

90. 1992 State of the Union Address, reprinted in *Congressional Quarterly Almanac,* 1992, 10E.

91. Lurie, "JOBS Implementation in 1991." States had trouble finding the money they needed to spend in order to receive matching dollars from the federal government; in FY 1992, states were able to "draw down" only about one-third of the federal money appropriated for the JOBS program because they could not provide the matching funds. States that had done relatively little with welfare-to-work programs before the Family Support Act was adopted were having an especially hard time. Researchers for the Rockefeller Institute of Government found that Michigan and Tennessee, two states that had not experimented with work programs before 1988, were able to spend less than 10 percent of the federal funds allotted them in FY 1991.

92. For a complete description of the proposal, see *Congressional Quarterly Almanac,* 1994, 365.

93. *Congressional Quarterly Almanac,* 1994, 364.

94. Eric Pianin, "Formerly United House Republicans Split over Welfare Reform Package," *Washington Post,* April 29, 1994, A37.

95. Gillespie and Schellhas, *Contract with America,* 65.

5

Making Masculine Mothers: Vanquishing Feminality

FIRST USED BY THE NATION'S FOUNDERS TO EXPLAIN WHY THEY did not need to "remember the ladies" in the constitutional foundation for citizen equality and later used to justify Aid to Families with Dependent Children (AFDC), mother-work has been the primary basis upon which women could make claims upon the state. Republican motherhood was the idea that women made a most important contribution to the polity as mothers by raising future citizens capable of making a contribution to the commonweal. In fact, this type of contribution was never easily extended to all women. In practice, republican motherhood has always had mythological dimensions. Class and race politics interfered with the ability of every woman to claim her mother-work was valuable. A white woman, married to a good enough white man, was always a subtext of republican motherhood, one that curtailed interpretations of worthiness.[1] Further, in classic liberal tradition, the concept was used to mark women as outside the body politic by not treating women the same as men. Nonetheless, in a masculinist system that systematically subjugated women, mother-work provided women one consistent basis for standing as citizens. Care of one's children was considered valuable work. No more in welfare policy is this true.

The 1996 welfare reform act and subsequent implementation ended republican motherhood. Welfare reform requires that everyone become breadwinners, that all able-bodied adults, including mothers, adopt this masculine role in order to be citizens in good standing. The feminale roles of caregiving and nurturing were no longer acceptable grounds for social citizenship. In this move from the complementarity paradigm to the individuality paradigm, masculine tenets negated feminalist ones, reflecting and reinforcing masculinist dominance generally. Paid employment was deemed to be work, an activity affording independence. The

107

direct, daily care of one's own children was defined as "not work." Thus, because mothers receiving welfare did not "work," they were by definition dependent. In turn, dependence was a condition not to be tolerated for adults. Because women who were mothers were adults, government policy would force them to engage in paid employment, to labor outside the home, in order to free them from dependence.[2]

Although many aspects of welfare reform in 1996 were conflictual, this denial of the feminale role of caregiving and the upholding of the masculine role of breadwinning was remarkably consensual. A defense of mother-work all but disappeared from the debate, with only welfare rights groups vigorously promoting the public support of mothering. Mothering was portrayed by many as a private activity, one that simply did not count when considering whether or not women contributed to the polity. For others, the mother-work done by women receiving welfare was detrimental to society, for they saw it as the root cause of most social problems. Race was an important aspect of the denigration of mothering. Through a number of stereotypes that disparaged poor mothers and their children, women receiving welfare were regularly portrayed as black.[3] These pejorative portrayals were not new. As we saw in Chapter 4, the deservingness of black women and their children has always been questioned in welfare policy. In the past, however, welfare was defended because it enabled mother-work, and advocates for black women could argue that their mother-work too should be recognized as beneficial for the broader good. Welfare reform and its reauthorization disparaged mother-work in general. Mothering, including that done by white women, no longer is considered an activity deserving of public support.

Instead, policymakers have championed the masculine role of breadwinning. Using gender ideologies from intersector to patriarchalism, policymakers agreed that welfare should be organized around the quest for independence through paid employment. Although they disagreed about what needed to be done to accomplish this aim and why the existing AFDC program was not succeeding, they shared the goal of women's autonomy and independence through paid employment. They presumed women would garner from paid employment economic and psychological rewards, including economic self-sufficiency, increased social status, and a sense of psychological autonomy that brings the self-confidence needed to "succeed" in life. They implicitly acknowledged, and hence to some degree legitimized, the existence of mother-only families and thereby recognized women as adult heads of households. Thus, welfare reform incorporated key tenets of liberal feminism, as it was more easily aligned with other political ideologies important to governing in the United States.

Because so many policymakers with different ideological arguments expressed their faith in the moral meaning and value of work, the coalition behind work was thus quite strong. But it was also fragile. All could agree that individuals should work, but they disagreed mightily about the extent of the rewards work should provide and government's role in facilitating work. The fact that the individuals required to work were women, and women with children, raised questions about using the masculine bread-winner role as the model for all adults. A potent conflict developed over child care, as feminale policymakers separated from their masculine counterparts to insist that government provide greater support for child care so that women would be similarly situated to their male counterparts in the labor market.

But other questions about work were papered over by upholding the myth of the male breadwinner, even though it does not withstand empirical scrutiny well. Although those advancing similarist and intersector arguments opened some of these questions when they demanded that government should "make work pay," few pursued these issues. After all, if government had to intervene to ensure that people could afford to work, what is the intrinsic value of work? How could work be equivalent to independence if government has to buttress work? If those who worked needed various kinds of government benefits, why were they not "dependent"? And if they were not dependent, why were welfare mothers? These questions were not asked, even though they follow logically from the very idea of "making work pay." They would have challenged the neoliberal capitalist underpinnings of the consensus around work, ideas rooted in the Protestant work ethic, Horatio Alger, and other boot-strap elements of American culture. More important, they would have challenged the notion that employment was the only significant and valuable way to contribute to society and would have allowed room for arguments consistent with republican motherhood, in particular the idea that women deserved to make claims upon the state for their work as mothers.

In this chapter we examine the debate among policymakers whose use of various gender ideologies led to the end of mother-work for women and the ascendance of the masculine mother. We consider first the adoption of welfare reform in 1996 and then turn to its implementation by the states. Even though the contours of the 1996 act were centered squarely in the individuality paradigm, the flexibility granted the states enabled them to fashion welfare programs consistent with the other paradigms. But states devised policies that advanced the individuality paradigm as they moved forward with programs emphasizing maternal employment. They readily accepted the notion of the masculine mother and did not try to resurrect mother-work as deserving of public support.

■ The Denigration of Mothering

The reform of welfare in 1996 denied mothering activities as a basis for the receipt of aid because mothering was understood as providing nothing worthwhile for individuals or the broader public. Women who received welfare were portrayed as persons who did nothing of value for anyone—for themselves, their children, or their communities—and consequently were devastated by their dependence and lack of worth. To make this depiction convincing, what women on welfare actually did had to be negated. Because AFDC was available primarily to single mothers with children and because most children receiving welfare were young, the condemnation of welfare required denying the mothering done by these women. *By disregarding the contributions of the feminale—to men, women, and children, but especially to broader society—it was easy to turn to the masculine world.* Market work then became the sole important source of individual growth and fulfillment, good parenting for children, and desired contributions to society.

Direct and impassioned criticism of the caregiving done by poor single mothers came from conservative policymakers advancing traditionalist and patriarchalist arguments, even as they claimed to esteem mothering activities. Because they believed that women could mother well only in the structure of marriage, single mothers would always be inadequate, no matter how hard they tried. Without a husband and father in the home, single mothers could not raise their children to lead law-abiding and productive lives. "Parenting is an art not fully understood by people on welfare," declared Representative Fred Grandy (R-IA).[4] Robert Rector of the Heritage Foundation asserted that "the very worst possible environment for raising a child, and we have overwhelming data on this, happens to be a single mother at home alone with an AFDC check."[5] Michael Horowitz from the Hudson Institute lamented giving aid to teen mothers because "taxpayers have suffered, but the children of those mothers have suffered most of all from this arrangement."[6] The chair of the House Ways and Means subcommittee on human resources, Representative Clay Shaw (R-FL), praised a witness for describing cash assistance to a teen mother as "federally funded child abuse" and remarking "that you wouldn't entrust your dog to some of these kids that are having kids."[7]

Although these policymakers used traditionalist and patriarchalist arguments to lament single motherhood in general, their specific criticisms highlighted black women and children. They did not do so by saying explicitly that black women were bad mothers; rather, they associated the problems facing urban poor communities with welfare and single-parent families.[8] Single mothers were portrayed as living in inner cities—in housing projects in particular—not in small towns and suburbs. They were described as permanently relying on welfare for all their family resources and refusing to work because of indolence. They and their children had numerous problems, including illegal drug use, juvenile delinquency, illiteracy, child abuse, and neglect. Indeed, these advocates attributed the social problems of poor, minority communities to single mothers and their children. Although their specific remarks identified minority women and children, their general explanation went beyond race and targeted single motherhood as the central cause of social problems. In their eyes, welfare enabled women to mother outside the confines of marriage and thus only helped to create and sustain a form of mothering detrimental to society.

Policymakers relying on similarist and universalist ideas were less likely to criticize directly the mothering done by poor women. More often their approach was to ignore mothering, to simply overlook it. Women receiving welfare were presented as doing nothing. "More something for nothing is not the answer," pronounced Donna Shalala, secretary of the Department of Health and Human Services (DHHS), as she argued that welfare recipients had an obligation to work in exchange for the public assistance they received.[9] As he described the assumptions behind the proposal offered by the National Governors' Association, Tommy Thompson, then governor of Wisconsin and later secretary of DHHS, explained "only work should pay; idleness should not be rewarded. The premise should be that everyone is truly capable of doing something."[10] Such language cast caring for one's own children as mere idleness. It simply disregarded the effort spent on daily care of children; caring for one's own children was not work.

In these similarist and universalist comments, when the care of children was mentioned, it was referred to as an activity that took little time and energy. Working mothers got up and took their children to day care or school before they went to work. For example, Governor Thompson explained, "The parents have to make sure that they get up in the morning, get them to school, get them to a day care center if they are pre-school age, that they have the responsibility to do so."[11] The care of children required—and expected—of women on welfare was not very demanding. In short, parents' most important responsibility was to turn their children over to others for care. Mothers would work outside the home, and workers paid for their labor would care for their children; mother-work could readily be commodified into market work. Thus, women who did not work did little or nothing, and they did not deserve public assistance. In a reversal of republican motherhood and federal policy since at least 1935, mothering should no longer be considered an activity for the public good or a way to demonstrate contributions to the community.

Although they ignored mothering as an activity, Democrats propounding similarist rhetoric ardently defended children. They denounced the Republican bill for punishing children for the failings of their parents. It was simply unfair, they argued, to penalize children "because of the happenstance into which they have been born," for those were circumstances over which children had no control.[12] Moreover, when their families reached the lifetime limits, substantial numbers of children would be denied aid, and that would "undoubtedly mean children in deep despair, and in deep poverty."[13] Something should be done to protect children, they argued, and they offered the idea of vouchers, payable to a third party rather than the child's mother, to provide for some basic needs for those children who would not be eligible for cash assistance under Temporary Assistance for Needy Families (TANF). Using odd language that implied children could care for themselves, Senator Tom Daschle (D-SD) explained that "we want to provide them [children] with every opportunity for rent, for clothing, for whatever other needs they have because it is not their fault they are in the position of needing assistance."[14]

Such arguments bolstered rather than refuted the notion that poor mothers were bad mothers, even though they were offered in an attempt to preserve some aspect of an entitlement. By proposing some aid for children but not for their mothers, this reasoning implicitly suggested that children could be disconnected from their families.[15] Somehow children's needs could be met by receiving aid equivalent to the child's portion of AFDC (which was never very much money), even as their mothers were denied aid in order to force them to work. Although this reasoning relied less on stereotypes of the black urban poor, the disregard for mothering activities meshed with a long tradition of ignoring black children's need for care and nurturing.[16] Those making similarist arguments were willing to contend that children needed material resources but not mothering. By asserting that children deserved some form of material assistance but their mothers did not because they should work, this use of similarist rhetoric simply reinforced the idea that mothers did nothing of import for their children.

Thus, these similarist arguments did little to unseat the notion that unemployed mothers were irresponsible adults who did not deserve assistance. Similarist beliefs equated paid employment with responsibility. Because all working women got up and got their children to day care or school before they went to work, women who did not readily do so were painted as abnormal, much as other stay-at-home-moms often lament.

Given these positions toward mothering, it was relatively easy for most policymakers, even though they made use of a range of gender ideologies from similarism to patriarchalism, to claim that paid employment would benefit both single mothers and their children. If women worked, they would be responsible and would contribute to society, giving something back in return for the welfare they received. They would have a chance to compete, to work hard and make something of themselves and their families. They would develop laudatory individual attributes and pass them on to their children. "Watching their parents come home from work at night will allow children to see the self-confidence that results from bringing home a paycheck and being self-supportive," asserted Senator Patrick Leahy (D-VT).[17] The "big winners" of welfare reform were "the children who watch their parents get up each morning, go to a job, and return home at night," argued Representative Bill Archer (R-TX), because the "virtues of work, not idleness" would be "instilled in them at a young age."[18]

Thus, policymakers no longer claimed that children needed the direct care and nurturing offered by loving mothers. Instead, they needed to watch their mothers go to work and come home at night. They needed role models they could observe, not caregivers who engaged directly with them. They needed the masculine mother, one who through her own diligence and effort exposed her children to the world of work, showing them how to compete in this world and transmitting to them discipline, self-control, and delayed gratification. These children would not be raised in welfare as a "way of life" but would have access "to hope, to independence, and to opportunity."[19] They would "now grow up in a different kind of atmosphere where, if they only have one parent, at least that parent will be working and contributing, as they will be expected to do as they grow older."[20] Changing the system would "give children of this country an opportunity and incentive to enjoy the American dream, to get off the welfare system, to know what the free enterprise system is all about."[21]

This acclamation of paid labor and the denigration of mothering occurred with very little conflict between proponents of feminale and masculine thought. Although many women used similarist and intersector arguments to passionately criticize welfare reform, few defended the mothering done by poor single women. Welfare rights groups, whose members are mostly women, defended maternal caregiving and contended that mothering should be supported publicly, but few others joined them. Without the backing of other proponents of feminale thought, the welfare rights groups could not gather enough support for mothering as a public activity whose value equaled that of paid employment.

Welfare rights groups ardently defended the mothering done by poor women. Mothering was work, they insisted. "Mothers are workers, mothers are working. Caregiving is work, the most valuable work in the United States," proclaimed Pat Gowens, from Welfare Warriors of Milwaukee, Wisconsin.[22] Mothering took considerable time and energy and benefited both children and neighborhoods. Moreover, poor women did an excellent job raising their children, and no one else could do as well. "We are the best people to be raising our children in this country, and we are going to continue to raise them. . . . I am the only person that cares about that and I am the only person who has given up everything I have to feed, clothe, and house my child," pointed out Sherry Honkala, of the Philadelphia Welfare Rights Project.[23]

Because they believed mothering was important and poor women were good mothers, members of welfare rights groups argued that it made little sense to require women to work and then pay others to care for their children. Doing so would transform the care of children into work by making it paid labor performed by an adult who was not the child's parent. But transforming this task into work did not improve the care provided and certainly did not replicate mothering, especially in poor neighborhoods that lacked highly paid care providers. To the contrary, it compromised the quality of care provided because workers who were paid badly and forced to work to get by could not be good caregivers. "Our children are being denied the right to loving caregivers," complained Gowens. "Our children are being carted around like luggage. . . . When you are being cared for by an enslaved worker, that is not a happy worker."[24] Mothering was valuable, even when done by poor, single, black women, and their children deserved to have this loving care rather than the compromised care provided when mothering was turned into a commodity purchased in the market.

In addition to compromising the direct care of children, requiring mothers to work did not enhance individual fulfillment. Asking single mothers to work and raise children was not going to increase self-esteem and happiness; rather, it would lead to overwork and stress. "The double work day is oppression, not liberation," argued Pat Gowens.[25] These groups, organized by and speaking for women receiving welfare, did not accept the notion that work was intrinsically good and the only worthwhile option for individuals. All too often, work was drudgery, paid badly, and offered no opportunity for self-fulfillment and growth. Because they thought that poor women were engaged in the important and valuable job of mothering their children, there was simply no reason to require them to labor at lousy jobs and send their children to be cared for by unhappy workers.

Occasionally, a legislator or interest group who shared the social democratic views of the welfare rights groups would speak up to defend mothering. Representative Maxine Waters (D-CA) reproached Representative Clay Shaw for his "irresponsible and outrageous statement disparaging welfare mothers" and then explained that there were "many solid responsible welfare recipients who love and care for their children, who attend church on Sunday," while working, searching for jobs, and going to school."[26] Referring to Marilyn Quayle's speech at the 1992 Republican National Convention, David Liederman of the Child Welfare League of America criticized the hypocrisy of expecting poor women to work yet applauding Quayle for announcing how important it was to forgo a career and stay home to care for children. Declaring that everyone knew parenting was hard work, Liederman embraced a broad antipoverty strategy focused on education, housing, and neighborhood improvement, rather than forcing mothers to enter the labor market.[27]

Welfare rights groups found few allies, however, among other feminale groups. Women's groups on the left were adamantly opposed to welfare reform. For example, National Organization for Women (NOW) President Patricia Ireland was arrested after protesting the Republican bill in March 1995. These groups' defense of welfare, however, tended not to rest on a vindication of mothering as a valuable societal activity. Rather, they defended the competence and capabilities of women who received welfare with respect to their employment histories and desire to work, not with respect to mothering. They rebutted a variety of widely used and often conflicting stereotypes about poor women on welfare. These included the notions that poor women were too lazy and irresponsible to work, that they were too dejected and despondent to work, and that they were shrewd and devious manipulators of the system who refused to work but still found ways to increase their welfare benefits, including having additional children in order to get larger monthly grants. They argued instead that women on welfare made a great effort to find work and exercised considerable initiative and perseverance as they searched for and held yet another low-paying job. "Women receiving AFDC are not lazy slackers," concluded Leslie Wolfe, from the Center for Women Policy Studies, as she continued on to explain that a significant number of women on welfare worked.[28] Roberta Spalter-Roth, of the Institute for Women's Policy Research, echoed this finding when she argued that "most welfare recipients are not pathologically dependent on welfare." Most women on welfare combined AFDC with income from other sources, including their own earnings and wages from other family members. Other women moved back and forth between welfare and work, leaving welfare when they found jobs and returning to the rolls when they could not work.[29] These groups argued that welfare receipt had more to do with the inadequacies of the labor market, particularly the nature of low-wage employment, and not women's irresponsibility, incompetence, or indolence. Thus the views of these women's groups fit into the intersector category.

These groups recognized that the jobs poor women held were generally not very good jobs because they were dead-end and had low wages and no benefits.[30] Their ideas about the causes of poverty and welfare receipt were similar to those of the welfare rights groups, but they did not reach similar conclusions about mothering. Because they did not recognize the tensions between mother-work and market-work, they did not compare mothering to working in lousy jobs and then conclude that both women and children would be better off if the United States provided public support for mothering. Instead, they held on to the idea that paid employment was the route to independence and self-sufficiency and that paid work led to individual fulfillment. For example, Cynthia Newbille, National Black Women's Health Project, urged Congress to "develop policies that facilitate the empowerment of women so that they can become self-sufficient."[31] Lori Karny, National Council of Jewish Women, explained that this organization's goal "has consistently been to provide a continuum of interrelated services to assist women towards self-reliance and self-empowerment."[32] Diana Pearce, from Wider Opportunities for Women, urged members of Congress to consider an alternative program, but one that would make welfare recipients "economically self-sufficient" and enable families to "become more responsible for themselves."[33] All focused on developing the mother as an adult individual, one who happened to be a woman and mother but whose adult life was not determined by these factors.

More conservative groups relying on the tenets of corporative feminalism were also disinclined to support mothering as an important public activity. Corporative feminalists feel that it is important to expect of women what Americans have long expected of men. Equal treatment meant requiring all individuals to support themselves through work and to strive for individual growth, development, and responsibility, not changing the rules to accommodate the feminale. Cathy Young from the Women's Freedom Network, a group "founded to promote an approach to women's issues that emphasizes individual rights and personal responsibility," argued that childrearing should not interfere with career development. It was commonplace for young women to "consider job skills to be just as essential as young men do, even if many plan to spend some time at home with their children full time." Caring for children was important, but mothering was something that women should plan for and handle themselves without the support of the state. Moreover, mothering provided little opportunity for personal growth and fulfillment. It was paid employment that built "discipline, self-confidence, and self-worth," and poor women needed to be drawn into the "women's movement into the workplace and toward economic self-determination."[34]

Despite their belief in maternal caregiving as crucial to children, new right feminalism was not used by conservative women's groups to defend publicly the mothering done by poor women. Concerned Women for America, for example, supported the feminale in the structure of private patriarchy, or in two-parent, married couples. Women who tried to establish households independently of men would find success elusive because mothering rested on the financial support and the moral authority of men. Concerned Women for America saw single mothers and their children as a major source of social problems and a family structure that should be discouraged. As a group, it believed welfare was a program that subsidized and encouraged illegitimacy, causing grave problems for children, and thus were not going to defend it as a program that offered invaluable public support for nurturing and caregiving. Although the organization did not endorse work requirements for women with preschool-age children, it did not fight them either, perhaps because individuals within the group were torn between their desire for maternal caregiving and their animosity toward welfare.[35] Instead, it wanted to shift the focus of welfare reform away from work and toward encouraging marriage and discouraging illegitimacy. Two-parent families were better for both women and children.

Thus, other than welfare rights groups, no feminale interest groups defended public support of mothering. New right feminalism trusted in separate roles for men and women and understood mothering as an activity that should occur within and be supported by private patriarchy. Traditional maternalism thought marriage was best, but if women were outside marriage, then they must provide good care and be the masculine breadwinner. Corporative feminalism and liberal feminism did not share this emphasis on two-parent families and acknowledged mother-only households, at least implicitly, as an acceptable family form. But both ideological perspectives perceived mothering as a private activity, and women who had children needed to support their households through their own market labor. Women could form independent households, but they should not expect the public to support their mothering. Women were individuals, and all individuals were responsible for the consequences of their actions; in this case, they were responsible for the children they had and the households they formed.

▆ The Value of Work

Once mothering was denied as an activity that established grounds for social citizenship, the masculine role of breadwinning endured as the appropriate activity for all adults. Understood as paid employment, work was perceived as desirable because it improved the moral character of the individual. Work meant self-sufficiency and independence. Work produced discipline and control. Work led to self-esteem and dignity. Those who worked were contributing members of society, not necessarily because they made or produced some tangible good society needed, but because they apparently took care of themselves and did not require someone else to care for them. Why work improved the individual or what conditions were necessary to make work fulfilling were unexamined questions. Ideas from the Protestant work ethic and Ben Franklin's secularized version of work as the way to success pervaded the debate without comment. Women's traditional work—labor largely done outside the capitalist system—was ignored. Work narrowed to mean employment, and it was intrinsically good.

Among Republicans, those advancing universalist arguments were especially likely to emphasize individual improvement through work. For example, elaborating on the importance of work to welfare reform, Representative Jennifer Dunn (R-WA) explained, "We want to give people self-respect. We want to restore their self-esteem through the dignity of holding a job."[36] "Responsibility brings dignity," Senator Olympia Snowe (R-ME) stated plainly.[37] When work was the issue on the table, Republicans articulating traditionalist and patriarchalist views backed the universalist position, even though they preferred that welfare reform center on family structure. They had long applied these tenets about work to men, and it was not difficult for them to extend them to women who were not married.

These conservatives were vague about precisely why work bestowed these enrichments, but discipline, daily routine and schedule, and the very act of offering one's labor in exchange for wages were crucial aspects of work's intrinsic value. "Work, as we know, is the evidence of an internal discipline. It orders and directs our lives," explained Senator Daniel Coats (R-IN).[38] Arguing that the work requirement was an opportunity, not a penalty, Senator Rick Santorum (R-PA) explained that welfare recipients would "learn what it is to get up in the morning and get their children ready for day care . . . and get yourself to a work site, work an 8-hour day, and get home and again provide for their children."[39]

The cachet of work was heightened by contrasting it with the denigrated alternative of welfare. By definition those who worked were independent and self-sufficient. Because mothering had no public value, women who received welfare did nothing and therefore were dependent on public largesse. This dependence was humiliating and sapped one's spirit. It destroyed one's self-esteem, so that even if an individual wanted to and thought she should work to get off the rolls, she would be unable to overcome her demoralization.[40] Dependence made one indolent and slothful. It destroyed self-control and determination, leading to licentiousness and depravity. It was common practice to link any number of social problems to welfare, including crime, drug abuse, early sexual activity, teen pregnancy, and poor educational attainment, and then conclude that it was welfare receipt itself that led to these problems. Welfare, Senator Snowe asserted, "has become a way of life, a culture of despondency, a tradition of dismay, and has bequeathed a sad inheritance of dependence for millions of our citizens."[41]

Even though they challenged other ideas voiced by Republicans, Democrats espousing similarist views agreed that work was a paramount activity for citizens. For example, Senator Joseph Biden (D-DE) emphasized the notion that work indicated individual responsibility when he proclaimed, "Citizenship is more than a bundle of benefits. It is also a set of responsibilities. And, *the primary responsibility* is to provide for yourself and your family by working" (italics added).[42] Highlighting the idea that employment brought pride and self-worth to mothers and their children, President Clinton relayed a conversation he had with a woman named Lillie Harden, who had been on welfare and then got off. "I said, 'Lillie, what's the best thing about being off welfare?' And she looked me straight in the eye and said, 'When my boy goes to school and they say what does your mama do for a living, he can give an answer.'"[43] Senator Barbara Mikulski's (D-MD) endorsement of the act rested on the belief that work was the route for all to achieve autonomy, independence, and self-fulfillment. "I believe in the capacity of people to better their lives and build a better future for themselves and their families," declared Senator Mikulski, as she explained why she would vote for the welfare reform bill.[44]

Because work was desirable and other activities clearly were not, anyone who *could* work, who was able-bodied, *should* work. Allowing an individual to choose whether she worked would mean that she also had a choice over the way in which she defined her life and her relationship to the broader society. After all, choice implies two or more desirable options and assumes that the individual can decide for herself which one is best. But because these policymakers did not perceive mothering by single women to be a valuable public activity, they had little reason to give these women a choice about engaging in paid employment. Moreover, single mothers had already made bad choices: in the eyes of those espousing similarist and universalist claims, single mothers had produced children without having the wherewithal to provide for them; for proponents of traditionalist and patriarchalist thought, they had produced children without marrying. Although the mothering done within the confines of marriage and private patriarchy was less suspicious, even the choice not to work by a married woman could be circumscribed. If her family received welfare, they became dependent, and states were allowed to require that both parents work when a two-parent family received TANF cash assistance.[45] An individual had to work—or be connected to work through an independent breadwinner—in order to be considered a viable member of the community. Ideas from 1970s liberal feminism about the need for a woman to be able to provide for herself pervaded the mindset; liberal feminism prevailed even though it had been appropriated and applied in ways it never would have initiated.

■ Policy Conflicts and the Individuality Paradigm

With work perceived as the only creditable activity for citizens, the framework of the Personal Responsibility and Work Opportunity Reconciliation Act (PRWORA) was centered squarely within the corporative individuality paradigm. Because only work would suffice, government had to demand work. Thus, work requirements and time limits on welfare were adopted and endorsed by policymakers advancing an array of ideological arguments, from similarist to patriarchalist. As Representative Howard McKeon (R-CA) explained, work requirements had to be backed up by time limits because "after five years, recipients face the ultimate work requirement, the end of all cash welfare, period."[46] Not to be outdone by Republicans, Democrats too ignored women's contributions through nonmarket care work and included work requirements and time limits in their alternative bill: "Hard work has built this Nation and hard work continues to sustain it," proclaimed Representative Neal Deal (D-GA). "Changing the institution of welfare and replacing it with work" was the goal because work was "the only long-term solution to welfare."[47] Nor did legislators adopting similarist positions shy away from requiring mothers of young children to work: "Everyone must work," declared Senator Mikulski, because "everyone must do something for benefits."[48]

Despite their agreement on the centrality of work, these policymakers disputed the conditions of work, the rewards of work, and the extent to which government should intervene in the labor market to help women work and reward those who did. The central tension was between the two versions of the individuality paradigm. Those articulating similarist and intersector views advanced policies consistent with civic individuality. Those making universalist arguments promoted corporative individuality and gained support from proponents of patriarchalist and traditionalist thought. With little defense of mothering, innovative policies toward work consistent with the complementarity paradigm never came on the agenda. And shifts toward the egality paradigm were limited both by the small number of legislators espousing intersector tenets as well as the constraints on new ideas imposed by the widespread embrace of work. Even with these paradigms on the sidelines of the discussion, though, conflict over the desired policies toward work took time to reconcile, especially when disputes emerged between proponents of masculine and feminale thought.

Republicans were content with policies of the corporative individuality paradigm. Because they believed the major social problem was dependency and not material deprivation, getting welfare recipients off the rolls was the goal. Requiring women to work, sanctioning them with benefit cuts if they did not, and then ending cash assistance entirely were all policy devices intended to force women to pull themselves up by their bootstraps. The responsibility of the state was to require that welfare recipients act in ways that would get jobs—search for a job, accept one if offered, or enter a community work program if no job was found. Thus, PRWORA included provisions that encouraged states to emphasize "work first," a term referring to immediate entry into the labor market.[49] This work first requirement was readily picked up by the states and later hailed as central to the success of welfare reform.

Behind these policies rested several assumptions about welfare recipients and the labor market, agreed on by Republicans espousing universalist, traditionalist, and patriarchal beliefs. They assumed that women were on welfare because they refused to work and lacked work experience. If they looked for jobs, they would find them, even in areas of high unemployment.[50] Entry-level jobs, even those involving unskilled labor with low wages, were fine because work was valuable, regardless of how well the jobs paid and the prospects of upward mobility. For example, grumbling about the purported need for job training, Representative Mark Foley (R-FL) argued that any job was a good job:

> What is wrong with work? I can't believe what people are saying here. Not enough job training. I worked as a dishwasher. I cleaned toilets. . . . I was a wrecker, an auto mechanic. I worked at a golf course. Now I am a proud Member of the United States Congress. No job is beneath me.[51]

Senator Phil Gramm (R-TX) argued that even if welfare recipients were engaged in workfare jobs such as picking up trash, cleaning parks, and washing windows, they would "be part of building a better country. And I believe they will be richer, freer, and happier for it."[52] Moreover, work experience provided sufficient upward mobility, they asserted. Poor women should expect to move first into entry-level jobs and not hold out for jobs with higher wages. Lamenting the attitude that women should be referred only to "jobs that start at $8 or $9 or $10 an hour," Senator Hank Brown (R-CO) asserted that "the way you do well in our economy is you start off on the ladder, and you climb it rung by rung by rung."[53] Those who were determined and diligent would fare well. Those who did not would at least have the satisfaction of contributing something to society.

Conservatives holding universalist, traditionalist, and patriarchalist tenets also had little patience with proposals to provide education and training for welfare recipients so they could land better jobs. Their belief that welfare mothers evaded work was so strong that any proposal not conforming to these assumptions was portrayed as an attempt to bypass work. Education and job training were simply devices to avoid work. There were "people who take advantage after advantage after advantage of the job training and other services, rather than having to go get a job in the private sector and work every day and do what they should do, support themselves and/or their families," exclaimed Senator Orrin Hatch (R-UT).[54] It was not acceptable to meet work requirements through education and training because those activities were not work. "Work means work," explained Senator Rod Grams (R-MN). "Any farm kid who rises before dawn for the daily chores can tell you that. Ask any of my brothers and sisters what 'work' meant on our family's dairy farm. It didn't mean sitting on a stool in the barn, reading a book about how to milk a cow. 'Work' meant milking cows."[55]

Like these Republicans, Democrats advancing similarist arguments also emphasized a work first strategy. They, too, had faith in the virtue of work, and their focus on individual effort, reward, and responsibility led them to also promote immediate job placement. But unlike conservatives, their confidence was moderated by similarist recognition of these adults as women with children, not simply generic workers, who faced particular barriers and needs in the labor market. Policymakers pressing similarist claims understood that women's welfare receipt was not due to evading work. Many women left welfare for work, they argued, only to return shortly to welfare, because the jobs they found often lacked health insurance and did not pay enough to cover the costs of child care.[56] Work had to pay enough so that women could work, they asserted. Ensuring that women stayed in the labor market was just as important as inducing them to work in the first place.

Despite being united around their faith in work, policymakers advancing similarist arguments differed from those espousing universalist positions because they felt that government had an obligation to help people find work and support them once they were in the labor force. They complained that the Republican proposal was antiwork because it did not expect states to do enough to make it possible for women to enter and stay in the labor market. Thus, legislators with similarist views wanted to add another layer of policies consistent with civic individuality; they wanted to place requirements on the states themselves, not merely on individuals, such as the demand that states continue to devote state money to welfare programs, in addition to the federal funds they received, a practice officially called "maintenance of effort."[57] Certainly government was warranted in expecting individuals to act as good citizens, but states also had a reciprocal obligation to make it possible for them to do so.

Although Democrats with similarist ideas acknowledged that women had difficulty finding good jobs, they shied away from a structural analysis of the labor market promoted by the tenets of intersectors. Like similarism, the intersector strand holds that there are not enough good jobs to enable women to be truly self-sufficient. Based on that realization, the intersector position offers a demanding assessment of the labor market and government's responsibility to ameliorate the conditions the market created. If the labor market does not produce a sufficient number of good jobs, then government should generate those jobs or protect those who cannot find such work. Thus, according to intersector tenets, welfare is necessary to compensate for the market's failings. Legislators articulating such positions wanted to retain the entitlement to welfare while enhancing government employment programs. But a broad proposal offered by Representative Patsy Mink (D-HA) failed overwhelmingly in the House, and narrower proposals introduced in the Senate also failed. By advancing an argument that exonerated poor women from blame, these Democrats used intersector tenets to challenge the concept of the autonomous individual made independent through paid employment. But they did not couple this argument with an affirmation of feminale care activities or an emphasis on the mother-work that could be supported by public assistance. Therefore, they offered no positive claim for public support of poor women and children through welfare. Without such a claim, an entitlement to welfare was difficult to promote, and the intersector argument could not garner enough support from Democrats advancing similarist ideas to make headway in Congress.

Democrats making similarist arguments were wary of policies that might be portrayed as exempting individuals from work, but they ardently promoted policies that facilitated work. "Make work pay" was the rallying cry for these judgments about government responsibilities. The strongest and most successful effort concerned child care. The arguments they advanced for more government support for child care united liberals and, more important, divided conservatives. Arguments about child care could appeal to universalist principles, particularly corporative feminalism, and efforts to promote child care funding gained crucial support from Republican women. Parting from their masculine counterparts, these Republican women saw the need for child care as a practical problem to be solved. Women could be required to take on the masculine role of breadwinning, but they were mothers nonetheless. Something would have to be done about their children.

The assault on the child care provisions in the Republican bill began when Senator Ted Kennedy (D-MA) dubbed it the "home alone program," claiming that women required to work would end up leaving their children alone when they could not find child care. The need for care was a straightforward, simple fact: "a single-parent with a pre-school-aged child cannot hold down a job if there is no one to care for that child."[58] Government funding of child care was an obvious, uncontroversial issue, with no legitimate reason for opposition. "If you do not understand the linkage between child care and welfare reform," asserted Senator Christopher Dodd (D-CT), "then you do not have the vaguest notion about welfare and what needs to be done to make it work better."[59] Without child care funding, welfare reform could not be achieved, and the work requirement in the Republican plan was a "hoax."[60]

Understanding the need for child care and believing that government should help with that expense was obvious to policymakers advancing both similarist and intersector arguments. Most of the adults on welfare were single mothers, and the majority of their children were young. They needed to be cared for while their mothers worked. "We want to provide welfare recipients with the tools to stay on the job. What the facts prove time and time again is that the most necessary tool is child care for children," explained Senator Mikulski.[61] Liberal feminists had long pushed for equal opportunity, and that meant the need to recognize and then remove barriers to employment faced by women. Sometimes, then, special treatment was needed to level the playing field and make women and men be similarly situated. Women could compete in the marketplace with men if they were more like men—not hampered by family responsibilities. The success of welfare reform, the opportunity for women to be self-sufficient through work, rested on child care.

Conservative men criticized such funding as just another form of dependency. Traditionalist tenets found common cause with new paternalism, the masculine variant of gender universalism. Arguing against the amendment, Senator Charles Grassley (R-IA) asserted that one "system breeds dependence. The other independence . . . We want people on welfare to assume responsibility and to move forward with life."[62] In order to be responsible and truly self-sufficient, people needed to succeed in the labor force on their own and not expect government to help them. If child care were fully funded, individuals would turn to government first and stop trying to handle child care by themselves. They would then come to rely on government to provide for their families. Moreover, government funding of child care was based on the pernicious assumption that "the welfare recipient might not be totally capable, or ought not to have the responsibility even, of making that decision" about child care.[63] In order to prevent this dependency, individuals needed to be challenged "to go out and work and find ways to provide for themselves and their families."[64]

To proponents of traditionalism and new paternalism, it was obvious that parents should handle child care themselves. Most Americans did so, even those with little money, and welfare recipients should not be treated any differently. Senator Grassley explained:

> They get up every morning and they take their children to child care. They go to a job where they work all day. They pick up their children in the afternoon and go home. That is what most American families do. That is what even most American families who are low income or "working poor" do without any concern by any bureaucracy. They just do it.[65]

If need be, parents could—and should—get help from extended family, neighbors, and friends. Historically, that is what people have always done, and these "networks of support" created a rich, interdependent fabric and culture of society. Government support for child care would only weaken these relationships, rendering parents more isolated from family and neighbors.[66]

Although the Kennedy-Dodd amendment to substantially increase the funding for child care—and provide a claim for such care until a child was twelve years old—was defeated in the Senate, that loss did not mean that the new paternalist and traditionalist views prevailed. Conflict continued because of tension between Republican women and Republican men. Exploring the tension between the masculine and feminale variants of universalism, new paternalism, and corporative feminalism sheds light on this rift, as the conflict emerged when Republican women separated from their male counterparts. Recognizing the demands on single mothers, these conservative women acknowledged that "the availability of safe, affordable child care is essential to successful welfare reform."[67] Simply expecting women to fall back on family and friends for child care, as the new paternalist and traditionalist position expected, was not practical. "Not everyone is fortunate enough to have a grandparent or an extended family member who can help with child care. In fact, many today do not have relatives that can or will care for their children," pointed out Senator Nancy Kassebaum (R-KA).[68] Moreover, it was not just families on welfare who needed help with child care. Many people already in the labor force needed child care assistance, and limiting the amount of money available would result in competition for child care subsidies among welfare recipients, the working poor, and low-income workers.

Drawing on the ideas of corporative feminalism, Republican women offered two important policy changes concerning child care. In a bow to the views of traditional maternalism, Senator Olympia Snowe first suggested granting an exemption from the work requirement if child care were unavailable and the child was five or younger. Exempting women from the work requirement was better than doing nothing, responded those Democrats advancing similarist ideas, because at least it meant they would not be caught in a bind, forced to choose between two unsatisfactory alternatives. But because it would exempt too many women from the work requirement, Democrats—particularly men drawing on the neo-fraternalist variant of similarism—still roundly criticized this solution to the problem. Asserting that "there is nothing that is more salutary for a family, a neighborhood, a community than work," Senator Dodd lamented that the Snowe amendment "gives people an excuse not to get from welfare to work."[69]

Although Democrats accepted the Snowe amendment as better than nothing, they continued to push for greater funding for child care in order to protect children, help women work, and preserve the true goal of welfare reform, moving women from welfare to work. The impasse was resolved when Senator Nancy Kassebaum pressed for both additional child care funding and combining all major federal child care programs into one program to make it easier for families leaving welfare or struggling to stay off welfare to receive such aid.[70] Eventually the Senate leadership worked out an agreement that added considerable funding for child care, although not as much money as Kennedy and Dodd had initially requested.

With their emphasis on paid employment as the marker of autonomy and independence, these legislators embraced policies consistent with the individuality paradigm. Still, significant differences arose among them regarding the government's role in insisting on work. Although compromise could often be reached, crafting the policy details that would smooth over rather than incite tension took time and energy. In these negotiations, proposals consistent with civic individuality could be portrayed as "weak on work." Thus, similarist arguments were more successful when they justified policies understood to be facilitating paid employment, such as greater funding for child care. Enhanced child care would situate women in the labor market in the same position as men and thus allow them to compete for all open positions. Recognizing that without child care there was no level playing field, Republican women with corporative feminalist arguments joined Democrats on this issue, even as they resolutely opposed them on so many others.

■ State Programs and Masculine Breadwinning

Although the broad contours of federal law clearly fit the corporative individuality paradigm, federal regulations and the flexibility of the block grant provided more leeway for states to adopt programs consistent with the other paradigms. Important federal restrictions do not apply to state funds demanded by the maintenance of effort (MOE) requirement, granting states considerable latitude in their use. Thus, states can allocate these funds so that families are not subject to work requirements, time limits, or even cooperation with child support enforcement. In addition, states can use federal TANF money to fund a variety of services for low-income families, even if these families have never received TANF cash assistance, and without counting this aid as part of their lifetime limit.[71] If states had the political inclination and sufficient funds (and most of them do not), state welfare programs could then conform to any of the paradigms we discuss, even the egality paradigm.

For the most part, though, states embraced and did not challenge the individuality paradigm that serves as the crux of the federal law. Moreover, with an emphasis on reducing caseloads and requiring work, most of the states' policies fell well within the corporative individuality paradigm. Most states adopted some kind of policy designed explicitly to reduce the number of people receiving cash assistance through TANF by making it more difficult to get on the rolls and to stay on the rolls. One policy required a job search before individuals could apply for aid. A second gave individuals some short-term emergency assistance to cover expenses such as repairs on cars and outstanding rent or utilities bills in exchange for not going on the TANF rolls for a certain length of time.[72] States also adopted policies to make it more difficult to continue receiving welfare, such as a lifetime limit of less than five years or an intermittent time limit, for example, allowing families to receive aid for only twenty-four months out of a sixty-month period.[73]

Most states also adopted requirements for work that were stricter than federal law demanded. These requirements demanded that women participate in work programs immediately or shortly after their families became eligible for assistance, rather than allowing them the full twenty-four month period provided under federal law. States also made it clear that these work requirements applied to mothers, and mothers with young children, by adopting relatively few exemptions. States reorganized their intake and orientation procedures to indicate to individuals applying for welfare that they need to find and accept employment as quickly as possible.[74] Lauding the achievement of the 1996 act, the Bush administration highlighted the increased number of single mothers in the workforce: "Here's the bottom line: welfare reform worked because single mothers left welfare and went to work in unprecedented numbers. Good for them. Good for their children."[75]

In order to enforce work requirements, states also adopted stricter sanctions than the federal government required. And in most states, the strictest penalty involves terminating welfare benefits for the entire family for an extended period, what is called a "full family sanction."[76] When families are sanctioned for not complying with work requirements under

TANF, many states also reduce or eliminate their Medicaid or food stamps.[77] Although some analysts portray sanctions as devices intended simply to induce compliance with work requirements, not to reduce caseloads, the structure of the penalties does exactly the latter. Moreover, conservatives lauded sanctions precisely because they reduced caseloads and thus, in their eyes, ended the culture of dependency.[78]

Clearly, the states embraced the notion that welfare receipt itself was the problem to be solved. Across the nation, caseloads declined dramatically in the late 1990s and more modestly in the early 2000s. This reduction was touted as the program's major success by policymakers at both the state and federal level. For example, boasting that Florida had the largest caseload decline among the fifty states, the director of the state's program asserted that welfare reform was "one of America's most successful social policy experiments. The state's welfare caseload plummeted from 150,000 to fewer than 30,000 in less than four years."[79] "Just the threat of a work requirement was moving people off of welfare, even before the 1996 law took effect," said one House Republican aide.[80] Even as poverty rates started to increase in the early 2000s, DHHS secretary Tommy Thompson lauded continued declines in TANF caseloads.[81] The reputed success of the stringent policies of the corporative individuality paradigm led Republicans to endorse even stricter work requirements in the reauthorization of TANF in hopes of reducing welfare caseloads even further. Endorsing the Bush administration's proposal that 70 percent of welfare recipients participate in work and work activities for forty hours a week, Representative Clay Shaw (R-FL) explained: "Now we expect the states to get more of their people on the work rolls. We have lowered the amount of people on welfare across this country by over 50 percent, but we are not through."[82]

Not surprisingly, the kind of employment emphasized in the states is immediate entry into the workforce; women are expected to take jobs for which their existing skills and work experience qualify. State policies insisting on a job search as part of the application process and imposing immediate work requirements both lead to this focus on work first. States have also curbed the use of education and training by restricting the kinds of educational activities that count toward the work requirement, limiting the amount of time individuals can devote to those activities, and providing little funding for educational services.[83] Although very little federal funding was devoted to education and training and few individuals participated in such activity, House Republicans hoped through reauthorization to restrict participation in educational activities even further.[84] Praising the states for getting women off the rolls and into the workforce as quickly as possible, they demanded that individuals receiving welfare satisfy the work requirement by partaking only in work activities, with participation in educational services allowed only after this work requirement was ful-filled.[85] When Congress finally passed reauthorization in early 2006, it adopted tighter work requirements, which are anticipated to restrict state flexibility in designing their programs.[86]

Although the corporative individuality paradigm served as the back-bone for many state initiatives and for reauthorization, challenges from the civic side of the individuality paradigm persisted through "make work pay" initiatives. In this tension between the corporative and civic versions of the individuality paradigm, policies that remove barriers to work or make it easier for women to work have been more widely accepted than policies that reward work. Simply put, policies that make work *possible* are more popular than policies that make work *pay*.

The major way in which states have facilitated work is through addi-tional funding for work support services, such as transportation services and child care. In addition to the Child Care Development Block Grant, states used federal TANF funds for child care, with reports on state resources indicating that child care was the second-largest use of TANF funds.[87] In a detailed study of spending on social services in sixteen states, the Rockefeller Institute and the Brookings Institution found that spending on child care increased more than any other service, with ten of the sixteen states at least doubling their expenditures in that area between 1995 and 1999.[88] Many states also adopted policies that increased the number of working parents eligible for some kind of child care subsidy, even though most still had limits below the federal ceiling.[89]

These changes did not indicate consensus about the need for and adequacy of child care funding. Disputes over child care were a major sticking point in reauthorization. Republicans highlighted the histori-cally high spending on child care and claimed the amount provided in their bill was adequate. Democrats insisted that large numbers of eligi-ble families were unable to receive child care assistance because of con-tinued funding shortages and that increased work requirements without concomitant increases in child care funding would leave women once again in an untenable bind. Faced with budget problems in the early 2000s, states started cutting back on their child care programs, and in Washington legislators continued arguing over appropriate federal fund-ing for child care.[90] Republican women who relied on corporative femi-nalism to push for greater child care funding in 1996 found themselves again attempting to broker a compromise.[91]

Policies that reward work by increasing the household income of those who labor have not been as popular among the states or advanced as persuasively by liberals during reauthorization debates. States have made it possible for families to hold more assets and still be eligible for TANF cash assistance, and they have adopted more generous earned income disregards, the technical name for a practice that reduces the welfare grant by less than the amount earned through work.[92] Theoretically, these policies are supposed to enable women to combine work and welfare and thus increase household income. But because caseloads declined significantly, few working mothers are eligible for cash assistance through TANF and thus do not benefit from these changes.[93] In addition, because maximum benefits remain low in most states and because their real value is still declining, even generous disregards mean that those working single mothers who receive some cash assistance through TANF do not receive much money.[94] Finally, although much was made of expecting both mothers and fathers to contribute financially to the care of their children, most states do not give collected child support to families receiving welfare. The tendency among the states was to end what is called the "child support pass-through," meaning that for a family receiving welfare, the state retains the money in its own coffers and does not "pass it through" to the families. Of those states that allot some of the child support to families, only four give to families all the funds collected. Thus, in most states a working mother would find it difficult to combine earnings from employment, welfare, and child support to boost her household income.

Because of these difficulties, income subsidies to men and women with low earnings have to come from programs outside of TANF and require expansions in programs serving the working poor, in particular food stamps, Medicaid, and the earned income tax credit (EITC). In dollar amounts, the EITC is now larger than TANF, and eighteen states have adopted a state EITC supplementing the federal program.[95] Food stamps were always available to the working poor, and eligibility for Medicaid is no longer contingent on receipt of welfare. Still, studies find that most women leaving TANF and other low-income mothers do not receive many government benefits. Many families leaving welfare do not receive food stamps or Medicaid, even though they are eligible, and state practices administering food stamps make it difficult for working parents to meet continuing eligibility requirements.[96] Moreover, the increase in the EITC was offset by a decline in benefits from welfare and food stamps. Several studies also found widespread unmet need for child care assistance and—again—state policies that make it difficult for low-income families to receive assistance.[97] Despite increased earnings from paid labor and increased cash assistance from the EITC, poverty rates for families headed by a working single mother remained constant from 1995 to 1999.[98] The stagnant job market in the early 2000s meant that more women leaving welfare struggled to find employment, let alone better-paying jobs.[99]

Studies of women receiving AFDC regularly found that women could find jobs and leave the rolls, but many could not earn enough while working to support their families and maintain a family income above the poverty line.[100] Studies of women leaving TANF have similar findings.

When women leaving TANF find jobs, they find jobs with low wages and few benefits, similar to those held by other low-income mothers.[101] Over time, wages sometimes increase, but they do so slowly or not at all, and many working mothers remain poor or have very low incomes.[102] In other words, the economic benefits of welfare reform for women, children, and families are limited. Moreover, studies cast doubt on the psychological and social benefits for women and children, as women continue to experience high rates of depression and few improvements in parenting practices.[103] The empirical evidence that women leaving welfare struggled economically was recognized during reauthorization debates, but Democrats did not push proposals to increase the rewards of work during reauthorization. They emphasized instead improvements in human capital through educational activities and facilitating work through funding for child care. Make work pay was the rallying cry, but it was a slogan that focused on enhancing the individual woman's capacity to compete in the extant labor market; the rewards she would garner from this employment would be determined by the market itself.

◾ Conclusion

Grounded in the individuality paradigm, PRWORA denied the feminale roles of caregiving and nurturing, with mother-work deemed at worst detrimental and at best a private matter for society. Masculinist tenets dominated, as only paid employment was deemed to be work. Even feminale arguments about the care of children were subsumed into masculinism. Child care could be purchased in the market, so that women could compete in the workplace. Mother-work could be commodified.

Autonomy and independence were the characteristics desired of good citizens, and by definition, individuals acquired these attributes when they worked. The value of paid employment was not questioned. By uncritically adopting the masculine model of breadwinning and making paid work the only valuable path to good citizenship, welfare reform vanquished mother-work. PRWORA overturned the tradition of republican motherhood present at the time of the founding of the United States; it ended one of the few policies that recognized and valued the feminale.

◾ Notes

1. Kann, *A Republic of Men;* Newman, *White Women's Rights;* and Feldstein, *Motherhood in Black and White.*
2. Mothers who were legally minors were required to go to school and live with adults so that they could prepare for their adult roles as workers.
3. Schram develops a similar analysis in *After Welfare.*

4. Representative Fred Grandy, Testimony before the House Select Committee on Hunger, *Rethinking Poverty Policy,* 102nd Cong., 2nd sess., 1992, 11.

5. Robert Rector, Testimony before the House Committee on Economic and Educational Opportunities, *Contract with America: Hearing on Welfare Reform,* 104th Cong., 1st sess., January 18, 1995, 64.

6. Michael Horowitz, Testimony before the Senate Committee on Governmental Affairs, *Reinventing Government,* 103rd Cong., 2nd sess., Jan. 25, 1994, 80.

7. Representative Clay Shaw, Jr., Testimony before the House Committee on Ways and Means, Subcommittee on Human Resources, *Contract with America—Welfare Reform,* 104th Cong., 1st sess., January 13, 20, 23, 27, and 30, 1995, 63.

8. Comments tying welfare and poverty to urban minorities were woven through legislators' remarks. Sometimes those remarks explicitly connected the issue to urban blacks, such as Representative Deborah Pryce's (R-OH) criticism of Democrats: "But it is these same Democrats who are standing in the doors of the Nation's ghettos, refusing to let people out." 104th Cong., 1st sess., *Congressional Record* 141 (March 23, 1995): H3578. Indirect connections between welfare, single mothers, and social problems were more common. For a discussion of the development and use of racial stereotypes over time, see Neubeck and Cazenave, *Welfare Racism;* and Solinger, *Beggars and Choosers.*

9. Donna Shalala, Testimony before the House Committee on Ways and Means, *Contract with America—Overview,* 104th Cong., 1st sess., January 5, 10, 11, and 12, 1995, 59.

10. Tommy Thompson, Testimony before the Senate Committee on Finance, *States' Perspective on Welfare Reform,* 104th Cong., 1st sess., March 8, 1995, 17.

11. Ibid., 19.

12. Senator Christopher Dodd (D-CT), 104th Cong., 1st sess., *Congressional Record* 141 (September 7, 1995): S12763.

13. Senator Barbara Boxer (D-CA), 104th Cong., 1st sess., *Congressional Record* 141 (September 7, 1995): S12773.

14. Senator Tom Daschle, 104th Cong., 1st sess., *Congressional Record* 141 (September 6, 1995): S12714.

15. Republican Senator Rick Santorum (PA) called the Democrats on this reasoning, explaining that he could not fathom the argument that an entitlement could be provided to children without benefiting their parents. "I do not know many 3-year-olds who fend for themselves," he explained. "The money is going to go to the parents and it is going to be support." 104th Cong., 1st sess., *Congressional Record* 141 (September 12, 1995): S13344.

16. Roberts, *Killing the Black Body.*

17. Senator Patrick Leahy, 104th Cong., 1st sess., *Congressional Record* 141 (September 11, 1995): S13191.

18. Representative Bill Archer, 104th Cong., 2nd sess., *Congressional Record* 142 (July 18, 1996): H7796.

19. Representative Phil English (R-PA), 104th Cong., 1st sess., *Congressional Record* 141 (March 21, 1995): H3362.

20. Howard Dean, Governor of Vermont, Testimony before the Senate Committee on Finance, *States' Perspective on Welfare Reform,* 104th Cong., 1st sess., March 8, 1995, 13.

21. Representative Donald Manzullo (R-IL), 104th Cong., 1st sess., *Congressional Record* 141 (March 21, 1995): H3348.

22. Pat Gowens, Testimony before the House Committee on Government Operations, Subcommittee on Human Resources and Intergovernmental Relations,

Ending Welfare as We Know It: Progress or Paralysis? 103rd Cong., 2nd sess., March 10, 1994, 37.

23. Sherry Honkala, Testimony before the House Committee on Economic and Educational Opportunities, *Contract with America: Hearing on Welfare Reform,* 104th Cong., 1st sess., January 18, 1995, 77–78.

24. Pat Gowens, Testimony before the House Committee on Government Operations, Subcommittee on Human Resources and Intergovernmental Relations, *Ending Welfare as We Know It: Progress or Paralysis?* 103rd Cong., 2nd sess., March 10, 1994, 38.

25. Ibid., 37.

26. Representative Maxine Waters, 104th Cong., 1st sess., *Congressional Record* 141 (March 23, 1995): H3578–H3579.

27. David Liederman, Testimony before the House Committee on Government Operations, Subcommittee on Human Resources and Intergovernmental Relations, *Ending Welfare as We Know It: Progress or Paralysis?* 103rd Cong., 2nd sess., March 10, 1994, 134–136.

28. Leslie Wolfe, Testimony before the House Committee on Ways and Means, Subcommittee on Human Resources, *Contract with America—Welfare Reform,* 104th Cong., 1st sess., February 2, 1995, 1129.

29. Roberta Spalter-Roth, Testimony before the House Committee on Ways and Means, Subcommittee on Human Resources, *Contract with America—Welfare Reform,* 104th Cong., 1st sess., February 2, 1995, 887–888.

30. Some groups mentioned the need to place women in nontraditional employment, but generally they did not emphasize sex segregation as the central cause of women's low wages. Most placed greater emphasis on investments in human capital through education and training than on integrating traditionally male blue-collar jobs.

31. Lori Karny, Testimony before the House Committee on Ways and Means, Subcommittee on Human Resources, *Contract with America—Welfare Reform,* 104th Cong., 1st sess., February 2, 1995, 1152.

32. Diana M. Pearce, Testimony before the House Committee on Education and Labor, Subcommittee on Human Resources, *Field Hearing on Welfare Reform,* 103rd Cong., 2nd sess., October 28, 1994, 40.

33. Diana M. Pearce, Testimony before the House Committee on Ways and Means, Subcommittee on Human Resources, *Contract with America—Welfare Reform,* 104th Cong., 1st sess., February 2, 1995, 901–903.

34. Cathy Young, Testimony before the House Committee on Ways and Means, Subcommittee on Human Resources, *Contract with America—Welfare Reform,* 104th Cong., 1st sess., February 2, 1995, 1237.

35. Duerst-Lahti, "Conservative Women's Political Thought," 21–23.

36. Representative Jennifer Dunn, 104th Cong., 1st sess., *Congressional Record* 141 (March 21, 1995): H3361.

37. Senator Olympia Snowe, 104th Cong., 1st sess., *Congressional Record* 141 (September 19, 1995): S13791.

38. Senator Daniel Coats, 104th Cong., 1st sess., *Congressional Record* 141 (September 13, 1995): S13498.

39. Senator Rick Santorum, 104th Cong., 1st sess., *Congressional Record* 141 (September 6, 1995): S12702.

40. For the argument that dependency politics characterizes politics concerning poverty, see Mead, *The New Politics of Poverty* and *Beyond Entitlement.*

41. Senator Olympia Snowe, 104th Cong., 1st sess., *Congressional Record* 141 (September 19, 1995): S13790.

42. Senator Joseph Biden, 104th Cong., 1st sess., *Congressional Record* 141 (September 7, 1995): S12791.

43. "Remarks by the President at the Signing of the Personal Responsibility and Work Opportunity Reconciliation Act and an Exchange with Reporters," August 22, 1996, reprinted in *Public Papers of the Presidents of the United States: William J. Clinton 1996 Book II* (Washington, DC: Government Printing Office, 1998), 1325–1328.

44. Senator Barbara Mikulski, 104th Cong., 2nd sess., *Congressional Record* 142 (August 1, 1996): S9388.

45. As of October 1999, nine states required both parents to work to meet the hourly work requirements for two-parent families. An additional twenty-five states allowed both parents to work to meet hourly work requirements, but only seven demanded that hourly work requirements be met by only one person. "State Policy Documentation Project," Center for Budget and Policy Priorities and Center for Law and Social Policy, 2000, www.spdp.org.

46. Representative Howard McKeon, 104th Cong., 1st sess., *Congressional Record* 141 (March 21, 1995): H3382.

47. Representative Neal Deal, 104th Cong., 1st sess., *Congressional Record* 141 (March 23, 1995): H3677. Representative Deal switched to the Republican party on April 10, 1995, after the House passed its welfare reform bill in 1995.

48. Senator Barbara Mikulski, 104th Cong., 1st sess., *Congressional Record* 141 (September 6, 1995): S12687.

49. PRWORA imposed participation requirements on the states, demanding that certain percentages of the welfare caseload be engaged in work activities in particular years. PRWORA also eliminated the Job Opportunities and Basic Skills Training Program (JOBS), adopted as part of the Family Support Act, that emphasized education and training.

50. Senator Santorum claimed that even in areas of high unemployment, "there are jobs out there, you just have to go out and find them and be willing to work and go do it." 104th Cong., 1st sess., *Congressional Record* 141 (September 6, 1995): S12701.

51. Representative Mark Foley, 104th Cong., 1st sess., *Congressional Record* 141 (March 21, 1995): H3367.

52. Senator Phil Gramm, 104th Cong., 1st sess., *Congressional Record* 141 (September 6, 1995): S12690.

53. Senator Hank Brown, 104th Cong., 1st sess., *Congressional Record* 141 (September 7, 1995): S12787.

54. Senator Orrin Hatch, 104th Cong., 1st sess., *Congressional Record* 141 (September 12, 1995): S13347.

55. Senator Rod Grams, 104th Cong., 1st sess., *Congressional Record* 141 (September 19, 1995): S13788.

56. Donna Shalala, Testimony before the House Committee on Ways and Means, *Welfare Reform Proposals, Including H.R. 4605, The Work and Responsibility Act of 1994*, 103rd Cong., 2nd sess., July 14, 26, 27, and 28, 1994, 32.

57. Senator John Rockefeller (D-WV) explained that "states and the Federal Government have always shared the responsibility for the poorest families and children who exist everywhere in America," and a maintenance of effort requirement demanded that states and the federal government continue to be "honest partners." 104th Cong., 1st sess., *Congressional Record* 141 (September 13, 1995): S13538.

58. Senator Ted Kennedy (D-MA), 104th Cong., 1st sess., *Congressional Record* 141 (September 8, 1995): S12919.

59. Senator Christopher Dodd, 104th Cong., 1st sess., *Congressional Record* 141 (September 8, 1995): S12923.

60. Senator Kent Conrad (D-ND), 104th Cong., 1st sess., *Congressional Record* 141 (September 11, 1995): S13163.

61. Senator Barbara Mikulski, 104th Cong., 1st sess., *Congressional Record* 141 (September 11, 1995): S13190.

62. Senator Charles Grassley, 104th Cong., 1st sess., *Congressional Record* 141 (September 11, 1995): S13149.

63. Ibid., S13148.

64. Senator Rick Santorum, 104th Cong., 1st sess., *Congressional Record* 141 (September 11, 1995): S13189.

65. Senator Charles Grassley, 104th Cong., 1st sess., *Congressional Record* 141 (September 11, 1995): S13148.

66. Senator Rick Santorum, 104th Cong., 1st sess., *Congressional Record* 141 (September 11, 1995): S13188, S13193.

67. Senator Nancy Kassebaum, 104th Cong., 1st sess., *Congressional Record* 141 (December 22, 1995): S19178.

68. Ibid., *Congressional Record* 141 (September 11, 1995): S13148.

69. Senator Christopher Dodd, 104th Cong., 1st sess., *Congressional Record* 141 (September 11, 1995): S13172.

70. For an account of legislative action and the motives of Kassebaum and other women in Congress, see Carroll and Casey, "Welfare Reform," especially 126.

71. Federal law permits states to use these funds to provide cash assistance beyond the federal lifetime limit and to establish separate state programs in which families would not be subject to a number of requirements, such as work or cooperation with child support. In addition, states can devote federal TANF funds to services for working poor families, even if they have never received TANF cash assistance, and this assistance does not count against the family's lifetime limit. For an explanation of these rules, see Jack Tweedie, Dana Reichert and Sheri Steisel, "Challenges, Resources, and Flexibility: Using TANF Block Grant and State MOE Dollars," September 1999, National Conference of State Legislatures, www.ncsl.org/statefed/welfare/flexblty.htm. Federal law also requires that states conform to the Fair Labor Standards Act, so that states have to pay minimum wage if they require welfare recipients to participate in community work experience programs. This requirement has limited the appeal of having welfare recipients work off their grant through community work experience.

72. Diversion programs spread quickly throughout the states. In 1996 only three states had diversion programs, but by 2002, twenty-nine states had such programs. At the time of application, sixteen states required a mandatory job search. Only twelve states adopted neither policy. For data on these state policies, see Gretchen Rowe, with Victoria Russell, "The Welfare Rules Databook: State Policies as of July 2002," Urban Institute, October 2004, http://urbaninstitute .org/UploadedPDF/311109_DP04-06.pdf, Tables I.A.1 and Table I.A.2.

73. US Department of Health and Human Services, Administration for Children and Families, Office of Family Assistance, "Temporary Assistance for Needy Families (TANF), Sixth Annual Report to Congress," November 2004, http://www .acf.hhs.gov/programs/ofa/annualreport6ar6index.htm, Table 12:10; and Rowe, "Welfare Rules Databook," Table IV.C.3.

74. US Department of Health and Human Services, "Temporary Assistance for Needy Families (TANF) Sixth Annual Report to Congress," Table 12.3; and Rowe, "Welfare Rules Databook," Table II.B.1; and Nathan and Gais, *Implementing the Personal Responsibility Act of 1996,* 2024.

75. White House Press Release, "Working Toward Independence," February 2002, http://www.whitehouse.gov/news/releases/2002/02/welfare-reform -announcement-book-all.html, 9.

76. Rowe, "Welfare Rules Databook," Table L7; and Pavetti and Bloom, "State Sanctions and Time Limits," 247.

77. Gais and Weaver, "State Policy Choices Under Welfare Reform," 35.

78. Rector, "Comment."

79. Phyllis Busansky, "Florida's Business Leaders Face Biggest Challenge in Welfare Reform," *Tampa Tribune,* September 2, 2000, 15. Busansky was the former director of Work and Gain Economic Self-Sufficiency (WAGES), for the state of Florida.

80. David Nather, "Welfare Overhaul's Next Wave," *CQ Weekly,* March 17, 2001, 585.

81. Department of Health and Human Services, Administration for Children and Families Press Office, "HHS Releases Data Showing Continuing Decline in Number of People Receiving Temporary Assistance," September 3, 2003, http://www.hhs.gov/news/press/2003press/20030903.html; and "Welfare Rolls Fall Under Two Million," October 7, 2004, http://www.hhs.gov/news/press/2004press/20041007.html.

82. Representative Clay Shaw, 107th Cong., 2nd sess., *Congressional Record* 148 (May 16, 2002): H2539.

83. About half of the states (twenty-six) have limited postsecondary education as an allowable work activity to less than two years full-time. Many states have curtailed even minimal educational services; twenty-two states have limited high school equivalency and English-language education as allowable first activities. See Gais and Weaver, "State Policy Choices Under Welfare Reform," 34. Even when states allow education as an acceptable activity, they provide few funds for these services. According to a study by the Center for Law and Social Policy, states used a miniscule amount of TANF and maintenance of effort (MOE) funds on education and training; even though almost all states reported spending some money on education and training, most spent very little. "Forty States Likely to Cut Access to Postsecondary Training of Education Under House-Passed Bill," Center for Law and Social Policy, June 19, 2002, http://www.clasp .org/publications/doc_Postsec_survey_06192.pdf.

84. Karin Martinson and Julie Strawn, "Policy Brief: Built to Last: Why Skills Matter for Long-Run Success in Welfare Reform," Center for Law and Social Policy, April 2003, http://www.clasp.org/publications/BTL_report.pdf.

85. Julie Strawn, "Why Congress Should Expand, Not Cut, Access to Long-Term Training in TANF," Center for Law and Social Policy, February 10, 2004, http://www.clasp.org/publications/TANF_Postsec.pdf.

86. For a summary of the provisions of reauthorization and a discussion of their likely effects on states, see Mark Greenberg and Sharon Parrott, "Summary of TANF Work Participation Provisions in the Budget Reconciliation Bill," Center for Law and Social Policy, January 18, 2006, http://www.cbpp.org/1-18-06tanf .htm; Elisa Minoff, "Participation in TANF Work Activities in 2004," Center for Law and Social Policy, March 23, 2006, www.clasp.org/publications/work_ participation_activities.pdf; and Sharon Parrott, "Conference Agreement Imposes Expensive New TANF Requirements on States and Will Result in Loss of Child

Care for Working Poor," Center on Budget and Policy Priorities, December 19, 2005, http://www.cbpp.org/12-18-05bud2.htm.

87. Mark Greenberg and Hedich Rahmanou, "TANF Spending in 2003," Center for Law and Social Policy, February 2, 2005, http://www.clasp.org/publications/fy2003_tanf_spending.pdf.

88. Donald J. Boyd, Patricia L. Billen, Phil Dearborn, Carol Meyers, and Jane McNeil, "The Fiscal Effects of Welfare Reform: State Social Service Spending Before and After Welfare Reform," Nelson A. Rockefeller Institute of Government and the Brookings Institution, March 31, 2002, http://www.rfs.rockinst.org/exhibit/110/Full%20Text/RIG_Brookings_ACF_Report_final.pdf.

89. In 2000, forty-seven states had limits below the federal ceiling. In some states the income of persons eligible for the child care subsidy could not be higher than 40 to 45 percent of the state median income. Gina Adams and Monica Rohacek, "Child Care and Welfare Reform," Brookings Institution, February 2002, 5, http://www.brookings.edu/dybodocroot/es/wrb/publications/pub/pub14.pdf.

90. "States' Rules for Child Care Are Reported to Be Stricter," *New York Times,* May 6, 2003, A26.

91. Senator Olympia Snowe (R-ME), at the time on the Senate Finance Committee, advocated increasing funding beyond the level supported by House Republicans. See Bill Swindell, "Working Through the Welfare Overhaul," *CQ Weekly,* March 14, 2005, 656. The final reauthorization provided some additional money for child care, but not as much as Snowe had pushed for. See Mark Greenberg and Sharon Parrott, "Summary of TANF Work Participation Provisions in the Budget Reconciliation Bill," Center for Law and Social Policy, January 18, 2006, http://www.cbpp.org/1-18-06tanf.htm.

92. For changes in these policies over time, see Rowe, "Welfare Rules Databook," Tables L4, L8, and L9.

93. Arloc Sherman, Shawn Fremstad, and Sharon Parrott, "Employment Rates for Single Mothers Fell Substantially During Recent Period of Labor Market Weakness," Center on Budget and Policy Priorities, June 22, 2004, http://www.cbpp.org/6-22-04ui.htm.

94. Gais and Weaver, "State Policy Choices Under Welfare Reform."

95. For a discussion of state EITC policies, see Joseph Llobrera and Bob Zahradnik, "A Hand Up: How State Earned Income Tax Credits Help Working Families Escape Poverty in 2004," Center on Budget and Policy Priorities, May 14, 2004, http:www.cbpp.org/5-14-05sfp.pdf.

96. Ed Lazere, Shawn Fremstad, and Heidi Goldberg, "States and Counties Are Taking Steps to Help Low-Income Working Families Make Ends Meet and Move Up the Economic Ladder," Center on Budget and Policy Priorities, May 18, 2001, http://www.cpbb.org/5-18-01wel.htm. For a discussion of administrative practices concerning Medicaid and food stamps, see Fossett and Gais, "A New Puzzle for Federalism."

97. States curbed outreach services and maintained administrative practices that made it difficult for working parents to apply for and maintain child care subsidies, such as requiring them to take time off from work in order to apply for benefits or prove continuing eligibility.

98. Kathryn H. Porter and Allen Dupree, "Poverty Trends for Families Headed by Working Single Mothers: 1993 to 1999," Center on Budget and Policy Priorities, August 2001, http://www.cbpp.org/8-16-01wel.htm.

99. Shawn Fremstad, "Recent Welfare Reform Research Findings: Implications for TANF Reauthorization and State TANF Policies," Center on Budget and Policy Priorities, January 30, 2004, http://www.cbpp.org/1-30-04wel.htm.

100. One of the more thorough studies is Edin and Lein, *Making Ends Meet.*

101. Pamela Loprest, "Families Who Left Welfare: Who Are They and How Are They Doing?" Urban Institute, July 1999, http:www.urban.org/publications/310290.html.

102. Sheldon Danziger et al., "Does it Pay to Move from Welfare to Work?" Working Paper 254, April 2002, Joint Center for Poverty Research, www.fordschool.umich.edu/research/poverty/pdf/v2workpays-danzetal.pdf; Pamela Loprest, "Families Who Left Welfare"; Denise F. Polit et al., "Is Work Enough? The Experiences of Current and Former Welfare Mothers Who Work," Project on Devolution and Urban Change, Manpower Demonstration Research Corporation, November 2001, http://www.mdrc.org/publications/74/overview.html; Shawn Fremstad, "Recent Welfare Reform Research Findings: Implications for TANF Reauthorization and State TANF Policies," Center on Budget and Policy Priorities, January 30, 2004.

103. Bruce Fuller et al., "New Lives for Poor Families? Mothers and Young Children Move Through Welfare Reform," Growing Up in Poverty Project, University of California at Berkeley, Teachers College at Columbia University, Stanford University, and Yale University, April 16, 2002, http://www.pace.berkeley.edu/pace_new; Kann, *A Republic of Men;* Newman, *White Women's Rights;* and Feldstein, *Motherhood in Black and White.*

6

Policy Casts Fathers: Deadbeats and Scofflaws, Good Guys and Promise Keepers

THE GOVERNMENT HAS ALWAYS HAD A STRONG INTEREST IN MEN and masculinity and created policies accordingly, including welfare policy. But which kind of man, and how does policy create such men? Although the Personal Responsibility and Work Opportunity Reconciliation Act (PRWORA) ended the last vestiges of republican motherhood, it pursued aspects of masculinity present at the founding, striving to create family men capable of being citizens and to reduce the number of dangerous bachelors and other disorderly men. Debates over welfare policy drew on themes that also harken back to the founding, such as using women to tame men and, conversely, enabling men to control women through private patriarchy.[1] Despite the oft-mistaken notion that gender and women are synonymous, men have gender too, and the government also creates masculinity through policy. In welfare policy, conflicts over men revolved around the extent to which government policies should enforce male involvement in families. The dispute centered not on *whether* government should be active in trying to induce biological fathers to assume various masculine roles, but on *which* roles should be encouraged, even required, by government.

This conflict played out in debates about enforcing the breadwinner role through stronger child support enforcement measures or moving beyond this straightforward economic role to encourage marriage and thus induce men to act as husbands and fathers. Not surprisingly, few proposals that reconfigured the idea of these masculine roles and questioned their centrality to families came forward because the ideas of intersectors and the gender left find few proponents in Congress. Broad support arose for policies that required men to contribute financially to the care of their children, an idea consistent with both similarism and universalism but one that can also mesh with the claims of traditionalism and patriarchalism. These measures also garnered support from adherents of feminalist and masculinist thought, as the policies could be justified both in terms of increased autonomy and independence for women, policies particularly important to liberal feminism and corporative feminalism, but also to all left of similarism. Further, the maintenance of the traditional masculine role of breadwinning could be seen as central to men's success as citizen-fathers and part of the sense of shared responsibility and fairness central to the ethic of rights supposedly important to men. Given the broad appeal of these ideas to adherents of different ideologies, criticism of the child support measures was difficult to mount, and what little emerged was easily ignored or neutralized.

Policies to foster and connect through marriage the male roles of husband and father were more conflictual. Various proposals were advanced initially by a group of Republican men who anchored their initiatives on patriarchal arguments. Consequently, the debate over men, families, and welfare reform in 1995 began with this attempt to center welfare reform around conservative variations of the complementarity paradigm. Despite considerable success within the House, these proposals became too controversial to serve as the center of welfare reform. Still, they survived in a less ambitious format, but one that left room for patriarchal and traditionalist arguments to resurge. As states implemented welfare reform and Congress debated reauthorization, policymakers used patriarchal and traditionalist ideology to promote marriage as a solution to poverty among women and children, even as most feminalists across the spectrum worried about domestic abuse and advocates of the egality paradigm were left reaching for positive opportunities within the complementarity framework.

As welfare reform was implemented in the states, initial research found that states were doing relatively little to advance the formation of two-parent families, focusing instead on implementing work programs for women. Reacting to this finding, a number of advocates proposed strengthening the male role in families. Rather than emphasize only punitive measures, these efforts focused on searching for programs that would encourage and support low-income men in finding jobs, paying child support, and becoming more emotionally involved in their children's lives. Commonly referred to as fatherhood programs, these policy initiatives have provoked little criticism, even though the justification for them is rooted in the complementarity paradigm. They are endorsed by conservatives using new patriarchalism to advance policies designed to reinstate men in two-parent families. They also have garnered support from those relying on similarist and universalist ideologies to portray child support payments as a means to help women and children financially; liberal feminist and corporative feminalist ideologies could see these measures as a means to improve individual men by demanding them to be responsible. In addition, similarist as well as intersector ideologies could envision a source of improved resources and opportunities if government strove to ensure upward mobility for all. One consequence of this focus on men's standing in the labor market, however, was to avoid and perhaps preclude questions about women's low wages and poor prospects for upward mobility, questions that would be readily apparent to intersectors and those on the gender left.

Consensus around fatherhood programs that could be achieved by ignoring certain questions was hindered during reauthorization, however, by a revived interest in marriage. When it advocated marriage promotion activities, the Bush administration shifted policy proposals concerning men toward the complementarity paradigm and away from the civic individuality paradigm. This shift had the advantage of drawing attention away from the need for government to shore up men's labor market prospects, a move that could be endorsed by all to the right of similarism. Still, it upset the tentative balance between the tenets of the complementarity paradigm and the policy tools of civic individuality that had gained support for fatherhood programs.

▪ Making Promise Keepers: The Complementarity Paradigm and Marriage

The preamble to PRWORA opens with a congressional finding that "marriage is the foundation of a successful society." Marriage is an "essential institution" for the promotion of children's interests, Congress continued, and children require "responsible fatherhood and motherhood" for a successful upbringing. Following these conclusions, the preamble details a litany of social problems that result when children are born out of wedlock and raised in mother-only families, including educational difficulties, juvenile delinquency, crime, poverty, and welfare receipt.

The preamble reflects the ideas of patriarchalism, whose proponents believe that a wide range of social problems originate in mother-only families. According to those making patriarchal arguments, mother-only families should not simply be seen as experiencing these problems but rather as the cause of them. For example, Senator Lauch Faircloth (R-NC) argued that the "root cause of the tragedy of welfare dependency is illegitimacy, the rise in out-of-wedlock births."[2] Representative James Talent (R-MO) declared, "the growth in illegitimacy is the single most important change in our country in the last generation. It is a fact so powerful that it annihilates all other facts."[3] Senator Phil Gramm (R-TX) even linked the rise in out-of-wedlock births to the decline of civilization and the greatness of the United States, proclaiming, "No great civilization has ever survived the destruction of its families, and I fear the United States of America will not be the first."[4]

Mother-only families were inherently flawed, these legislators argued, because they lacked a man to act as husband and father. When men became husbands and fathers, they fulfilled the breadwinner role, and their employment provided economic security and independence for the entire family, the woman/mother included. When men became husbands and fathers, they provided control, authority, and discipline, necessary attributes for raising children who would conform to societal rules and expectations. "When young boys are deprived of a model of responsible male behavior, they become prone to violence and sexual aggression," and young girls were "far more likely to have children out of wedlock," explained Senator Dan Coats (R-IN).[5] Mothers offer children unconditional love and acceptance; men are "the protector, provider, teacher, and authority figure."[6] Because only females can provide love and only men have authority and a capacity to protect, provide, and teach, children needed the presence of a father in the household in order to become law-abiding, well-behaved adults.

In these patriarchal arguments, welfare reform oriented around work would fail because the cause of the problem was mother-only families themselves.[7] The masculine characteristics of independence, discipline, and authority necessary not only to raise children but to support the very foundation of American civilization could not be accomplished by requiring single mothers on welfare to work. Though a work-oriented approach implicitly accepted the existence of mother-only families and tried to incorporate masculine roles and traits into families through women's employment, in the tenets of patriarchalism, biological sex and gender were inextricably linked, and therefore any attempt to capture masculine attributes through women was foolhardy. Such an endeavor would never succeed because females cannot achieve such attributes.[8] Only by eliminating mother-only families and reinstating two-parent families could the societal benefits provided by the husband and father be achieved.

That this approach minimized the importance of caretaking and nurturing provided by women was fine for these advocates. Tension between the masculine and feminale variants of patriarchalism did not emerge in these debates. Women's groups that espoused new right feminalist arguments also supported these measures emphasizing male rather than female contributions to families.[9] In their eyes, too many women had taken on the role of mother without the benefits of private patriarchy. Therefore, despite strong concerns about very young children, they felt these mothers were obligated to provide for their children. In a position that echoes Carol Gilligan's ethic of responsibility, women propounding traditional maternalist and new right beliefs concluded that to be good mothers, women must first take care of themselves and that work was the route to such self-development.[10] Because the feminale activities of caretaking and nurturing were valuable only in the structure of a two-parent family, government policies should not encourage women to establish single-parent families.

The advocates of such beliefs generated a host of ideas about ways to incorporate men into families through marriage. In the 1995–1996 welfare reform debate, policy initiatives centered on eliminating the alleged incentive to form a mother-only family through a nonmarital birth.[11] This incentive was supposedly embedded in Aid to Families with Dependent Children (AFDC) because it provided public aid to unwed mothers and their children. Arguing that "you get what you pay for," legislators advancing new patriarchalism maintained that this cash assistance paid for and subsidized illegitimacy. Welfare encouraged young men and young women to be irresponsible about sex and then encouraged young women to forgo marriage and establish independent households when they became pregnant. Welfare encouraged young men to abandon their responsibilities to provide for and protect these women and children. Welfare made husbands and fathers dispensable and lured women into having children without marrying.

Given this line of thought, ideal solutions were straightforward. Withdraw this incentive, and illegitimacy would decline. The primary proposals at the heart of this complementarity orientation to welfare reform were distinctly masculinist—the penalties were directed at women rather than men. Targeting women's childbearing, the two main initiatives would have required states to deny aid to unwed teen mothers and their children and imposed family caps, a term referring to the practice of refusing to increase benefits if a child is born to a woman already receiving public assistance.[12]

An additional measure focused on paternity and would have denied benefits to any child for whom paternity was not established, even when the child's mother had cooperated with the state government in its efforts to identify a child's biological father. Even though it might seem unreasonable to penalize women for something they have no control over, this proposal indicated the extent to which proponents of new patriarchalism believed in the importance of legal fatherhood and "legitimate" children. Children who did not have legal fathers—men identified and acknowledged by the government as fathers—should not receive public support.

New patriarchalist arguments claimed that the financial disincentives inherit in these proposals would hinder the formation of single-parent families by inducing women to forgo childbearing or to marry before or during pregnancy. If young, unmarried women did not have children, they would not be poor, and there would be fewer poor children. If young men and women married, men would work hard, families would be independent, and children would be raised with proper virtues. The nation would "return to the teachings of the moral obligations: self-sacrifice, social conformity, and abstinence."[13] It was crucial that the federal government require the states to adopt these measures. Despite the general conservative inclination to grant more authority and decisionmaking power to the states, an inclination that prevailed in other aspects of the legislation, proponents of new patriarchalism argued that in this instance, the intrusion of the federal government was warranted. Because of the overriding national interest in curbing illegitimacy, the federal government needed to intervene and restrict state autonomy.[14]

Although these legislators wanted to advance marriage, their proposals focused on disincentives for out-of-wedlock births rather than incentives to marry, a move that could have appealed to the traditionalist's pragmatism and the universalist's and similarist's penchant for choice. As a solution to the alleged antifamily bias of AFDC, extending benefits to two-parent families had been proposed in both the 1960s and 1970s, but those articulating new patriarchal views advanced no such proposal. They did not even consider building on recent state experiments with modest financial incentives to marry, dubbed "bridefare" or "wedfare" by pundits.[15] Support from the state for two-parent families would simply be another kind of welfare, public assistance that undermined the very attributes of independence and discipline that men should impart to families. Inside the confines of marriage and private patriarchy, men should become good guys who held up their end of the family bargain or promise keepers who gave strong leadership to and provided for their families.

Although many opposed these measures, their criticism did not rest on a defense of single mothers. Legislators making similarist and universalist arguments did not refrain from lamenting the rise in the out-of-wedlock birthrate. After all, the pressures of mothering diminished women's capacity to compete in the world as an independent adult. For example, Representative Barbara Kennelly (D-CT), who took an active role in trying to blunt the force of the initial measures, explained, "all of us want to lower the number of out-of-wedlock births. There is no doubt about it. It has gone beyond acceptability, it has gone beyond what we can handle."[16] They instead centered their criticisms on the unjust punishment of children that would result from these measures. Children could not possibly be held responsible for the circumstances of their birth, opponents complained, and thus did not deserve to be punished for being born out of wedlock, to a woman already receiving welfare, or without a legally identified father.[17] Even if the punitive measures had some impact on out-of-wedlock births, children would continue to be born in these circumstances. Denying them benefits would merely worsen their already impoverished living conditions.

Yet it was not punitive measures per se that these critics of patriarchalism opposed, for they advanced their own set of punitive measures that would deny or reduce benefits provided to children. They endorsed denying benefits to women who did not cooperate with the government in identifying the fathers of their children and legally establishing paternity.[18] They endorsed restrictions on the aid provided to mothers who were minors, including prohibiting them from establishing independent households and requiring them to live with parents or in group homes.[19] These initiatives would also punish children for the actions of their parents, but they were grounded in the individuality paradigm rather than complementarity. Rather than penalizing single mothers for not being married, they penalized single mothers who did not act in prescribed ways intended to establish households independent from government support.

■ From Deadbeats to Good Guys: The Individuality Paradigm and Child Support

Opposition to the conservative Republicans' family formation proposals rested on different ideas about proper gender roles and the desirable government policies to advance them. Rather than viewing gender roles through the ideas of patriarchalism, Democrats making similarist arguments and Republicans relying on universalism wanted all adults, including single mothers, to become good citizens by achieving autonomy and independence. For these legislators, the primary vehicle to achieve this goal was employment. Their views shared with patriarchalism a concern about the social problems corresponding with poor mother-only families, but saw work—breadwinning—rather than marriage as the solution. Thus, when conservative Republicans advanced the complementarity paradigm by introducing measures to reduce the formation of mother-only families, Democrats and other Republicans responded with policies consistent with the individuality paradigm. Through paid employment, women would assume the masculine role of breadwinner and bring to families all its corresponding benefits. Roles gendered as the province of one sex would be open to both men and women.

Relying on new patriarchal arguments, many policy actors lampooned this approach for treating men as irrelevant. In their eyes, if women are presumed to be able to support independent households through their own labor, then men do not have a unique role in families. Rather than share gender roles with women, men would forsake their families. Perceiving themselves as unnecessary and replaceable, men would not assume any duties and responsibilities within the family.[20]

But these Democrats and Republicans were not ignoring men. To the contrary, an emphasis on equal treatment and the assumption of responsibilities by all individuals led them to promote work requirements for mothers. It also justified a concomitant set of policies aimed at noncustodial fathers. Just as women should work to support themselves and their children, so should men. Fairness demanded it. Although this perspective did not extend to reinforcing through marriage the roles of father and husband, it definitely included imposing on men the role of breadwinner through child support enforcement. Government need not compel men to become husbands, but it should oblige them to assume the parental role of providing financially for their children and thus share masculine advantages with them.

Consequently, the child support provisions of PRWORA applied the tenets of the individuality paradigm to men, incorporating aspects of both civic and corporative individuality. Implicitly drawing upon complementarity by assuming that men already worked and so already should be breadwinners, the act built on earlier federal laws concerning child support enforcement.[21] It added several new requirements for state governments, pushing them to establish the administrative capabilities to collect more child support from more people. Steeped in the equal treatment language of individuality, these requirements included adopting procedures to increase the number of noncustodial parents who were legally obligated to provide support, the amount of support they were expected to provide, and the likelihood of collecting that support. Targeting state governments rather than individuals, many of these provisions conform to civic individuality. They aim to have government establish the infrastructure that enables people to act as good citizens. For example, one of the provisions required states to adopt procedures at hospitals to establish paternity voluntarily. Such a policy rests on the belief that individuals will act as good citizens—men will acknowledge their offspring—when given the opportunity to do so. Men would have a chance to be good fathers too.

The more widely touted provisions, however, rested on negative rather than positive assumptions about individuals. These were the provisions that added a new round of penalties for men who did not pay child support, such as denying them food stamps and revoking their driver's and professional licenses. The act also required states to develop procedures to require noncustodial parents who were behind in their child support to work or develop a payment plan. Consistent with corporative individuality, these policies presume that individuals will evade rather than assume their responsibilities. Government, then, must use its power to force individuals to fulfill these obligations.

As we discuss more extensively in Chapter 8, these child support proposals were initiated by a bipartisan group of women legislators who used their institutional positions to advance proposals consistent with the individuality paradigm. Democratic and Republican women worked together to urge the Republican leadership to include additional rigorous procedures and strict penalties for child support enforcement in welfare reform. They were initially thwarted in the House Ways and Means Committee, but this bipartisan coalition of women legislators persevered and used hearings, comments on the floor, and the amendment process to insist that child support measures be a critical part of welfare reform.

Although the Republican leadership of the House Ways and Means Committee was reluctant to shift the central focus regarding men from proposals rooted in the complementarity paradigm, the child support measures were remarkably consensual once they made it on the congressional decisionmaking agenda. Indicating the powerful appeal of the individuality paradigm, they could be justified in ways that garnered support from legislators articulating a range of ideological arguments. Similarist and universalist tenets validated equal treatment and individual responsibility without arousing friction between their masculine and feminale elements. Intersector arguments that child support enforcement would enable women and children to gain resources, much to their material advantage, appealed to Democrats on the left. These justifications in turn appropriated the patriarchal arguments about the importance of men made by conservative Republicans, making it difficult for them to oppose the proposals outright and allowing them to accept child support enforcement without having to compromise their underlying beliefs.

The similarist and universalist justification for child support enforcement that enabled Democrats and Republicans to cooperate had three central parts. First, crucial to these efforts was the argument that individuals were responsible not only for providing for themselves but also for their offspring, an idea consistent with both similarist and universalist tenets, albeit for somewhat different reasons, because anything else would be inconsistent with the ethic of rights. For universalism especially, "good" autonomous, independent individuals did not expect others to care for their children. Providing for children was a parental rather than a public duty. Moreover, for similarism especially, if men would do their share, then women could be autonomous individuals, independent of the state. Government's role was to ensure that individuals met these obligations and did not foist them onto others. If noncustodial fathers did not pay child support, the public would have to provide financially for their children. That simply was not fair and constituted "sticking taxpayers with the tab," a phrase used frequently by·a host of political actors.[22] In the individuality paradigm, caring for others was not an obligation adopted by citizens in order to achieve civic equality, but a burdensome duty imposed on taxpayers. Ironically, this tenet of individuality that destroyed republican motherhood's emphasis on women's civic duty for care work emerged in a policy plank that actually dealt primarily with men and fathers.

Second, claims about equal treatment accompanied this argument about individual responsibility. Noting gender conditions, similarist arguments contended that changes in societal expectations for women should be accompanied by comparable changes in expectations of men.[23] "Ultimately, anything we ask of mothers we should also ask of fathers," declared David Ellwood, assistant secretary for planning and evaluation in the Department of Health and Human Services, as he explained the Clinton administration's endorsement of tough child support enforcement measures.[24] Policy should ensure that men and women are similarly situated. If mothers were expected to work to support their children financially, so should fathers. Not inclined to flag gender, universalist arguments simply stated that all parents were responsible for their offspring. Ascribed gender roles of mother and father were secondary to the capacity of each household to decide, in the privacy of its home, how parenting would be handled. However, children must be raised, and if the households failed, government would enforce this obligation.[25] Like women, men had created children and therefore had the responsibility to provide for them.

Finally, legislators making similarist and universalist arguments agreed on the necessity of stringent and punitive policy tools to effect compliance. This reliance on penalties rather than inducements rested on a specific explanation about why noncustodial fathers did not pay support. Although many men from inner-city black communities would more aptly be labeled "embarrassed dads" due to their inability to meet the breadwinning standard of "good men," the dominant account was the "deadbeat dad" image, a picture of men who were able but unwilling to assume their responsibilities as fathers.[26] These men were more likely to be portrayed as middle- or upper-middle-class divorced fathers rather than poor, never-married fathers who faced radically different material conditions. They were "scofflaw or runaway dads,"[27] professionals or capable tradesmen who kept up with car payments but not their child support.[28] Women and children ended up on welfare because these men would not pay child support.[29] Some men would claim they were out of work and could not afford to pay, but court-ordered work programs would call their bluffs, and suddenly they would remember they could get a job.[30] Thus, even if deadbeat dads were poor and unable to pay support, their destitution was voluntary. If they wanted to and tried hard enough, they could find work and fulfill their male breadwinning roles by paying child support.

Because for these proponents, nothing but personal irresponsibility prevented these men from paying child support, policies that penalized men for noncompliance were ideal. Penalties would accomplish the goal of actually collecting the support due because men would pay when forced to do so. Moreover, these men supposedly could afford to pay support, so the approach was worthwhile because it would actually make women and children better off economically. Penalties would also foster a sense of individual responsibility by declaring societal expectations and transmitting them to the public, even to children.[31] They would also make it clear that there was no valid reason to not fulfill this responsibility. Even men who did not have jobs could be required to enroll in work programs, an opportunity that would later be supported by proponents of policies in the egality paradigm. If individuals were not autonomous and independent, they could be made so, both women and men.

A challenge to these arguments from the left did not emerge. Intersector tenets recognized the deep structural inequities in the labor market that reduced women's earnings, making them more vulnerable economically, and thus in need of financial support from males. Fighting for structural change of the labor market so that women could earn higher wages or promoting public assistance to compensate for the failure of the labor market was impractical. But the left was bound by the demise of comparable worth efforts in the mid-1980s and the market-driven new Democrats. Further, masculinist dominance overwhelmed. Few in Congress recognized how the labor market was structured by sex, and the idea that government should adopt labor policies to enable women to raise their children without financial support from fathers was too challenging to masculinism.[32] The dominance of the individuality paradigm—in particular, the idea that individuals should support their own children—constrained the ability to challenge these policies from the left.[33] Concerns drawing on social democratic or social-liberal feminism and their stronger orientation toward an ethic of care were not raised. Working within the policy options presented, then, legislators using intersector ideas saw in child support enforcement a glimmer of improved material conditions for poor women and children.

Support from Republicans attuned to traditionalism and patriarchalism was attained by emphasizing the conservative underpinnings of child support enforcement and downplaying the possible rift between feminalist and masculinist perspectives. Liberal feminist arguments for child support enforcement that emphasized enabling women to successfully head single-parent families clashed with patriarchal tenets that understood mother-only families to be the root cause of social problems. Conservative Republican men were not going to support policies under the guise of advancing women's autonomy in forming families. Child support enforcement measures that accepted mother-only families as a legitimate family form implied that masculine roles could be met simply through a check and undermined the notion that men were crucial to families.[34]

Yet patriarchalist arguments about the importance of men to families left these Republicans no room to argue convincingly against child support enforcement policies centered in the corporative individuality paradigm. They could not criticize the proposals for being too punitive when they had already endorsed tough penalties for women who did not cooperate with the state in its efforts to establish paternity. They could not very well argue that men did not earn enough to pay child support, given that they had already argued that work could be found, if only women would look for and accept jobs. Once confronted with the issue of child support enforcement, patriarchal ideas about gender roles constrained their arguments, and they had to acknowledge that if men were so important to families, they should at least have to meet a minimal breadwinner duty of paying child support.

In accounting for their endorsement of stringent child support enforcement measures, these Republicans did not stray from their faith in two-parent families and the belief that children needed the gendered parenting of a mother and a father. They instead used patriarchalism to revamp the understood need for child support enforcement, presenting it as a policy weapon that would curtail illegitimacy and reestablish the primacy of two-parent families. The chairman of the House Ways and Means Committee, Representative Clay Shaw, Jr. (R-FL), explained, "Oh, I can tell you, I think the best way to stop out-of-wedlock births is to get the dad . . . we are going to identify them, we are going to find them, and we are going to make them pay."[35] Because child support orders rest on knowing paternity, child support enforcement measures secure the use of the law as a tool to ascertain who is the father of a child, rather than relying on the man's initiative in claiming a child as his own. Fatherhood was not only a biological or social act, but also a legal one. The state needed to use the law to compel fatherhood, first by establishing legal paternity and then by ordering and enforcing child support.[36]

This legal creation of fatherhood was a crucial device for establishing and reinforcing responsibility. Similarist and universalist arguments saw *individual* responsibility as the watchword, whereas patriarchal tenets were committed to *paternal* responsibility. In patriarchal ideology, the cornerstone of male involvement in the family was the responsibility to provide for and protect women and children. "It is unforgivable, it is wrong to walk out on a mother and child," explained Representative Shaw in his opening remarks before the house hearing on child support enforcement. "It is even worse to do so and not adequately provide for them."[37] Patriarchalist arguments could be used to ignore the possibility that child support enforcement would enhance women's autonomy and instead advance men's responsibility to assume the masculine roles in the family.

Because patriarchalist arguments located paternal responsibility in providing child support, opposition to this enforcement policy rooted in concerns about the distribution of power and authority in the family did not emerge from the masculine right. The feminale left also raised few concerns about how child support enforcement would affect the distribution of power and authority in families. Few women's groups raised questions about this issue. Groups advancing maternalist and corporative feminale views saw such decisions as purely a private matter; groups with social-liberal and social democratic views believed that increased enforcement of child support laws would improve economic conditions for poor women.[38] Most embraced the importance of establishing paternity and pursuing child support orders, although they wanted procedural protections for women who did not want to identify a child's father because they were afraid of domestic violence. They did not express qualms that men might try to use legally established paternity and compliance with child support orders to exert more control over children or press forward with custody claims in court.[39] They did not challenge the notion that it would be good if men became more involved in their children's lives and thus did not strain the cooperation between feminalist and masculinist adherents.

Men's rights groups, such as the American Fathers Coalition and the Children's Rights Council, were more insistent on connecting child support enforcement to broader struggles between men and women over control of families. Their claims aligned with patriarchal ideas that fathers were critically important to families and that welfare wrongly rewarded mother-only families. However, their primary focus was not on policies that would reinstate two-parent families but on reviewing and altering a host of policies and institutional structures in the legal system that they felt unfairly advantaged women in obtaining custody of children.[40]

Although these men's rights groups tended to analyze family law through structural systems and group dynamics, their ideas about the relationship between the market and government were more similar to traditionalism and patriarchalism. They tended to assert that women were poor because they were irresponsible and that men should have custody of children more often because they had jobs and could support them. But in contrast with patriarchalism, they wanted to upset rather than preserve traditional gender roles. This desire to dismantle gender might have led them to form alliances with enlightened left and liberal masculinists, but their conservative views of the market-state relationship and their refusal to see economic structures as the primary cause of material hardship limited their ability to forge connections with liberal groups.[41] Nonetheless, their complaints that child support enforcement did not address the real issue were handled easily by providing demonstration programs concerning visitation. Thus, their attempts to open up and upset the consensus behind child support enforcement made little headway as PRWORA was adopted.

■ State Implementation and the Individuality Paradigm

Child support enforcement policies consistent with corporative individuality were reinforced and strengthened as PRWORA was implemented by the states. In 1996, through executive order, President Bill Clinton ordered federal agencies to refuse a number of loans, including home, farm, and small business loans, to persons delinquent in their child support payments. In 1998, by adopting the Deadbeat Parents Punishment Act with little opposition, Congress created two new categories of felonies, with penalties of up to two years in prison, if noncustodial parents were found guilty of traveling across state lines with the intent to evade child support payments. Criminalizing the failure to pay child support was presented as necessary in order to enforce the parental obligation to provide for children. "The abdication of moral and legal duty by deadbeat parents calls for unequivocal social condemnation," explained Representative Bill McCollum (R-FL).[42] Government could not force parents to be "loving, nurturing, and involved," to fulfill the feminale, but it could force them to be providers, to fulfill the masculine role of breadwinning.[43] "This measure sends a clear message to deadbeat dads and moms: ignore the law, ignore your responsibilities, and you will pay a high price. In other words, pay up or go to jail," declared Senator Herb Kohl (D-WI).[44] Moreover, government needed to criminalize the failure to provide, to construct it as a felony rather than a misdemeanor or a civil act, because of the additional penalties and moral censure attached to a felony conviction. "A felony conviction carries more than just a jail term," explained Representative Marge Roukema (R-NJ). "A convicted felon loses the right to vote, to be licensed in many professions, to hold public office and many other rights."[45] Indeed, because this approach was so crucial to the enforcement of parental obligations, Roukema argued that the federal government should insist that states also make the failure to pay support a criminal offense. This approach limited civil citizenship. Men who failed to fulfill their social roles faced conditions of civil and political citizenship similar to women who, at the time of the founding, were restricted in property and voting rights and could not hold office. This approach also returned to notions prevalent during the founding that fathers were "good enough men" to be citizens.[46]

States have not shied away from these punishments and indeed have developed their own innovations.[47] For example, the state of Virginia launched a KidsFirst Campaign, arresting parents with outstanding warrants for not complying with child support orders. Then the state began installing car boots when parents were delinquent in their payments, with pink car boots for girls and blue boots for boys.[48] In a symbolic action implying that noncustodial dads were not just deadbeats but also criminals, Massachusetts resurrected the "most wanted" posters, highlighting the "Five Most Wanted of the Month."[49]

Child support enforcement policies that directly applied to custodial mothers also fit the corporative individuality paradigm. Federal law required that states reduce welfare benefits if the state decided that a woman was not cooperating in establishing paternity or collecting child support, but the law allowed states to adopt stricter penalties if they desired. Most states opted for stricter penalties. Only fourteen states adopted the minimum penalty of benefits reduction. All other states adopted policies that led to more severe sanctions for noncompliance. One state, Nebraska, reduced benefits and then terminated medical coverage. Other states moved to terminate cash assistance entirely, with eighteen states terminating assistance outright and fourteen states first reducing benefits and then subsequently terminating benefits if a woman was considered to be noncompliant.[50]

In addition, states chose to direct money collected through child support enforcement to the state rather than to women and children receiving Temporary Assistance to Needy Families (TANF). Under the 1988 Family Support Act, states were required to pass through to families $50 a month per child, keeping for the state only what was collected beyond that. The 1996 act eliminated this requirement, allowing states to decide if they would keep the money in the state coffers or pass it through to families. A majority of states retained all support collected while a family received cash assistance, and about one-third passed through $50 or less. Other states passed through greater amounts to the families, with varied policies about how this money affects the amount of welfare benefits they could collect.[51] Proposals to increase the amount of money received by families have been introduced in Congress, but they have concentrated on arrears accrued before and after a family received welfare benefits. They continued to require that women receiving welfare assigned their child support to the states and left it to states to decide how to handle these funds.[52] Representative Patsy Mink's reauthorization bill challenged conventional child support policies by prohibiting states from requiring women to cooperate with government efforts to establish paternity and child support orders and by insisting that states pass through child support payments to families receiving cash assistance.[53] But these ideas from the gender left have not been discussed seriously in Congress. Because the state had to pick up the breadwinning role, fathers whose children received welfare owed the state. The underpinning of the individuality paradigm—the notion that individuals were responsible for providing for their family members—was upheld by requiring fathers to reimburse the state for public aid.

Even as policies consistent with the individuality paradigm thrived as states moved ahead with tough child support measures, policies from the complementarity paradigm received less attention from states. As states developed and implemented their welfare programs, none centered their programs on the punitive policies concerning out-of-wedlock births underpinned by new patriarchalism during the congressional debate. Some policies concerning eligibility were adopted by the states, but they were not bundled together into a comprehensive scheme to reward two-parent families and penalize single-mother families. Moreover, in the states that did consider such an approach, opposition was fierce, and not enough support could be generated for the proposals.

One policy change concerning family structure that spread rapidly and widely through the states was removing the barriers for eligibility imposed on two-parent families. During AFDC, three restrictions on eligibility applied to two-parent families, but under TANF, more than two-thirds of the states eliminated all those restrictions.[54] Because procedures adopted by the states discourage all families from receiving welfare, the impact of these changes on particular families is minimal. But ideologically, they indicate equal treatment of two-parent and single-parent families and a willingness, at least on paper, to extend cash assistance to able-bodied men, a shift hinting at the egality paradigm.

Although states changed their eligibility policies so that they did not disadvantage two-parent families, states opted not to deny aid to unwed mothers and their children, an idea pushed vigorously through patriarchal arguments in the House debate. About half the states (twenty-one) adopted a family cap in various forms, with the most common policy to be the straightforward denial of an increased grant if a child was born to a woman already receiving public assistance.[55] Although much of the rhetoric justifying the family cap centered on preventing out-of-wedlock births and promoting childbearing within marriage, the cap applied to both unmarried and married women. Some proponents tied the cap to individuality rather than complementarity by emphasizing the importance of having children only if one could support them. In this view, having a child while receiving welfare, whether or not one is married, should be discouraged. For example, then New Jersey governor Christine Todd Whitman defended the cap by asserting "it's about accepting responsibility for your actions, and personal responsibility."[56] The commissioner of the state's Department of Human Services, Michele Guhl, elaborated on the administration's reasoning: "We think the family cap says to a family, 'If you want to have another child while you are on welfare, that is certainly your choice, but it is also your responsibility—and not that of the public—to financially care for that child.'"[57]

In some states, legislators introduced family formation proposals as the heart of the state's welfare program. But they were too controversial, and states moved away from them to more consensual work programs. Even in conservative states known for meager welfare benefits, patriarchal tenets could not justify punitive proposals rooted in complementarity as the heart of welfare policies. For example, in Mississippi, the early (1992) welfare reform bill included proposals to implant "female AFDC recipients with four or more children with the birth control drug Norplant," impose a family cap, and offer "a thousand dollar 'reward' to women who married and left the rolls."[58] Designating it a "pro-family" bill, State Senator Gunn said the primary intent was "'to restore sanctity to the family and dignity to the individual.'"[59] Governor Kirk Fordice invoked the complementarity paradigm when he argued that the cap would prevent births to teen mothers and thus "the continual production of children that nobody seems to want to take responsibility for raising," and would thereby get "right to the root cause of crime in Mississippi."[60] But there was strong opposition from the State Legislature's Black Caucus and a variety of advocacy and religious groups, and the bill eventually died after the chair of the House Appropriations Committee refused to consider it, saying that he "didn't want to put the House through the misery of debating this bill."[61] Though the final bill retained the cap, the new proposal focused instead on work and self-sufficiency, with an emphasis on immediate attachment to the workforce.

■ Reviving Complementarity in Reauthorization

Defenders of the states' focus on work often argued that work requirements and time limits were sufficient to fulfill the family formation goals outlined in PRWORA. Enamored of the notions of individual responsibility and accountability in the individuality paradigm, these advocates believed that work would structure women's lives and thus lead them to control—and limit—their own childbearing.[62] Tough child support enforcement policies would have similar effects on men, they argued. But advocates of the complementarity paradigm were discomfited by policies that ceded such leeway to individuals and treated decisions about family formation and structure as secondary, rather than primary, consequences. Conservative Republicans were not content with relying on child support enforcement alone to compel men to take on a host of masculine roles in the family. Moreover, they feared precisely what liberal feminism wanted—if child support enforcement were successful, it would enhance women's autonomy by providing them greater financial resources to support a family without marriage. But their efforts to advance punitive policies within the complementarity paradigm had failed, and they looked to advance proposals concerning family formation that could gain more political support from others.

They turned first to fatherhood programs, a shorthand label referring to programs that offer services to men in hopes of encouraging them to take on masculine familial roles. Fatherhood programs can be designed in ways that tap into all of the paradigms, but they are most compatible with the complementarity paradigm. Fatherhood programs are based on the idea of gendered parenting and the gendered transmission of this knowledge. Advocates are interested not just in having fathers provide financially for children, but also in establishing more direct involvement in children's lives. They believe that, as fathers, men play a pivotal role in children's upbringing that cannot be filled by any other person, certainly not a mother. Moreover, men have to be taught how to be fathers by other men. Fathering is a male role, and one that is culturally and socially transmitted by men.[63]

Fatherhood programs are based on the idea that men want to, but cannot, care for their children, both financially and emotionally, in contrast to child support enforcement measures, which assume that men can, but will not, support their children. No longer are these men deadbeat dads who will not pay support unless forced to do so by the government. Now they are "deadbroke" dads who simply do not earn enough money to cover their own living expenses and those of their children. They do what they can by providing in-kind support and intermittently slipping money to the child's mother when they have it. Moreover, they want to be good fathers, but they do not know how to do so, for they were not taught or shown how to be fathers.[64] Unless there is some intervention, over time, they will drift away from their children and their children's mothers. Fatherhood programs assume that these men are basically good people who want to do the right thing and just need to be helped along.

All fatherhood programs share this assumption, but they differ in the kinds of changes they think men have to undergo and thus the kinds of services offered. This variation can make the general idea of fatherhood programs consistent with a broad range of ideological strands. Programs like Charles Ballard's Institute for Responsible Fatherhood appeal to patriarchalism and traditionalism. With its emphasis on individual conversion and personal morality, Ballard's program holds out the promise that even the most disreputable and dejected man can be changed, and its use of married couples as counselors places a central focus on marriage as the ultimate place for fatherhood.[65]

Programs that offer employment services in order to increase men's earnings and thus their child support contributions coincide with elements of the individuality paradigm and thus appeal to both universalism and similarism. In addition, highlighting government programs that help low-income fathers gain employment needed to pay child support, similarist arguments emphasized the need to increase material resources for women and children. For example, Representative Benjamin Cardin (D-MD) insisted that "without such an effort, we are condemning custodial mothers near the poverty level to bear the entire burden of raising their children."[66] Because most programs rely on some element of coercion to induce men to participate, universalist tenets highlight the application of the corporative individuality paradigm to men. For example, participation in a fatherhood program is an alternative to jail time in Houston; part of probation or parole requirements in Wisconsin; and necessary to obtain flexible child support payments in Kansas City, Minneapolis, and Yakima, Washington.[67] Just as the work requirements and time limits of PRWORA demanded that women become breadwinners, so too could fatherhood programs: "all our program does is to level the playing field by making similar services available to men," explained Representative Nancy Johnson (R-CT).[68] "This is the ultimate in women's liberation, that we should begin seeing women and men actually the same way as human beings, with certain requirements and needs and capabilities."[69] Thus government policies help men, women, and children by requiring men to be good upstanding citizens.

Fatherhood programs were more problematic for legislators relying on intersector tenets because the programs ignored structural impediments in the labor market. Emphasizing such problems, intersector arguments could portray fatherhood programs as a misguided policy intervention, one that should be replaced by broad-based economic and social policies. "If we are really serious about improving the quality of fatherhood and motherhood in our country, let us do something about the minimum wage. Let us bring out a bill that will give us national health insurance. Let us really do something for parents so that they can be strong, competent, capable parents, raising their children in competent and capable ways," exhorted Representative Maurice Hinchey (D-NY).[70] But for legislators working within extant policy alternatives, fatherhood programs could still be presented in a manner that made them difficult to oppose, even through intersector arguments. Programs such as the Fragile Families Initiative were designed to extend services to poor black men. They were also very inclusive regarding family structure because they urged services for all unwed couples with children, regardless of the state of their involvement.[71] Tilting toward the egality paradigm, these programs extend the US welfare state to a group generally ignored.

Because fatherhood programs can be designed with different goals, services, and interventions, they can fit all the paradigms and gain endorsement through an array of ideological arguments. Complementarity can strengthen men as fathers, individuality improves men as individuals, and a rare nod toward the egality paradigm is seen in the unusual incorporation of poor men and, in particular, black men as worthy. Moreover, the issue has been set up in such a way that explicit opposition, particularly from feminalism, is tricky; it is hard to present feminalist arguments against programs depicted as helping poor and low-income men live up to their civic duties.

Despite this apparent consensus for fatherhood programs, state programs remained small, tended to be pilot or demonstration programs, and were also cut as states battled budget deficits in the early 2000s. Although states can develop fatherhood programs within the confines of existing law, advocates of fatherhood pushed for an explicit funding stream from the federal government in order to encourage the states to expand existing programs and develop new initiatives. Because Congress did not pass such a program before 2002, these efforts moved to the reauthorization of welfare reform. The Bush administration emphasized marriage, not simply fatherhood, in its reauthorization proposal, and the major bills debated in Congress included some funding for some sort of programs aimed at masculine familial roles. Indeed, the bill passed by the House was dubbed the Personal Responsibility, Work, and *Family Promotion* Act of 2002 (italics added).

The debate in the House centered on questions about work requirements, education and training, and child care, and legislators made comparatively few remarks concerning marriage and fatherhood. This relative quiet, however, concealed considerable conflict simmering behind the proposals focused on men. The very fact that the fatherhood programs can be arranged to fit with all of the paradigms and appeal to an array of ideologies also means that disagreements can emerge quickly, particularly when political rhetoric about proposed details and purposes tilts toward a specific gender paradigm.

The Bush administration opened such disagreement by focusing its reform proposal on marriage and heightening the complementarity paradigm. Making the patriarchal argument that fatherhood needed to rest within marriage to be successful, the Bush administration proclaimed, "cohabitation is not equivalent to marriage in promoting the well-being of children." The state needed to advance marriage because men would act as fathers only if they were husbands too. Calling for revisions in the preamble of TANF to give more weight to the goal of promoting "healthy two parent married families and responsible fatherhood," the Bush administration also requested funding for marriage promotion activities in state welfare programs.[72] The Republican-sponsored House bill obliged by including funding for activities that would exhort people to marry, such as public advertising campaigns on the value of marriage, and various kinds of education efforts centered on improving relationship skills.[73] Disputes over the centrality of marriage promotion activities in TANF continued as reauthorization quarrels persisted into 2005, with House Republicans promoting legislative language that demanded states include marriage promotion in their TANF programs and Senate Republicans favoring more flexibility.[74]

These efforts were not benign when viewed through the tenets of intersector and similarist thought. Similarism perceived unwarranted government intrusion into people's lives, with liberal feminism particularly concerned about undermining women's autonomy. Policies such as Oklahoma's practice of requiring women receiving TANF cash assistance to attend "marriage skills" classes were not simply irrelevant to their lives but potentially damaging because of domestic violence.[75] Preceding marriage with the word "healthy" was the attempt by the Bush administration and Republican leaders in Congress to signal their awareness of and concern for domestic violence; these efforts might have quieted Republican women who would support their party, but Democratic women had little reason to be hushed.

A second source of conflict rested in intersector and similarist arguments that marriage promotion activities would be ineffective because they did not deal with underlying economic problems. Trying to shoehorn the egality paradigm into these efforts, Democrats in Congress pushed for statements proclaiming that reducing child poverty was the goal of TANF, not just changing the structure of the families in which they lived. They also promoted a policy that would *require,* not simply encourage, states to treat one- and two-parent families equitably and therefore formally allow two-parent families access to cash assistance. Unwilling to allow Republicans to dominate the issue of fatherhood, they also included a grant program targeting family formation in their substitute bill. But it focused on what they saw as the real issue—jobs— so that noncustodial fathers could pay child support, rather than an "experimental marriage counseling program" with "no information on whether it even works."[76] "Deadbroke" dads needed jobs, not exhortations to marry.

All these proposals would create rather small programs with minimal funding. Indeed, the reauthorization of TANF slipped into the budget agreement in early 2006 provided $150 million per year for marriage and fatherhood initiatives.[77] Such an approach is probably a crucial strategy for maintaining sufficient consensus to pass legislation. Patriarchal and traditionalist arguments maintain that fatherhood, like mothering, needs to occur in the confines of marriage to be successful. Similarism lauds policies designed to induce men to be citizen-workers but is loath to involve government in efforts to induce marriage. Universalism endorses individual autonomy and freedom and thus would not validate government intervention regarding marriage and fatherhood, but legislators whose positions ally with universalism are willing to tolerate small programs out of support for their party. Because intersector thought sees a government responsibility to compensate for the failures of the market so that all persons can develop fully, legislators advancing such arguments seek ways to expand and extend the welfare state to poor men but are uncomfortable with solutions focused on marriage and fatherhood rather than the market. Even though these mainstream ideologies agree that government needs to do something about the men who are fathers of poor children, they do not all agree on what that something should be.

■ Conclusion

With a consensus around tough child support enforcement policies persisting through the adoption, implementation, and reauthorization of welfare reform, welfare reform efforts centered on cementing the notion that men should provide for their children. Although this idea has long been important in the United States, AFDC represented a willingness—however grudging—to publicly care for children who lacked a male breadwinner. Welfare policy now focuses on enforcing male breadwinning. If men and women would not marry or sustain marriage, government would require men to assume at least one masculine familial role.

The success of this endeavor and the dominance of the individuality paradigm rested on the assumption that all men were breadwinners. Men worked and acquired material resources, and even poor men could be successful breadwinners, if they only put their minds to it. Interestingly, when they looked at the implementation of strict child support enforcement policies, the fact that not all men fared well in the labor market was recognized by many, from legislators making universalist arguments to those advancing patriarchalism. But the implications of this finding were too serious to consider for long. Fatherhood programs run the risk of laying bare the myth of the male breadwinner, as they highlight the presence of men with low earnings and few job prospects and thus open the door to questions about the government's intervention in the market. Fatherhood programs indicate the seriousness with which mainstream gender ideologies perceive individual and masculine responsibility for their offspring. But the very need for such programs threatens the consensus that produces them. Thus, fatherhood programs continue to be small, with minimal funding. Child support enforcement policies within the individuality paradigm remain ascendant by keeping off the table questions about why women need support from men in order to provide for their children and why these men are "deadbroke" and not simply deadbeat.

The Republican attempt to rely on new patriarchalism to center welfare policy around punitive policies of the complementarity paradigm fared badly as states developed their welfare programs but did not prevent continued attempts to promote complementarity. Focusing now on efforts to induce marriage more than prevent out-of-wedlock births, policymakers sympathetic to new patriarchal beliefs continued to promote private patriarchy as the solution to poverty among women and children. Ironically, the success of the individuality paradigm helps to keep these efforts alive. Women's earnings are not high enough to compensate for the cash assistance withdrawn by welfare reform, and so it is to men that women and their children are supposed to turn.

▩ Notes

1. Kann, in *A Republic of Men,* writes of the founders' gendered legacy in which they asked "which men" should have rights and be citizens. He analyzes their treatment of bachelors, the family man, the better sort, and the heroic man. One suspects that most male members of Congress consider themselves to be "the better sort." See also Kann, *The Gendering of American Politics,* for the continuing consequences of the initial gendering of politics.

2. Senator Lauch Faircloth, 104th Cong., 1st sess., *Congressional Record* 141 (September 13, 1995): S13508.

3. Representative James Talent, Testimony Before the House Committee on Ways and Means, Subcommittee on Human Resources, *Causes of Poverty, with a Focus on Out-of-Wedlock Births,* 104th Cong., 2nd sess., March 5, 1996, 19.

4. Senator Phil Gramm, 104th Cong., 1st sess., *Congressional Record* 141 (September 13, 1995): S13488.

5. Senator Dan Coats, 104th Cong., 1st sess., *Congressional Record* 141 (September 13, 1995): S13499.

6. Popenoe, *Life Without Father,* 183.

7. Murray, "Keeping Priorities Straight on Welfare Reform," 10–12.

8. Staff at conservative women's groups disagree with their masculinist kindred that women could not possess such attributes, yet they seldom put this forward as the organization's position for a public policy because they agree that mother-only families are undesirable. Further, they believe that women should cultivate such attributes before having children and in case of the need to support oneself, but that children are a mother's most important calling. See Duerst-Lahti, "Conservative Women's Political Thought."

9. The largest new right feminalist interest group is Concerned Women for America. See testimony by Penny Young, the legislative director of this group, before the House Committee on Ways and Means, Subcommittee on Human

Resources, *Contract with America—Welfare Reform Part 2,* 104th Cong., 1st sess., February 2, 1995, 823–825.

10. Duerst-Lahti, "Conservative Women's Political Thought."

11. For an example of the types of proposals suggested, see Wade Horn and Andrew Bush, "Fathers, Marriage, and Welfare Reform," Hudson Institute, March 1997, http://www.welfarereformer.org/articles/father.htm.

12. Legislators advancing new patriarchal arguments also advanced abstinence-only sex education, or sex education that teaches abstaining from sex until marriage and does not teach about birth control. They also agreed with the time limits, work requirements, and block grant provisions advanced by others in welfare reform. Because they did not propose denying aid to all unwed mothers and their children—a proposal that would have been consistent with patriarchal ideas about the ideal family structure—they needed to champion policies that treated all unmarried mothers harshly and expected them to struggle with the market if they did not marry. Doing so also enabled them to build connections with legislators whose traditionalist arguments stressed a more pragmatic worldview and thus recognized the many working mothers who were forced to work by life circumstances or economic necessity. Of course, such women often fill the traditional feminale jobs such as clerical posts or teaching assistants that enable them better to reconcile their mother-work with their market work.

13. Senator Charles Grassley (R-IA), 104th Cong., 1st sess., *Congressional Record* 141 (September 13, 1995): S13509.

14. House Committee on Ways and Means, *Welfare Transformation Act of 1995,* 104th Cong., 1st sess., 1995, H Rept. 104-81 Part 1, 22.

15. For a summary of these state initiatives, see Bryner, *Politics and Public Morality,* 266.

16. Representative Barbara Kennelly, Testimony Before the House Committee on Ways and Means, Subcommittee on Human Resources, *Contract with America—Welfare Reform Part 1,* 104th Cong., 1st sess., January 13, 20, 23, 27, and 30, 1995, 169.

17. See the minority report issued by Democrats, House Committee on Ways and Means, *Welfare Transformation Act of 1995,* 104th Cong., 1st sess., 1995, H Rept. 104-81 Part 1, 363–364.

18. For the administration's views on paternity and child support, see David Ellwood, Assistant Secretary for Planning and Evaluation, Department of Health and Human Services, Testimony Before the House Committee on Ways and Means, Subcommittee on Human Resources, *Child Support Enforcement Provisions Included in Personal Responsibility Act as Part of the CWA [Contract with America],* 104th Cong., 1st sess., February 6, 1995, 33–35, 50.

19. See the minority report issued by Democrats, House Committee on Ways and Means, *Welfare Transformation Act of 1995,* 104th Cong., 1st sess., 1995, H Rept. 104-81 Part 1, 369.

20. Popenoe, *Life Without Father;* and Blankenhorn, *Fatherless America.*

21. National legislation was adopted initially in 1974. It required states to establish administrative systems to pursue child support for those women and children receiving public assistance and provided federal funds to help cover the cost of these activities. Subsequent acts adopted in 1980, 1984, and 1988 expanded and strengthened these programs. For example, the 1974 act required that mothers cooperate with state efforts to establish paternity and collect child support as a condition of receiving AFDC. Provisions of the 1984 and 1988 acts focused on noncustodial parents, generally understood to be fathers, and adopted

some penalties for those who were delinquent in the payment of their child support. For a discussion of the politics behind these earlier acts and changes in policies over time, see Crowley, *The Politics of Child Support in America.* For a discussion of the normative and political underpinnings of child support policy in the United States, see Josephson, *Gender, Families, and State.* For a discussion of the behavioral consequences of these policies, see Beller and Graham, *Small Change.*

22. President Clinton used this phrase in an address to the American Nurses Association. See John F. Harris and Judith Havemann, "Clinton Vows Tougher Rules on Welfare Fathers," *Washington Post,* June 19, 1996, A2. See also Representative Clay Shaw, Jr.'s (R-FL) statement announcing hearings on child support enforcement, Testimony Before the House Committee on Ways and Means, Subcommittee on Human Resources, *Child Support Enforcement Provisions Included in Personal Responsibility Act as Part of the CWA,* 104th Cong., 1st sess., February 6, 1995, 2.

23. In initial hearings on welfare reform by the House Ways and Means Committee, Representative Barbara Kennelly took the lead in this effort, frequently using her question time to point out that the Contract with America placed all the responsibility for out-of-wedlock births on women and did not address men. See comments and exchange with Bill Bennett, Testimony Before the House Committee on Ways and Means, Subcommittee on Human Resources, *Contract with America—Welfare Reform Part 1,* 104th Cong., 1st sess., January 13, 20, 23, 27, and 30, 1995, 170 and 177.

24. David Ellwood, Testimony Before the House Committee on Ways and Means, Subcommittee on Human Resources, *Child Support Enforcement Provisions Included in Personal Responsibility Act as Part of the CWA,* 104th Cong., 1st sess., February 6, 1995, 35.

25. Duerst-Lahti, "Conservative Women's Political Thought."

26. William Martin (executive director of Employment Solutions, the second-largest Milwaukee W-2 provider), interview by Georgia Duerst-Lahti, February 17, 1999.

27. Representative Sam Gibbons (D-FL), Testimony Before the House Committee on Ways and Means, Subcommittee on Human Resources, *Contract with America—Welfare Reform Part 1,* 104th Cong., 1st sess., January 13, 20, 23, 27, and 30, 1995, 506.

28. Representative Constance A. Morrella (R-MD), Testimony Before the House Committee on Ways and Means, Subcommittee on Human Resources, *Child Support Enforcement Provisions Included in Personal Responsibility Act as Part of the CWA,* 104th Cong., 1st sess., February 6, 1995, 22.

29. Representative Marge Roukema (R-NJ), Testimony Before the House Committee on Ways and Means, Subcommittee on Human Resources, *Child Support Enforcement Provisions Included in Personal Responsibility Act as Part of the CWA,* 104th Cong., 1st sess., February 6, 1995, 8.

30. Richard Hoffman, president, Child Support Enforcement, and Marilyn Ray Smith, president, National Child Support Enforcement Association, Testimony Before the House Committee on Ways and Means, Subcommittee on Human Resources, *Child Support Enforcement Provisions Included in Personal Responsibility Act as Part of the CWA,* 104th Cong., 1st sess., February 6, 1995, 95.

31. David Ellwood, Testimony Before the House Committee on Ways and Means, Subcommittee on Human Resources, *Child Support Enforcement Provisions*

Included in Personal Responsibility Act as Part of the CWA, 104th Cong., 1st sess., February 6, 1995, 31.

32. There was concern that tough child support enforcement might place *some* women in vulnerable positions, specifically those women facing domestic violence. But the idea that women as a group should not and need not rely on male financial support was not voiced.

33. Proposals to provide for a system of child support assurance have been introduced in Congress but have received relatively little attention and support. Even though a variety of interest groups and organizations indicated support for such a system in their congressional testimony, they did not push for it or spend much time and energy advocating it. In a system of child support *assurance,* in contrast to enforcement, government would provide a minimum level of support to all children in single-parent families whose noncustodial parent did not make this contribution. This government support would not be means-tested or tied to the earnings of the custodial parent. Thus, it would provide a greater level of public support to children than a system of child support enforcement. However, because it would support only children in single-parent families, it would provide less public support than policies to provide economic security to all children, regardless of family structure. For a discussion of such a policy, see Garfinkel, "Bringing Fathers Back In."

34. Blankenhorn, *Fatherless America.*

35. Representative Clay Shaw, Jr., Testimony Before the House Committee on Ways and Means, Subcommittee on Human Resources, *Causes of Poverty, with a Focus on Out-of-Wedlock Births,* 104th Cong., 2nd sess., March 5, 1996, 94.

36. For an example of this line of thought, see remarks by Senator Rick Santorum (R-PA), 104th Cong., 2nd sess., *Congressional Record* 142 (July 18, 1996): S8076. Republican women who played a critical part in advancing child support enforcement measures reinforced this idea. See the exchange between Representatives Jennifer Dunn (R-WA) and Marge Roukema, Testimony Before the House Committee on Ways and Means, Subcommittee on Human Resources, *Contract with America—Welfare Reform,* 104th Cong., 1st sess., January 13, 20, 23, 27, 30, and February 2, 1995, 687.

37. Representative Clay Shaw, Jr., Testimony Before the House Committee on Ways and Means, Subcommittee on Human Resources, *Child Support Enforcement Provisions Included in Personal Responsibility Act as Part of the CWA,* 104th Cong., 1st sess., February 6, 1995, 2.

38. Duerst-Lahti, "Conservative Women's Political Thought."

39. For example, see Nancy Duff Campbell, Co-President, National Women's Law Center, Testimony Before the House Committee on Ways and Means, Subcommittee on Human Resources, *Child Support Enforcement Provisions Included in Personal Responsibility Act as Part of the CWA,* 104th Cong., 1st sess., February 6, 1995, 174–175. For a discussion of power struggles between women and men during divorce, see Mason, *The Custody Wars.*

40. They believed that the legal system wrongly perceived women as nurturers, too readily granted them custody of children, and pushed men away from their children. The judicial system, they argued, was biased against men in making decisions about child custody and support orders, and the child enforcement system only reinforced that bias. For a discussion of attempts by fathers' rights groups to reform these systems, see Crowley, *The Politics of Child Support in America.*

41. It is difficult, in fact, to place men's rights groups on any ideological scale. On any given issue, they seem to take the position that favors men, even if that means they are not consistent on questions about the economy, individual responsibility, and government authority. Perhaps they are the ultimate masculinists because ideas about other institutions and systems do not constrain their positions. For example, see Stuart A. Miller, American Fathers Coalition, Testimony Before the House Committee on Post Office and Civil Service, Subcommittee on Compensation and Employee Benefits, *H.R. 3694, The Child Abuse Accountability Act, and H.R. 4570, The Child Support Responsibility Act,* 103rd Cong., 2nd sess., July 12, 1994, 69–71; and David Burgess, American Fathers Coalition, Testimony Before the House Committee on Ways and Means, Subcommittee on Human Resources, *Contract with America—Welfare Reform Part 2,* 104th Cong., 1st sess., February 2, 1995, 1245–1246. For a discussion of the internal dynamics and ideas of various groups involved in fatherhood politics, see Gavanas, *Fatherhood Politics in the United States.*

42. Representative Bill McCollum, 105th Cong., 2nd sess., *Congressional Record* 144 (May 12, 1998): H3042.

43. Representative Steny Hoyer (D-MD), 105th Cong., 2nd sess., *Congressional Record* 144 (May 12, 1998): H3044.

44. Senator Herb Kohl, 105th Cong., 1st sess., *Congressional Record* 143 (November 13, 1997): S12667.

45. Representative Marge Roukema, 105th Cong., 2nd sess., *Congressional Record* 144 (May 12, 1998): H3045.

46. Kann, *On the Man Question.*

47. For an example of one state's provisions, see Roper, "Hitting Deadbeat Parents Where It Hurts."

48. Teresa A. Myers, "States Get Creative with Child Support Enforcement," *State Legislatures Magazine* 24 (December 1998).

49. Ibid.

50. Department of Health and Human Services, Administration for Children and Families, Office of Planning, Research and Evaluation, "Temporary Assistance for Needy Families (TANF) Program Third Annual Report to Congress," August 2000, http://www.acf.dhhs.gov/programs/opre/annual13.doc.

51. Michelle Ganow Jones, "Child Support Issues in Welfare Reform Reauthorization," TANF Reauthorization Resources, Welfare Information Network, May 2002, http://www.financeproject.org/Publications/childsupportissuetanfreauth_trn.htm.

52. Ibid. See also Vicky Turetsky, "Reauthorization Issues: Getting More Child Support to Children," Center for Law and Social Policy, February 2002, http://www.clasp.org/publications/getting_more_child_support.pdf.

53. *TANF Reauthorization Act of 2001,* HR 3113, 107th Cong., 1st sess., *Congressional Record* 147 (October 12, 2001): H6780.

54. The barriers were limits on work hours, work history requirements, and waiting periods. Four states retained all three of the AFDC barriers, and one state provided no cash assistance under TANF to two-parent families. Gretchen Rowe, with Victoria Russell, "The Welfare Rules Databook: State Policies as of July 2002," Urban Institute, October 2004, http://urbaninstitute.org/UploadedPDF/311109_DP04-06.pdf, Table L2.

55. Shelley Stark and Jodie Levin-Epstein, "Excluded Children: Family Cap in a New Era," Center for Law and Social Policy, February 1999, http://www.clasp.org/publications/excluded_children_pdf. Controversy over the family cap

erupted in 1998 over a disputed evaluation released by the state of New Jersey. Concerned about the finding that the cap increased abortions, legislators in both the state of New Jersey and the US Congress introduced bills prohibiting states from adopting the family cap under their TANF programs.

56. Ovetta Wiggins, "Family Cap Stays Despite Abortion Rise," *The Record,* November 3, 1998, A1.

57. Cheryl Wetzstein, "Welfare Policy Gets Credit for Reduction in Births," *Washington Times,* November 3, 1998, A1.

58. Mississippi Field Research Report 3, Nelson A. Rockefeller Institute of Government, Albany, New York, 1998, 3.

59. Ibid., 4.

60. Ibid., 5.

61. Ibid., 9.

62. Wisconsin Field Research Report, Nelson A. Rockefeller Institute of Government, Albany, New York; Deborah A. Orth and Malcom L. Goggin, "How States and Counties Have Responded to the Family Policy Goals of Welfare Reform," report to the US Department of Health and Human Services, Administration for Children and Families, Nelson A. Rockefeller Institute of Government, December 2003, http://www.rockinst.org/publications/federalism/ ACFFinals1203.pdf.

63. For a discussion of the need for, logic behind, and kinds of fatherhood programs, see Senate Committee on Labor and Human Resources, Subcommittee on Children and Families, *Encouraging Responsible Fatherhood,* 104th Cong., 2nd sess., May 23, 1996. In its opposition to same-sex marriage, Focus on the Family lays out explicitly the need for gender-based parenting. See "Helping Boys Become Men, and Girls Become Women," http://www.focuson yourchild.com/develop/art1/A0000683.html.

64. Dana Reichert, "Broke But Not Deadbeat: Reconnecting Low-Income Fathers and Children," National Conference of State Legislatures, July 1999. See also opening comments by Representative Nancy Johnson (R-CT), Testimony Before the House Committee on Ways and Means, Subcommittee on Human Resources, 106th Cong., 1st sess., *Fatherhood Legislation* (October 5, 1999), 4–5.

65. See Charles A. Ballard, President, National Institute for Responsible Fatherhood and Family Development, Testimony Before the Senate Committee on Labor and Human Resources, Subcommittee on Children and Families, *Encouraging Responsible Fatherhood,* 104th Cong., 2nd sess., May 23, 1996, 21–23. See also opening comments by Senator Dan Coats, pp. 1–4.

66. Representative Benjamin Cardin, 106th Cong., 1st sess., *Congressional Record* 145 (November 10, 1999): H11872–11873.

67. Karin Martinson, Jon Trutko, and Debra Strong, "Serving Noncustodial Parents: A Descriptive Study of Welfare-to-Work Programs," Urban Institute and Mathematical Policy Research, December 2000, pp. 19–23, http://fatherhood.hhs .gov/ncp_wtw_d00report.pdf.

68. Representative Nancy Johnson, 106th Cong., 1st sess., *Congressional Record* 145 (November 10, 1999): H11889.

69. Representative Nancy Johnson, Testimony Before the House Committee on Ways and Means, Subcommittee on Human Resources, 106th Cong., 1st sess., *Fatherhood Legislation* (October 5, 1999): 13.

70. Representative Maurice Hinchey, 106th Cong., 1st sess., *Congressional Record* 145 (November 10, 1999): H11873.

71. See Ronald B. Mincy, "What About Black Fathers?" *American Prospect,* April 8, 2002, 56.

72. Office of the President, White House Press Release, "Working Toward Independence," February 2002, 19–21, http://www.whitehouse.gov/news/releases/ 2002/02/welfare-reform-announcement-book-all.html.

73. Jodie Levin-Epstein, Theodora Ooms, Mary Parke, Paula Roberts, and Vicki Turetsky, "Spending Too Much, Accomplishing Too Little," Center for Law and Social Policy, June 11, 2002, 16, http://www.clasp.org/publications/HR _4737_family_form_analysis_061102.pdf.

74. For a comparison of legislation in the House and the Senate, see Paula Roberts, "A Brief Comparison of the Marriage-Related Provisions in Welfare Reauthorization Bills Passed by the Senate Finance Committee and the House Human Resources Subcommittee," Center for Law and Social Policy, June 2005.

75. Peg Tyre, "Giving Lessons in Love," *Newsweek,* February 18, 2002, 64. For a description of Oklahoma's marriage initiative, see http://www.governor.state .ok.us.

76. Representative Ron Kind (D-WI), 107th Cong., 2nd sess., *Congressional Record* 148 (May 16, 2002): H2581.

77. For a discussion of reauthorization provisions, see Sharon Parrott, "Despite Inclusion of 'Marriage Promotion' Funding, Budget Bill Would Penalize States That Provide TANF Assistance to Poor Married Families," Center on Budget and Policy Priorities, January 31, 2006, http://www.cbpp.org/1-31-06tanf.htm; and Alex Wayne, "Budget Ups Federal Role in Promoting Marriage," *CQ Weekly,* January 16, 2006, 170–172.

7

Gender Ideology in Practice: The Case of Wisconsin's Legislature

BEFORE THE US CONGRESS PASSED THE PERSONAL RESPONSIBILITY and Work Opportunity Reconciliation Act (PRWORA), Wisconsin Governor Tommy Thompson had already signed, in early 1996, an aggressive new welfare reform act into law. Wisconsin Works (W-2) ended the state's guarantee of providing welfare checks to low-income mothers and their children and is considered the model used for the design of the PRWORA and its reauthorization package. An examination of the passage of W-2 by the Wisconsin legislature is, therefore, a good place to begin the search for gender ideology in welfare reform. By examining the motivations and behavior of Wisconsin state legislators who were responsible for passing W-2, we can demonstrate that the compound model of ideology employed throughout this book has a solid basis among the proposals and ideas put forth by real legislative policymakers.

With a long history of initiating welfare reform efforts and a reputation as a twentieth-century laboratory for the development of social policy, Wisconsin attracted national and world attention when it began to reform welfare as early as 1969.[1] Wisconsin legislators have experimented with and invested more time on welfare reform than any other body of state elected officials. Wisconsin moved toward legislation that encouraged maternal employment through "make work pay" strategies in 1969, when the conservatives in the state Assembly orchestrated a reduction in Aid to Families with Dependent Children (AFDC) payment levels.[2] The state set a steady pace for reform by the late 1980s, when Wisconsin first implemented Learnfare, requiring Wisconsin teens and teen mothers on AFDC to stay in school. In 1987, more legislation was passed that required the state to automatically initiate proceedings to establish paternity for children born to unmarried mothers. Then in 1992, the state extended its focus on marriage and paternity with the "bridefare" program, which was designed to support "legitimate" two-parent teen families with job training. The reform movement tried a new approach in 1993, with a two-county demonstration project called Work-Not-Welfare that was presented as the first small-scale example of workfare in the nation.[3] Finally, in 1995 Governor Thompson officially announced his intention to "end welfare as we know it" and replace it with workfare. It is this kind of reform legislation in Wisconsin that prefigured national legislation and ultimately served as the model for the PRWORA.

Wisconsin's long history of supporting autonomous mothers and two-parent families allows us to analyze the relationship between governing ideology and gender ideology in the state that first conceived of such a reform plan. In this chapter, we use statistical analysis to uncover the ideological orientation of the ideas and arguments used by the Wisconsin legislators when they designed and passed W-2 on April 25, 1996. By uncovering that ideological orientation, we can demonstrate how gender operates as a distinct part of the conventional governing ideology. We use factor analysis on data from a survey of Wisconsin state legislators who passed W-2 to show that the interpretive analysis presented thus far in the book can withstand statistical scrutiny. Application of the compound model of gender ideology allows us to see that both male and female legislators in Wisconsin use gender as well as conventional governing ideologies to shape public policy decisions about the gender paradigms Americans promote as a nation.

Statistical analysis of a compound model of gender ideology challenges the traditional ways of measuring decisionmaking inside legislatures. Legislative scholars have argued that a single, unidimensional, liberal-conservative voting pattern structures legislative voting and that political party is the most important influence on decisionmaking.[4] Those who focus their research on dimensions of legislative voting behavior, however, have a tendency to discount the importance of any secondary dimensions, including gender. Scholars who identify one dominant liberal-conservative voting continuum argue that the second dimensions uncovered so far provide only marginal explanatory power to a voting model.[5] Keith T. Poole and Howard Rosenthal argued that adding more dimensions to a model "does not appreciably add to our understanding of the political process."[6] Similarly, William R. Shaeffer argued that other dimensions exist "but are not central to understanding the ideological orientations" of lawmakers.[7] Thus, the influence of gender assumptions on legislative behavior and policy outcomes has more or less been ignored when studying democratic legislatures in the United States, except by those who exclusively study women legislators.[8]

Assertions against secondary dimension studies stand in marked contrast to the entire subfield of political theory, whose purpose, among others, is to understand the important nuances of the theories guiding ideologies relevant to governing and to explore ideas important to politics and policymaking more generally. For example, feminist theorists suggest that issues of gender have a significant effect on policy and politics beyond the traditional ideological concerns of the left and right. They have long argued that sex/gender relations are an independent field of power that structures both societal and governmental arrangements and decisions made by men and women.[9] Feminist theorists do not suggest we discount ideology as the dominant voting cue, but instead suggest that our complex beliefs about gender roles may also influence the structure of decisionmaking in this policy area.

A handful of scholars have begun to challenge the traditional ideological analysis of legislative behavior. Eric R.A.N. Smith, Richard Herrera, and Cheryl Herrera reported that traditional left-right voting models do not capture abortion voting well. Norton discovered that both male and female legislators used gender-related voting cues when voting on pregnancy, family leave, child care, and abortion legislation. Even Poole and Rosenthal have acknowledged that an important exception to unidimensional voting exists for the issue of slavery (1860–1875) and civil rights legislation (1941–1971).[10]

Here we intend to further extend the analysis of multidimensional voting by using welfare reform to show that the chasm need not remain between those who theorize complex political ideology and those who rely upon particular measures to show unidimensionality.

Uncovering Evidence of Gender Ideology in Wisconsin

Wisconsin voting patterns initially indicate that a liberal-conservative continuum or governing ideology was at work when the members of the legislature voted on W-2. On March 7, 1996, 74 percent of Wisconsin's state Assembly voted for W-2 (Assembly Bill 591); and on March 13, 1996, 82 percent of the state Senate voted for the bill. A few months before the reform passed, Assembly Minority Leader Walter Kunicki (D-Milwaukee) predicted overwhelming support for W-2 when he told the *Milwaukee Journal Sentinel* that people were afraid *not* to vote for it. He noted, "no one wants to go on the record voting against welfare reform."[11] The reform was supported not only by large majorities of the Wisconsin legislature but also by Republicans and Democrats alike. Only a few liberal Democrats voted against the bill, with six Democratic senators and twenty-five Democratic members of the assembly voting to oppose welfare reform.[12] These patterns suggest that identification of gender ideology as a protoideology in relationship to powerful conventional governing ideologies will be no easy task, especially since gender ideology remains outside the scope of most conscious awareness.

Our approach to uncovering or untangling gender ideology must, therefore, include the use of multiple sources of data and several modes of analysis. The use of multiple sources and methods will help us dig deeper into the basis for the welfare reform ideas advocated by the Wisconsin legislature and help us validate the results of our search at the same time. Further, by carefully distinguishing the data and methods that help us uncover the influence of conventional ideologies on welfare policymaking and the data and methods that help us uncover the influence of gender ideology embedded in welfare policymaking, we can show that a nuanced analysis requires a more complex or layered examination than is traditionally used when studying legislative behavior. After identifying the types of data we present in this chapter, we divide the analysis into two distinct sections. In the first section, we identify and acknowledge the power of the liberal-conservative voting pattern at work during the design and passage of W-2. In the second section, we identify the concomitant influence of gender ideology at work during the debate over this legislation.

The decade-long legislative history of W-2 and the passions evoked during its design and passage provided us with a plethora of survey and archival data for review and analysis. When Work-Not-Welfare came before the Wisconsin legislature for authorization in 1993, an amendment offered by an inner-city Milwaukee legislator added the stipulation that AFDC must end before December 1998 and the governor must propose a replacement for it by December 1995. This step led to a paper trail of news reports, legislative committee reports, and repeated votes on early variations of W-2. For example, a special legislative joint Committee on Welfare Reform was formed with three senators, three assembly members, and three executive appointments in an attempt to build a new replacement system that would be implemented statewide. This committee held six public hearings across the state and, in October 1995, introduced AB591 (W-2) into the Assembly with forty-nine Assembly cosponsors and thirteen Senate cosponsors. W-2 and a handful of amendments were voted into law in March 1996, signed by the governor in April, and implemented in September 1997. Wisconsin had become the first state to end a guarantee of welfare to low-income mothers and children. Nearly all parents would be required to work in order to receive benefits, with the exception of parents of children less than three months of age. Participants would generally be limited to two years in any of the government-assisted positions and to five years of benefits through the overall system.[13]

▓ Data and Approach

Documents and the Official Record

First, we gathered relevant government documents to chart the process of policy formulation and passage through the various legislative stages noted above. These include information on prior policies, public hearings, and the bill's general legislative history, published in Wisconsin's official *Journal of the Senate* and the *Journal of the Assembly*. With these documents we were able to construct a complete record of official action. Second, we tracked the press reports on W-2 in the *Milwaukee Journal Sentinel* and the *Wisconsin State Journal*. These newspaper reports were used to augment our understanding of the official legislative record on W-2.

Survey of Legislators

A survey questionnaire, entitled "Political Beliefs and Legislative Decisionmaking," was mailed to all of the 132 Wisconsin state legislators who had been in office during the 1995–1996 legislative session. Sixty legislators responded to the questionnaire, which asked legislators about their personal background, their approach to legislation, their basic political beliefs, and their key votes during the 1995–1996 legislative session. The response rate of 45.4 percent provided us with a good sample of legislators. Table 7.1 compares the characteristics of the survey sample to the characteristics of the Wisconsin State Legislature in the 1995–1996 legislative session, showing that our sample provides a good snapshot of those who were involved with welfare reform in Wisconsin at that time. The legislators responding to the survey were asked to reveal several aspects of their ideological approach to governing. These types of questions provide us with a variety of ways to observe the traditional liberal-conservative voting patterns of the Wisconsin legislature. First, we asked the legislators whether they considered themselves liberal, moderate, or conservative when voting on social and fiscal policies. Second, they were asked to identify their preferences on a set of core political beliefs that might guide their legislative decisionmaking on issues like taxes, the market, and racial discrimination. Finally, in order to uncover the gender ideology embedded in the legislative decisions surrounding welfare reform, we also asked several questions about each legislator's beliefs about gender and family roles. For example, we asked legislators if they believed "women should support themselves" or if "traditional gender roles are best"; if "men should be caregivers too" or whether "traditional gender roles are best"; and "if good families come in many forms" or if

Table 7.1 Characteristics of Survey Sample Compared to Wisconsin State Legislature, 1995–1996

Characteristics	Survey Sample % (N)	Wisconsin Legislators, 1995–1996 % (N)
Republicans	57 (34)	52 (68)
Democrats	43 (26)	48 (64)
Male	72 (43)	76 (100)
Female	28 (17)	24 (32)
Married > 1 time	93 (51)	75 (99)
Single	6 (9)	25 (33)
White	96 (58)	94 (124)
Nonwhite	4 (3)	6 (8)
Total	N = 60	N = 132

Source: Wisconsin State Blue Book, 1995–1996.

the "traditional family was best." (See Appendix A, which lists the questions used to survey Wisconsin legislators and the variables we created for the analysis.)

Wisconsin Key Vote Index and Staff Ideology Rating

In addition to using the legislators' self-reported ideology provided by the survey responses, we used two other measures of ideology to help validate our findings. We constructed a "Wisconsin Key Vote Index" for each legislator, using ten key votes we selected from the 1995–1996 legislative session. This type of voting index is traditionally used by legislative scholars to observe the liberal-conservative voting patterns of legislators (Appendix B lists the ten votes used to construct the Key Vote Index). Additionally, we interviewed twenty staff members who worked for the legislators in our sample and asked them to rate all the 1995–1996 session legislators on a left-right continuum. We wanted to see if the staff could clearly rank the legislators on this continuum. These data were used to supplement and help validate other measures of ideology we use in the analysis.

■ Evidence of Conventional Governing Ideology at Work in Wisconsin

Even a cursory glance at the evidence we collected indicates that conventional governing ideology was a powerful force shaping the final draft of W-2. The official record, voting records, news reports, and our legislative survey all indicate that a traditional liberal-conservative voting and decisionmaking pattern was at work during Wisconsin's welfare reform effort in 1996. Although later in this chapter we demonstrate that a more nuanced explanation of a legislator's ideology shapes policy preferences, we cannot deny the strong correlation between conventional governing ideology and legislative policy preferences for W-2.

The official record shows that during the legislature's Joint Finance Committee debate over W-2, all amendments proposed by Democrats were rejected on party-line votes. In two days of nonstop committee votes, the Republican legislators killed dozens of changes pushed by Democratic legislators from urban Milwaukee, many of whom were African Americans.[14] A week later, when the bill reached the Assembly floor, the Democrats continued to attempt to amend the bill. A *Milwaukee Journal Sentinel* article, titled "W-2 Rolls Through Assembly: Bids to Alter Welfare Plan Fail," reported that all twelve changes proposed by Democrats were rejected, primarily on party lines.[15] Similarly, the Democrats in the Senate attempted to make thirty-five amendments to the bill, only to be routinely turned back by party-line cohesion.[16] In the end, the bill passed the Assembly on a 73–25 vote and in the Senate on a 27–6 vote. Although a few Democratic legislators broke party ranks, none of the Republicans voted against the passage of W-2.

Analysis of the news reports also provides support for an argument that a conventional ideology was at work. Opposition to W-2 was expressed by Democrats who espoused social liberal positions, and support was expressed by Republicans who espoused libertarian conservative and traditional conservative positions. In other words, most Democrats considered themselves to be liberal, and most Republicans considered themselves to be conservative. For example, Gwendolyn Moore (D-Milwaukee), an African American state senator from urban Wisconsin, vowed to fight W-2 without compromise. In one of her many public appearances speaking against welfare reform, Moore exhorted the audience that she "would not tolerate any compromise on welfare reform that put children in harm's way."[17] Similarly, another urban Democrat, Assembly member Rebecca Young (D-Madison), argued in the press that W-2 was unacceptable because it did not recognize the need for more education and training opportunities,[18] and yet another urban Democrat, Senator Gary George (D-Milwaukee), claimed that the Republicans were only giving the appearance of caring for the poor when supporting W-2.[19]

Republicans, however, tended to make public statements supporting the classic libertarian and traditional conservative positions. Assembly member Dan Brancel (R-Endeavor), a dairy farmer from rural Wisconsin, praised W-2, saying it "accomplishes the goals of helping people help themselves."[20] Similarly, Senator Carol Buettner (R-Oshkosh) claimed that "in W-2 we're giving people the opportunity and resources to work—they want to work."[21] Finally, the Assembly majority leader, Scott Jensen (R-Brookfield), noted that Wisconsin had set a national standard with W-2 by breaking the culture of dependency and changing it to "the only thing we know that works, and that is work itself."[22]

A quick look at our "Political Beliefs and Legislative Decisionmaking" survey paints a similar picture of the legislators' strong ideological orientations. Democrats from primarily urban districts who consider themselves mainline Protestants were the most likely to vote against W-2. Republicans from rural districts with small cities who consider themselves evangelical Protestants or Catholic were the most likely to vote for W-2. For example, a female senator from Madison with a law degree who identifies herself as a social liberal best represents the Democratic respondents who voted against welfare reform, whereas a male Assembly member from rural Wisconsin who is a conservative Christian and identifies himself as a traditional conservative best represents the Republican respondents who voted for welfare reform.

Table 7.2 allows us to look more closely at the relationship between the self-identified ideological orientations of the legislators and their party identification, their vote on W-2, and their votes on the Key Vote Index. Examination of the data indicates that legislators' governing ideology affected voting and party identification in Wisconsin during the 1995–1996 legislative term. For example, in the first column we can see that 100 percent of the respondents who identified themselves as strong liberals (social democrats or social liberals) also identified with the Democratic Party. Sixty-nine percent of the Democrats surveyed voted against W-2, and 89 percent of the Democrats surveyed scored a liberal ranking on the Key Vote Index. In the fourth column, we can see that 95 percent of the respondents who identified as strong conservatives (traditional conservatives and social conservatives) were also Republican; none of them voted against W-2; and 54 percent scored a conservative ranking on the Key Vote Index.

Finally, Table 7.3 presents staff ratings of state legislators' ideological positions in the 1995–1996 legislative term. As noted earlier, staff aides in each chamber were asked to rate legislators on the liberal-conservative continuum we present in Chapter 3 (Table 3.1). It is interesting to see that the staff aides were clearly able to identify the ideological variant associated with 132 of the Wisconsin legislators without any difficulty. Although these data are only descriptive, they show how these legislators distribute along the standard continuum. Further, the data show that staff were able to distinguish a range of conventional governing ideology variants for both male and female legislators.

Table 7.2 Relationships Among Ideology, Party, and Policy Priorities in Wisconsin

	Wisconsin Legislators' Ideology, 1995–1996			
	Strong Liberal % (N)	Moderate Liberal % (N)	Moderate Conservative % (N)	Strong Conservative % (N)
Party				
Democrat	100.0 (13)	46.1 (6)	46.1 (6)	5.3 (1)
Republican	0.0 (0)	53.9 (7)	53.9 (7)	94.7 (18)
n = 58; X² = 28.04, df = 3, p < .001				
Vote on W-2				
No	69.2 (9)	15.4 (2)	33.3 (2)	
Yes	8.9 (4)	24.4 (11)	66.6 (4)	100.00 (19)
n = 58; X² = 22.6, df = 3, p < .001				
Key Vote Index				
Liberal (0–33%)	88.9 (8)	11.1 (1)		
Moderate (34–66%)	28.6 (4)	35.7 (5)	28.6 (4)	7.1 (1)
Conservative (67–100%)	2.9 (1)	20.6 (7)	23.5 (8)	52.9 (18)
n = 57, Gamma = .84, p < .05				

Source: Political Beliefs and Legislative Decisionmaking Survey of Wisconsin State Legislators, 1995–1996; Wisconsin Legislative Reference Bureau, 1995–1996 Key Votes.

Table 7.3 Staff Rating of Legislators' Governing Ideology

Ideological Variant	All % (N)	Women % (N)	Men % (N)
Social democrat	20.8 (25)	40 (10)	60 (15)
Social liberal	19.2 (23)	27.4 (4)	82.6 (10)
New (neo) liberal	10.8 (13)	15.4 (2)	84.6 (11)
Libertarian (neo) conservative	6.7 (8)	50 (4)	50 (4)
Traditional conservative	33.3 (40)	12.5 (5)	87.5 (35)
Social conservative	9.2 (11)	27.3 (3)	72.7 (8)
Totals—All	100 (120)	23.3 (28)	76.6 (92)

Source: Survey of staff aides to 132 Wisconsin legislators, March 1998.

Again, all the indicators suggest that party and governing ideology contribute to the design of legislative policy preferences and proposals. Initial examination of the official record, news reports, voting records, and survey data point toward a liberal-conservative continuum as the primary basis for developing the ideas legislators used for welfare policy design. At first glance, it appears that there might not be room for a nuanced explanation for the theories guiding ideological development.

■ Evidence of Gender Ideology at Work in Wisconsin

To identify gender ideology as a protoideology in relationship to a governing ideology is no easy task, especially given the strength of the traditional ideological dialogue in the United States. In addition, previous chapters have emphasized that the national dialogue surrounding welfare and welfare reform has been particularly partisan and ideological in nature. A more thorough examination of the press reports, survey responses, and key votes in Wisconsin, however, suggest that ideas about gender were deeply embedded in the policy preferences and voting patterns of the Wisconsin legislature when W-2 was passed in 1996 and can be teased out with further analysis.

The press reports we referred to earlier in this chapter emphasize the traditional liberal-conservative split over welfare reform: Democratic legislators made statements against W-2, and Republican legislators made statements for W-2. Still, closer inspection of the statements made to the press show that many Wisconsin legislators were keenly aware of the implications W-2 held for women and their children. In a report announcing the impending Assembly vote on W-2, Senator Gary George (D-Milwaukee) is quoted as saying the reform plan "bashes poor women and would hurt their children."[23] After the Senate passed W-2 two weeks later, the *Milwaukee Journal Sentinel* printed the following report explaining George's disappointment with the final vote:

> George said that the W-2 program will be good only for "bottom-feeding, scum sucking employers who want a slave pool of women laborers." He (George) argued that the new welfare program would harm poor children because if their mothers were penalized, their children would have to do without food and other necessities. "It's no different from Caesar's time," he said of the program's message to poor unmarried mothers. "If you don't work, we will kill your children."[24]

Gwendolyn Moore (D-Milwaukee), a woman of color who had once been on welfare, similarly condemned the bill immediately after the Senate vote, observing that W-2 would primarily hurt women of color. She denounced the bill as "racist and sexist, evil, and mean spirited," claiming that all her efforts to help women and children by amending W-2 were finally thwarted on the Senate floor.[25]

These gendered statements are apparent in the occasional news reports about a legislator's beliefs and preferences, but they still do not show us that beliefs about gender roles and motherhood are important and distinct influences on each legislator. Closer scrutiny of the survey and voting data show us two new ways to think about the ideological belief patterns of the Wisconsin legislators. First, a reexamination of the data presented in Table 7.2 shows us that not all legislators fit neatly into conventional liberal-conservative patterns. Another glance at the table reveals that Democrats did not all identify themselves as strong liberals; conversely, Republicans did not all identify themselves as strong conservatives. In fact, 45 percent of the Wisconsin legislators surveyed considered themselves to be moderate, regardless of whether they were Democrats or Republicans. Further, Table 7.2 shows that several self-identified strong liberals and strong conservatives crossed over the conventional ideological lines during the 1995–1996 legislative session. For example, when looking at each legislator's party, we see that one Democrat identified himself as a strong conservative; when looking at each legislator's vote on W-2, we see that four self-identified strong liberals voted for W-2; and when looking at the Key Vote Index, we see that one strong liberal had a conservative ranking (scoring above 67 percent) and that one strong conservative had a moderate ranking (scoring below 67 percent). In each instance noted here, these legislators crossed the traditional ideological divide, indicating that other ideological patterns may be at work.

Second, a review of individual legislators' responses to questions in our Political Beliefs and Legislative Decisionmaking Survey about gender and family roles suggests that gender beliefs may serve as the "other" ideological pattern at work during the passage of W-2.[26] The traditional liberal-conservative ideological patterns simply do not explain every legislator's approach to the bill. If conventional patterns were closely related to gender belief patterns, we would expect liberal Democrats to identify with the ideas of the gender left or the intersectors gender ideology strands outlined in Chapter 3, and we would expect conservative Republicans to identify with the ideas of the gender traditionalist or patriarchalist gender ideology strands.

For the most part, these expected patterns hold true for the legislators who responded to our survey. Two female Democrats in the state Assembly, who voted against W-2, responded that both men and women should care for the home and children equally and that good families come in many forms. In contrast, two male Republicans in the state Assembly, who voted for W-2, responded that traditional gender roles and traditional families were always best.

Despite the apparent relationship between gender and ideology, several respondents did not match this pattern. For instance, two senior male Democrats who voted for W-2 actually responded in ways we would expect a gender traditionalist or a patriarchalist to respond on the gender beliefs questions. Both men indicated that traditional gender roles and traditional families are best, emphasizing that separate gender spheres are more desirable and that each household should have a male bread-winner. On the contrary, several Republican legislators from both the state Assembly and Senate voted for W-2 but did not emphasize a patri-archalist or gender traditionalist approach. In fact, four of these Repub-lican legislators noted that women needed to support themselves, even though they still preferred traditional family structures. These Republi-cans held gender beliefs that expect women to compete with men on the same terms in the open market. Their approach was not traditionally conservative. Instead, they appear to support ideas of the similarist or gender universalist strands.

■ Moving Beyond Outliers: A Systematic Analysis of Gender Ideology at Work

The reexamination of the patterns of party and ideology data in Table 7.2 and the initial exploration of responses to our gender belief questions in the survey of Wisconsin legislators suggest that gender ideology may have operated as a unique second dimension during the design, debate, and passage of W-2. Still, we have looked only at the outliers who have crossed over ideological strands when gender beliefs are brought into the debate. A more systematic analysis of the Wisconsin legislature is neces-sary to confirm suspicions about multidimensional legislative behavior. Factor analysis is the statistical technique most often used to identify the liberal-conservative ideological pattern that structures legislative behav-ior. We use factor analysis here to show that gender ideology did indeed structure the beliefs systems of those legislators voting on W-2.

The factor analysis was conducted on seven of the eight political belief questions asked in the survey: taxation scale, market regulation scale, race discrimination scale, government support scale, government entitlement scale, female gender role scale, male gender role scale, and family structure scale (see Appendix A for a description of each). If leg-islators were simply structuring their beliefs on governing ideology, fac-tor analysis of the basic political beliefs would show that a liberal-con-servative continuum was the one factor accounting for all the variance among the seven sets of beliefs. If, however, a second dimension struc-tures any part of the legislators' beliefs, there should be more than one factor accounting for those beliefs.

Our analysis confirms that at least two dimensions structured the belief systems of Wisconsin state legislators in 1995–1996. Table 7.4 shows that a single factor accounts for 46.3 percent of the variance (eigen-value = 3.24) and a second factor accounts for 18.2 percent of the variance in the seven sets of legislators' beliefs (eigenvalue = 1.27). Scholars of roll-call voting dimensionality tend to discount second factors that only explain 6 percent of the variance and have eigenvalues of less than 1. The second factor we have uncovered far surpasses those statistical thresholds.

The factor loadings on Table 7.4 reveal the significance of this two-factor relationship.[27] Factor 2 *accounts for all the gender-related personal and political beliefs* of the legislators, whereas Factor 1 accounts for all of the conventional personal and political beliefs, including the question of race. More specifically, the survey questions that begin with the progressive statements that "women should support themselves" (women's gender roles), "men should be caregivers" (men's gender roles), and "good families come in many forms" (family structure) all load on the same factor. The factor loadings are not strong, but they show two dimensions, with one distinctly related to the gender belief questions. In other words, a set of gender beliefs operates independently of the liberal-conservative ideological pattern, confirming observations made earlier in the chapter.

This finding indicates that gender mattered for the Wisconsin legislators who designed and debated the most comprehensive welfare reform package in state history. It does not, however, indicate that gender was a more important influence than party or ideology for these legislators. Instead, the discovery of two factors at work in Wisconsin shows that gender ideology and conventional ideology are part of a whole compound ideology—each working in tandem when a policy involving gender roles is put before the legislature. This finding is fully consistent with our attempts to theorize gender ideology as a foundational ideology that underpins conventional governing ideology.

To better understand this second factor, we took our investigation one step further by examining legislator responses to the three gender belief questions included in our factor analysis. First, we found that some legislators who voted yes on W-2 and reform held traditional beliefs, but some held progressive beliefs about men's gender roles. This discrepancy indicates that there was no clear consensus about the role men and fathers should play in welfare reform. Twenty of the legislators in favor of W-2 strongly believed that traditional gender roles were best, while another twenty-four in favor of W-2 strongly believed that men needed to take care of the home and the children. In contrast, we found no relationship between the W-2 vote and beliefs about women's gender roles. A majority of legislators indicated that women needed to be self-sufficient. Regardless of other beliefs, votes, and priorities, a majority of Wisconsin legislators agreed with the statement "women need to support themselves," rather than "traditional gender roles are best." Only one type of

Table 7.4 Factor Analysis of Wisconsin Legislators' Personal and Political Beliefs

Personal and Political Belief Scales	Factor 1	Factor 2
Taxation scale (government should provide services vs. keep taxes low)	.89	.18
Market regulation scale (government should regulate markets vs. markets produce good effects)	.59	.29
Race discrimination scale (enforce antidiscrimination laws vs. discrimination not a problem)	.78	.19
Government entitlement scale (many people need helping hand vs. individual effort makes sense)	.88	.17
Female gender roles scale (women need to support selves vs. traditional gender roles)	.14	.98
Male gender roles scale (men should be caregivers vs. traditional gender roles)	.32	.37
Family structure scale (good families come in many forms vs. traditional families best)	.39	.43
Eigenvalue	3.24	
Second eigenvalue	1.27	
Percentage of variance	46.30	18.20
Total variance	64.50	

Source: Political Beliefs and Legislative Decisionmaking Survey of Wisconsin State Legislators, 1995–1996.

Note: Maximum likelihood factor analysis, with factor loadings subjected to varimax rotation. Number of observations = 60.

legislator consistently indicated that males should be the breadwinners and women should stay at home. They tended to be the younger and more rural legislators who identified themselves as religious fundamentalists and indicated that their spouses were homemakers. These nuances suggest that gender beliefs have an effect on policymaking, but they also suggest that gender beliefs have a unique effect, depending on whether male or female gender roles are at stake.

▪ Conclusion

In this chapter, we have uncovered gender ideology operating in state legislative decisionmaking as a second factor in addition to the dominant liberal-conservative factor that structures legislative behavior. By reviewing press reports, the official record, the survey of Wisconsin legislators, and the Key Vote Index, we demonstrate that a compound model of gender ideology shaped the beliefs of these legislators responsible for the design and passage of W-2.

Although we have uncovered the influence gender has on structuring political beliefs in Wisconsin, we still need to understand how those beliefs translate into political action and policy outcomes. In other words, we have shown that Wisconsin legislators are independently influenced by gender, but we have not shown how nuanced beliefs about male and female gender roles affected the kind of policy that was ultimately written into law. We know through our analysis of the gender belief questions that a majority of the legislators agree women should support themselves. We also know that these same legislators do not share identical beliefs about the role of fathers or the structure of the family. Further, we know that there were a significant number of patriarchalists or gender traditionalists who believed in a fixed gender complementarity and who voted with the majority for W-2.

We still need to understand how these complicated sets of beliefs translate into public policy. Our findings only hint at the connection between a compound ideology and the gender paradigms that were ultimately supported and passed into law in Wisconsin. In Chapter 8, we investigate the relationship between gender ideology and public policy outcomes by analyzing the design, debate, and passage of PRWORA in the US Congress. Not only does the analysis of PRWORA provide further evidence of a compound gender ideology at work, but it also allows us to explore the connection between ideology and policy outcomes with a larger data set. The more complete record of committee meetings and the larger number of legislators at the national level make it possible to see the connection between gender beliefs and the ideas, amendments, proposal, and votes for PRWORA. In the next chapter, we show that gender matters in the US Congress and we demonstrate how those who shared a common gender ideology strand structured the final version of PRWORA. More specifically, we show how the gender universalists worked with the patriarchalists to produce a national welfare reform package that includes elements of both the individuality and complementarity gender paradigms.

▓ Notes

1. Corbert, "Welfare Reform in Wisconsin"; Sarah Harder, "Welfare Reforms: Undoing the Wisconsin Idea?" in *Speaking Out: Women, Poverty, and Public Policy. Proceedings of the Twenty-Third Annual Women's Studies Conference, University of Wisconsin Women's Studies Consortium, October 29–31, 1998,* edited by

Katherine A. Rhoades and Anne Statham, 56–61, Madison: University of Wisconsin System Women's Studies Consortium.

2. Kaplan, "Wisconsin Works."

3. Ibid.; and Monson, "Ties That Bind."

4. See the discussion of the liberal-conservative dimension in Poole and Daniels, "Ideology, Party, and Voting in the U.S. Congress"; Poole and Rosenthal, "On Dimensionalizing Roll Call Votes in the U.S. Congress"; Poole and Rosenthal, *Congress.* See discussion of party power in Kiewiet and McCubbins, *The Logic of Delegation;* Kingdon, *Congressmen's Voting Decisions;* and Cox and McCubbins, *Legislative Leviathan.*

5. Kritzer, "Ideology and American Political Elites."

6. Poole and Rosenthal, "On Dimensionalizing Roll Call Votes."

7. Shaeffer, "Rating Congress."

8. See the discussion of women legislators' policy preferences in Rosenthal, *When Women Lead;* Thomas, *How Women Legislate;* Thomas and Welch, "The Impact of Gender on Activities and Priorities of State Legislators."

9. See Brown, *Manhood and Politics;* Jonasdottir, *Why Women Are Oppressed;* Duerst-Lahti and Kelly, *Gender Power, Leadership, and Governance.*

10. Smith, Herrera, and Herrera, "The Measurement Characteristics of Congressional Roll-Call Indexes"; Norton, "Uncovering the Unidimensionality of Gender Voting in Congress"; and Poole and Rosenthal, *Congress.*

11. Amy Rinard, "Big Margin Predicted for W-2 Passage," *Milwaukee Journal Sentinel,* January 23, 1996, 1.

12. See Wisconsin's *Journal of the Assembly,* March 7, 1996; and *Journal of the Senate,* March 13, 1996.

13. Jeffery L. Katz, "House Passes Wisconsin Waivers," *Congressional Quarterly Weekly Report,* June 8, 1996, 1598; Jean J. Rogers, "Making Welfare Work," *New Statesman,* 126:43–49, August 29, 1997, 17; and, Kaplan, "Wisconsin Works," 108–109.

14. See articles by Amy Rinard, "Working on Welfare: Democrats Fail to Delay Welfare Plan," *Milwaukee Journal Sentinel,* March 1, 1996, 1; and Steven Walters, "Working on Welfare: W-2 Sent to Assembly," *Milwaukee Journal Sentinel,* March 2, 1996, 1.

15. Amy Rinard, "W-2 Rolls Through Assembly: Bids to Alter Welfare Plan Fail," *Milwaukee Journal Sentinel,* March 8, 1996, 1.

16. Amy Rinard, "Senate Passes W-2 Plan: Sweeping Welfare Reform Plan Sent to Governor," *Milwaukee Journal Sentinel,* March 14, 1996, 1.

17. Margo Huston, "This Is Raw Politics: Moore Gives Welfare Warning," *Milwaukee Journal Sentinel,* February 10, 1996, 5.

18. Amy Rinard, "Participants Would Have to Pay," *Milwaukee Journal Sentinel,* February 21, 1996, 5.

19. Amy Rinard, "Working on Welfare: Democrats Fail to Delay Welfare Plan," *Milwaukee Journal Sentinel,* March 1, 1996, 1. Young, from Madison, is white, and George, from Milwaukee, is black. News coverage suggests strongly that African Americans were more passionate than whites about W-2. Wisconsin's demographics were very white in 1996. No Latinos or Asians held a post in the legislature then. Unless indicated otherwise, all legislators quoted are white.

20. Steven Walters, "Working on Welfare," 1.

21. Amy Rinard, "Senate Passes W-2 Plan," 1.

22. Amy Rinard, "W-2 Rolls Through Assembly," 1.

23. Steven Walters, "Working on Welfare."

24. Amy Rinard, "Senate Passes W-2 Plan," 1. This pattern of debate corresponds with Hawkesworth, "Congressional Enactments," in that black legislators definitely took more vigorous stands on W-2 legislation than they did on issues in which race is less implicated.

25. Mike Flaherty, "Senate Oks W-2 Welfare Reform Plan," *Wisconsin State Journal,* March 14, 1996, 1A.

26. Despite being a statewide issue, in some regard welfare reform—much like other issues, such as school choice—was constructed as "Milwaukee versus the rest of the state." Not incidentally, the state's small African American population is concentrated in the southeastern corner, which includes Milwaukee. Our survey asked one question concerning race, which did not produce significant quantitative results. Perhaps these political elites are not likely to say anything that suggests their own racism on a written survey. Given the conflation of welfare and race discussed throughout this book and the nature of statements recorded in press, we have no doubt that race beliefs served as another ideological pattern at work during the passage of W-2. The state legislature does not have an equivalent of the *Congressional Record,* so we could not analyze actual floor debate.

27. Factor loadings are the numbers that show the relationships among the questions or variables in the analysis.

8

Measuring Gender's Influence in Congressional Policymaking

WHEN THE PERSONAL RESPONSIBILITY AND WORK OPPORTUNITY Reconciliation Act (PRWORA) was signed into law in 1996, members of Congress promised that the deficit would be reduced, social policy would be returned to the states, and one promise of the Republican Contract with America would be fulfilled.[1] Like Wisconsin legislators, however, our national policymakers gave little explicit attention to the underlying gender paradigms that they were also helping to create and legitimate. Analysis of the compound model of gender ideology allows us to see that both male and female members of the US Congress use gender as well as conventional governing ideologies to shape public policy decisions about the gender paradigms we promote as a nation.

A review of the national legislative process during consideration of PRWORA shows that a handful of Congress members designed the national welfare reform package that eventually passed. These legislators allowed some ideas to emerge and others to be submerged as they exercised agenda-setting power on the committees with jurisdiction over welfare policy and on the House and Senate floors. Analysis of the records for the 104th Congress show that several gender ideologies converged during the design and debate of welfare reform to promote the gender paradigm that shaped PRWORA. In this chapter, a close inspection of the policymaking process in the House of Representatives and the Senate shows how gender ideology and gender identity both played a role in creating welfare policy.

The theoretical model discussed in Chapter 3 and the empirical analysis of the Wisconsin legislature in Chapter 7 prepare us for an evaluation of the concomitant influence of conventional governing ideologies and gender ideologies on the creation of gender paradigms by the US Congress. The framework diagrammed in Table 3.3 and the analysis of the passage of Wisconsin Works help us to move beyond a unidimensional liberal-conservative explanation for policy and paradigmatic choice in Congress. In this chapter, however, we go a step further than we did with the analysis of the Wisconsin legislature. Here we use our knowledge that gender ideology operates as a distinct part of the conventional governing ideology to show how it guides the design of social policy and to explain the contest over the three gender paradigms during the 104th Congress: complementarity, individuality (civic and corporative), and egality.

Despite the fact that most votes for PRWORA split along party lines, analysis of the House and Senate records clearly indicates that adherents of several gender ideologies worked in coalition to design a welfare policy that advocated individuality but that concurrently supported elements of complementarity.

■ Uncovering Evidence of Gender Paradigms in Congress

During consideration of PRWORA, the appropriate gender roles for men and women were debated at length on the House and Senate floors. Embedded in the committee and floor debate over votes and amendment proposals were distinct ideological and paradigmatic approaches. A few legislators who favored egality approaches argued for job training, career education, and increases in a minimum wage for both male and female welfare recipients; legislators who favored civic individuality approaches made speeches about expanding the welfare reform package to "make work pay" by improving child care, health care, and food stamp provisions for recipients; legislators who favored the corporative individuality approach focused their arguments on welfare reform that would make individuals responsible for their own poverty through strict child support enforcement and work participation requirements; and, finally, those who made passionate speeches for the complementarity approach wanted welfare reform to be more about marriage than about work by supporting family caps, denial of aid to teenage mothers, and efforts to reduce out-of-wedlock births.

Discovering how these debates over votes and amendments intersect with distinct gender paradigms is complicated, not unlike following clues in a detective novel or breaking an encrypted code. Many avenues can be investigated, and several alternatives weighed in multiple stages of analysis. One of the complicating factors is that the gender-related provisions for framing the welfare reform package were made not only on the floors of Congress but also deep inside committees and subcommittees with jurisdiction over welfare reform. Factions inside the committees fought bitterly to frame the direction of welfare reform legislation. Some factions fought to shape an egalitarian role for families where mothers *and* fathers were responsible for caregiving, but others assumed that complementary roles were best because mothers should be responsible for child care. Thus, complete analysis of the influence gender ideology has in Congress requires close observation of the policy preferences of the committee members with welfare reform jurisdiction, as well as observation of House and Senate floor amendment activity. Since committee position enables legislators to influence a bill at all steps of the policy-making process, a better understanding of the ideological orientation of the legislators with committee jurisdiction will help us understand how gender ideology informs and intersects with the gender paradigms incorporated into public policy.[2]

A three-part analysis of the preferences and policy decisions of both committee members and floor activists will show the interaction between conventional and gender ideologies in Congress. In the first stage of analysis, a review of the voting behavior of committee members with welfare policy jurisdiction in the House shows that both a legislator's sex and his or her gender issue preferences influenced a series of welfare votes in the 104th Congress. Similar to the analysis conducted in Chapter 7, we establish that a relationship between gender ideology and welfare policy voting exists for the welfare reform activists sitting on committees of jurisdiction. For example, we show that committee members who disapproved of increased occupational and educational opportunities for women would be more likely to vote for a welfare reform package, whereas committee members who approved of governmental supports for women would be more likely to vote against welfare reform altogether.

After demonstrating an interrelationship among sex, gender ideology, and welfare reform policy for members of the US Congress, we show how gender paradigms were ultimately embedded in PRWORA in the second stage of the analysis. A review of the entire set of amendments proposed to the Committee on Rules in the House and formally offered on the House and Senate floors provides a glimpse of the gender paradigms that were either introduced and ushered through the policymaking process or introduced and dropped from further consideration. An examination of the content of both the House's and Senate's successful and unsuccessful amendments proposed and the personal characteristics of amendment authors helps to uncover a distinct pattern of the kinds of gender paradigms that were used to create welfare reform policy in the 104th Congress.

Finally, in the third stage of the analysis, we show how evaluation of both voting behavior and amendment proposing activity helps to uncover the relatively unique role played by female Congress members working on welfare reform. Their efforts indicate collaboration based on feminalist concerns against a backdrop of masculinist normality. The record indicates that congresswomen in both the House and Senate reframed the welfare debate at many steps of the legislative process, using the civic individuality paradigms more consistently than their male colleagues to frame their amendments to the proposed legislation.

This three-stage analysis, which uses both votes and amendments made in committees and on the floors of Congress, requires examination of the passage of two bills: H.R. 4 (1995) and H.R. 3734 (1996). The emphasis of the analysis here will be on H.R. 4, however, because most of the work on welfare reform was done on this original bill proposed in 1995. Even though President Bill Clinton eventually vetoed H.R. 4 because it included a contentious provision to revamp Medicaid, the agenda was set, and the majority of programs were designed in this first draft of the legislation.[3] In the first stage of the analysis outlined above, we have searched for roll-call voting patterns of the members of the three House committees with welfare reform jurisdiction. The bill was initially divided into three House committee jurisdictions for hearings and markup: Ways and Means assessed eligibility and work requirements; Economic and Educational Opportunities examined child care and job training; and Agriculture considered food stamps and nutrition. In the second and third stages of the analysis, our focus expands to include an examination of the amendment process on the floors of both the House and Senate for H.R. 4.

■ Stage One: Analysis of Committee Members' PRWORA Preferences

Committee Member Voting Behavior

The argument that committees matter to policy design and passage in Congress is well accepted.[4] Thus, examination of the relationship between gender ideology and the welfare policy positions of the 123 committee members who had welfare reform jurisdiction in the 104th Congress is important because it will help us show that gender ideology influenced committee members who designed and ushered the welfare reform bill onto the House floor and through the final conference committee. This part of the analysis will not tell us which gender paradigm was adopted in the final welfare reform package—we save that for parts two and three of this chapter—but it will tell us if gender ideology is independently related to welfare policy making, as it was for the legislators who designed the W-2 welfare bill in Wisconsin.

Here we hypothesize that gender ideology and the factors responsible for constructing differences in gender ideology are strongly correlated with welfare reform voting. Assuming that differences in sex, political party, religion, and family responsibility help to construct differences in gender ideology and that voting on other gender-related issues is associated with gender ideology, we can use these indicators to see if a committee member's gender ideology correlates with welfare reform voting patterns. For example, we can begin to see whether a connection exists between the gender left adherents and an egality approach, or between the gender traditionalists or patriarchalists and a complementarity approach, or whether the factors that construct difference in gender ideology are unrelated to voting on welfare reform. Empirical analysis of committee members' voting preferences allows us to test for positive or negative correlations between gender ideology and welfare reform voting. Not only will this measure provide evidence of gender ideology at work, but also it helps us verify our earlier findings about a concomitant gender ideology in Wisconsin.

If welfare reform and gender ideology intersect, we would expect to find, for example, Republican male legislators belonging to fundamentalist religions, with weak voting records on women's issues and only one or two children, to be more likely to favor welfare reform (e.g., gender traditionalists and patriarchalists). This profile mirrors the characteristics of many of the "new right" legislators elected into the 104th Congress who were committed to reforming welfare as part of the Contract with America but who wanted to see mothers as the primary caregivers for children. We would also expect male and female Democrats from nonfundamentalist religions and with strong voting records on women's issues to be more likely to disapprove of the welfare reform package (e.g., gender left and intersectors). Historically, these kinds of legislators have been more supportive of job training, educational programs, and the use of other economic options to reduce poverty and welfare receipt.

To identify a link between gender ideology and welfare reform voting patterns, we created an index of twenty welfare votes taken during the debates over H.R. 4 and H.R. 3734 to serve as our dependent variable. This variable acts as a proxy for a member's welfare reform preferences.[5] Use of a welfare reform preference index allows us to see how Congress members voted on an entire series of welfare votes, instead of relying on the more partisan final votes for bill passage. Committee members in favor of all reform options, including family caps, paternity reporting requirements, and denial of aid to minor or unmarried parents, were indexed between 76 and 100 percent and are considered to be more interested in supporting a complementarity gender paradigm; committee members who voted for most reforms, including strict child support enforcement programs, but who did not always support family caps and denial of aid to the unmarried, were indexed between 50 and 75 percent and are considered to be more interested in supporting the corporative individuality paradigm; committee members who generally opposed reform but who compromised with several amendments to soften reform by encouraging child care, food stamps, and health care improvements, were indexed between 25 and 49 percent and are considered to be more interested in supporting a civic individuality gender paradigm; and committee members who opposed reform and offered alternatives to reform were scored between 0 and 24 percent and are considered to be more interested in an egality gender paradigm.

A regression analysis shows that gender-related factors did indeed correlate to welfare reform voting for PRWORA—the "new right" legislator who opposed abortion and women's rights issues was much more likely to favor welfare reform, whereas the gender left was clearly less likely to support any reform proposals. Table 8.1 displays the results of the regression analysis, which uses both gender-related and non-gender-related independent variables to explain welfare reform voting patterns. The set of variables used in the regression analysis are listed and explained in Appendix C.

Not surprisingly, Table 8.1 shows that "political party" had the greatest influence on welfare reform voting, with Republican legislators far more likely to vote for reform proposals. Still, the evidence shows that several factors other than party influence welfare reform votes. A close look at the four gender-related variables indicates a relationship among personal characteristics, gender ideology, and welfare reform in the regression model. The four gender-related variables—a legislator's sex, "women's issue" voting, family responsibility (number of children), and partial-birth abortion vote—can all be considered closely related or statistically significant in the analysis.

First, the independent variable used to represent a Congress member's gender ideology was the American Association of University Women's (AAUW's) voting index for the 104th Congress. The AAUW index has been established as a gender-related measure of a Congress member's voting behavior and not a proxy for the conventional liberal-conservative voting dimension.[6] Members who had a high women's issue (AAUW) score were those who strongly favored gender equity and reproductive rights legislation, whereas those who had a low score rarely supported this kind of legislation. The regression analysis shows that legislators with a high AAUW score were simply not likely to vote in favor of PRWORA reform proposals

Second, Table 8.1 shows that a Congress member's sex also affects welfare reform voting. Male Congress members were significantly more likely to vote in favor of welfare reform proposals than were female Congress members. Evidence presented later in this chapter will validate

Table 8.1 Regression Analysis of Congress Members' Welfare Reform Index Scores

	Unstandardized Coefficient		
	B	Std. Error	t
Party (Republican = 1)	32.36	4.08	.00[c]
Sex (male = 1)	5.82	2.97	.05[b]
Women's issue index (pro–women's issues = 100%)	–.19	.05	.00[c]
Number of children (1–10)	–2.39	.99	.01[b]
Vote for partial-birth abortion ban (yes = 1)	–3.39	3.18	.28
% in district nonwhite	–.09	.04	.06[a]
Religion (fundamentalist = 1)	3.56	1.71	.04[b]
(Constant)	37.25	7.01	.00[c]
R square	.88		
Adjusted R square	.87		
F	177.25[c]		
n = 54			

Notes: Welfare Reform Index Score (100% = pro-reform).
a. $p < .10$.
b. $p < .05$.
c. $p < .001$.

this finding by showing that Republican women were less likely to support welfare reform, unless it included provisions designed to "soften" reform with feminale-oriented amendments for state-funded child care and domestic violence exceptions to paternity reporting requirements.

Third, the fewer family responsibilities legislators had, the more likely they were to support reform. Specifically, members with fewer than three children were more likely to support all aspects of reform. Legislators with fewer children may not be as sensitive to the demands and expenses of rearing children as those who have more. The regression analysis clearly indicates that Congress members who raised more children were much less likely to support the work requirements and reform proposed in PRWORA.

Finally, those who voted for the "Partial-Birth Abortion Ban" were also more likely to vote for welfare reform. This variable allows us to see how members who took the antifeminist position on the gender issue with the most media attention in the 104th Congress voted on the welfare proposals. Although that is the only gender-related variable that was not statistically significant in the analysis, the data indicate a relationship, albeit a weak one, between a yes vote on the partial-birth abortion ban and a yes vote on welfare reform.

Several non-gender-related characteristics were also considered in the regression analysis to fully model the concomitant relationship between conventional gender ideologies. Table 8.1 clearly shows what we would expect, that Congress members' party identification and religious affiliation, as well as the racial and ethnic demographics of their district, were significantly related to their welfare reform votes. At the same time, Table 8.1 shows that gender-related influences work side by side with conventional influences on legislative decisionmaking.

Of course, these initial results do not tell us yet which gender ideology strands led committee members to make their voting choices or which gender ideology strands were combined to structure the paradigm adopted in the final version of PRWORA. But they do tell us that sex and gender issue preferences affected voting choice for the welfare policy committee members in the House of Representatives. These results allow us to speculate about the kinds of gender ideology at work during the design of this policy. They also suggest that gender left and intersectors were more likely to oppose a welfare reform proposal that did not include an egality approach, whereas the gender traditionalists and patriarchalists were more likely to support a strong welfare reform proposal that included a complementarity approach.

More precisely, the regression analysis tells us that a Congress member who strongly supported welfare reform was more likely to be a religious fundamentalist, to be from a district with a high percentage of white residents, and to disagree with the AAUW positions on gender issues. That suggests a pattern of voting behavior in which the "new right" conservatives, with visions of mothers as caregivers, two-parent families, and a strong work ethic, were much more likely to support a welfare reform that encouraged corporative individuality and complementarity; conversely, a nonfundamentalist in a mixed-race district with preferences for equality between the sexes was much more likely to support welfare proposals that encouraged egality.

The Committee Activists

Another way to analyze committee member preferences for welfare reform is to explore the relationship between welfare proposals and gender-issue voting for the committee activists. According to experts on the congressional committee system, only a small percentage of those within the committee have the motivation, experience, and expertise to work on developing specific policy programs.[7] A complete review of the passage of PRWORA confirms these findings, showing that only a few motivated subcommittee and committee activists worked exclusively on these welfare bills. By closely examining the voting preferences of these committee activists, we will find out whether they also held distinct policy preferences for gender-related welfare reform issues. By doing so, we will come closer to identifying the gender paradigms supported by those who actively crafted the final draft of PRWORA.

A review of the subcommittee, committee, and floor amending activity for members of the Ways and Means and Economic and Educational Opportunities Committees shows that those from the gender left who favored egalitarian families, reproductive rights, and economic opportunities for men and women typically lost their bids to restrict the scope of welfare reform through amendment. The gender universalists or the traditionalists who supported the minimalist state or the patriarchal family, however, were often much more successful in their amending activity. For example, liberals like Charles Rangel (D-NY) and Barbara Kennelly (D-CT), both on the Ways and Means Committee, worked unsuccessfully to expand child care programs for low-income families and to improve work, education, and training activities for low-income adults. Conservative Ways and Means committee chair Bill Archer (R-TX) and fellow committee member Jim McCrery (R-LA) easily succeeded in adding their amendments for family caps and strict paternity reporting requirements to the committee bill.[8] In the following analysis, we will see that active legislators in committee typically shared similar welfare and gender issue voting patterns in the 104th Congress, with advocates of egalitarian reform failing and advocates of complementarity succeeding in amending the welfare policy legislation.

Tables 8.2 and 8.3 display the relationship between the gender-issue voting index and welfare reform preference index for members of the Ways and Means and Economic and Educational Opportunity Committees. The correlation between the two indexes is strong and statistically significant (gamma = .62; $p < .001$). Rather than describing the relationship between gender and welfare voting with numbers here, we have actually placed the names of the Congress members in the cells that identify the correlation between a member's gender voting and welfare reform voting patterns. That allows us to simultaneously identify the names of the activists and their voting patterns. Instead of using all four gender paradigms that we used in the regression analysis above, the welfare reform index was collapsed into the three broader paradigms. The labels *equality support, individuality support,* and *complementarity support* were assigned as values to make interpretation of the tables easier. Equality

Table 8.2 Welfare-Reform Voting and Gender-Issue Voting, Ways and Means Committee

Welfare-Reform Voting	Gender-Issue Voting					
	Gender Left		Universalists		Gender Traditionalists	
	Male	Female	Male	Female	Male	Female
Egality	Matsui (D-CA), Stark (D-CA), Gibbons (D-FL), Lewis (D-GA), Jacobs (D-IN), Cardin (D-MD)[a], Levin (D-MI)[a], Rangel (D-NY)[a], Coyne (D-PA), Ford (D-TN)[a], Payne (D-VA), McDermott (D-WA)[a]	Kennelly (D-CT)[a]	Neal (D-MA)[a]			
Individuality	Kleczka (D-WI)[b]		Shaw (R-FL)[b], Houghton (R-NY)	Johnson (R-CT)[b]	Thomas (R-CA), Nussle (R-IA)[a], McCrery (R-LA)[a], Camp (R-MI), Johnson S. (R-TX)	
Complementarity			Ramstad (R-MN), Zimmer (R-NJ)[b]	Dunn (R-WA)[b]	Herger (R-CA), Collins (R-FL), Crane (R-IL), Bunning (R-KY), Hancock (R-MD), Christensen (R-NE), Ensign (R-NV)[a], Portman (R-OH), English (R-PA), Archer (R-TX)[b]	

Sources: Congressional Quarterly Weekly Reports, 1995–1996; Congressional Record.
Notes: a. Member made amendments. b. Member made successful amendments.

Table 8.3 Welfare-Reform Voting and Gender-Issue Voting, Economic and Educational Opportunities Committee

Welfare-Reform Voting	Gender-Issue Voting					
	Gender Left		Universalists		Gender Traditionalists	
	Male	Female	Male	Female	Male	Female
Egality	Miller (D-CA)[a] Becerra (D-CA)[a] Martinez (D-FL)[a] Reynolds (D-IL) Clay (D-MO) Williams (D-MT) Payne (D-NJ) Owens (D-NY) Engel (D-NY)[a] Sawyer (D-OH) Reed (D-RI)[a] Scott (D-VA)	Woolsey (D-CA)[a] Mink (D-HI)[a]	Roemer (D-IN)[a] Kildee (D-MI)[b] Andrews (D-NJ)			
Individuality			Gunderson (R-WI)[b]	Roukema (R-MD)[b]	Cunningham (R-CA)[a] Knollenberg (R-MI) Barrett (R-NE) Ballenger (R-NC) Greenwood (R-PA)	Meyers (R-KS)
Complementarity			Fawell (R-IL)		Goodling (R-PA) Hutchinson (R-AK)[a] Riggs (R-CA) McKeon (R-CA) Weldon (R-DE) Norwood (R-FL) McIntosh (R-IN) Souder (R-IN) Hoekstra (R-MI) Talent (R-MO)[b] Funderbunk (R-NC) Graham (R-SC) Petri (R-WI)	

Sources: Congressional Quarterly Weekly Reports, 1995–1996; Congressional Record.
Notes: a. Member made amendments. b. Member made successful amendments.

supporters were identified as those who scored between 0 and 25 percent on the welfare reform index; individuality supporters (both civic and corporative) scored between 26 and 75 percent; and complementarity supporters scored between 76 and 100 percent. The gender-issue voting index was similarly collapsed into three distinct categories. The label *gender left* was used for those who had high scores on the women's issue index; the label *universalist* was used for those who had moderate scores on the index; and the label *gender traditionalist* was used for those who had low scores.[9] Representatives who scored as adherents of the gender left and supported egality welfare proposals can be found in the top left-hand cell in each of the tables; representatives who scored as universalists and supported individuality proposals can be found in the center cell; and representatives who scored as gender traditionalists and supported complementarity proposals in each index can be found in the bottom right-hand cell. Very few legislators were ranked with mixed scores on each index. The mixed scores, which highlight the convergence of several gender ideologies and paradigmatic approaches, will be explored further in stage two of the analysis presented in this chapter.

These two tables include several pieces of information about the identity of each Congress member. In addition to listing the names, the tables identify the party, sex, level of committee activism, and level of successful committee activism for each committee member with welfare jurisdiction. A quick glance at the tables initially shows that Democratic members ranked as gender left/egality supporters and Republicans ranked as gender traditionalist/complementarity supporters. Moreover, a legislator's sex appears to be unimportant in relation to party identification—most Republican women preferred complementarity approaches, and most Democratic women preferred the egality approach.

When the activists on the subcommittees and committees are identified by name, however, a new pattern emerges. We can see who took the most vocal role in shaping welfare reform by identifying and counting the number of amendments made by each member while debating in subcommittee, committee, and eventually on the House floor. Each of those who made more than one amendment in all three locations is noted on the tables. The new pattern that emerges shows that only a handful of committee members with distinctly gender left or gender right approaches finally contributed to the design of welfare reform legislation.

A look at the success rate for those activists who offered a large number of amendments helps us to better identify this emerging pattern. Activists with more than one successful amendment are also noted in Tables 8.2 and 8.3. The success rates now reveal that members who ranked as gender universalist/individuality supporters were more likely to present *successful* amendments in committees and on the House floor than were gender left/egality or gender traditionalist/complementarity supporters. For example, Matthew Martinez (D-CA) from the Economic and Educational Opportunities Committee and Carl Levin (D-MI) from the Ways and Means Committee both ranked as gender left/egality supporters on welfare and gender issues. But the record shows that the egality amendments they offered to expand low-income child care funding, to eliminate prohibitions on cash benefits for children born out-of-wedlock, and to delete a five-year cap on benefits never passed.[10] Similarly, Asa Hutchinson (R-AK) from the Economic and Educational Opportunities Committee and Jim Ensign (R-NV) from the Ways and Means Committee both ranked as strong gender traditionalist/complementarity voters on welfare and gender issues. But the record shows that they too were unsuccessful in getting amendments passed to reduce benefits while simultaneously encouraging marriage.

Those committee members who were ranked as universalist/individuality supporters or who had mixed scores, however, were successful at getting their amendments passed. Clay Shaw (R-FL), Nancy Johnson (R-CT), and Jennifer Dunn (R-WA) were the most active and successful Ways and Means Committee members. Shaw was responsible for the introduction and bill management of both H.R. 4 and H.R. 3734. Johnson and Dunn both offered successful amendments to improve child support and child care services associated with the bill. The same pattern holds true for the Economic and Educational Opportunities Committee. The universalist/individuality supporters on those committees were also the most active and the most successful members highlighted on Table 8.3—Marge Roukema (R-MD), Steve Gunderson (R-WI), and Dale Kildee (D-MI). Thus, Shaw, Johnson, Dunn, Roukema, Gunderson, and Kildee's names were all noted on Tables 8.2 and 8.3 in order to emphasize their success at amending the welfare reform bill with their policy preferences.

The fact that each committee had even one successful gender traditionalist in their ranks should not be ignored. Both Tables 8.2 and 8.3 show that complementarity was indeed supported because proponents of complementarity approaches passed amendments to welfare reform. The Ways and Means Committee chair, Bill Archer (R-TX), was a critical player in the passage of PRWORA, and conservative James Talent (R-MO) played the same role on the Economic and Educational Opportunities committee. Both were successful in placing a statement about the value of marriage, the two-parent family, and the immorality of out-of-wedlock births in the preamble to PRWORA.[11] The success of Archer and Talent helps to explain how both individuality and complementarity gender ideologies influenced welfare reform simultaneously.

In summary, this part of the analysis shows that those who preferred individuality approaches played a greater part in designing and amending a bill that assumed masculinized individuality for women. Those who preferred complementarity approaches like Talent and Archer played a lesser, but still important, part by assuring that the complementary roles of female caregivers and male breadwinners were not forgotten in the final version of the legislation. Further, the gender traditionalist activists who supported complementarity were also successful at incorporating language into the bill that gave states the discretion to pursue policies consistent with complementarity.

■ Stage Two: Analysis of House and Senate PRWORA Amendment Proposals

Until this point, we have presented only "circumstantial" evidence of a relationship between gender ideology and welfare reform. Although voting indexes and interest group ratings have been widely accepted as valid proxies for ideology,[12] they are not precise enough to uncover the full dimensions of gender voting and policymaking.[13] Voting studies do not uncover the nuances or multiple explanations for legislative behavior. To understand the extent of the relationship between gender ideology and welfare reform proposals, we need to uncover even more evidence about how gender ideology influences welfare reform.

We can learn more about the gender paradigms advocated by the welfare reform activists during consideration of PRWORA by carefully examining the kinds of ideas they proposed for debate on the House and Senate floors instead of simply looking at their votes. In the House, 148 amendments were filed with the Committee on Rules in the hope that they would be "made in order" on the floor.[14] The Rules Committee accepted thirty of these amendments (20.3 percent) for debate on the House floor. The Senate has no similar kind of gatekeeper. Thus, eighty-six welfare reform amendments were fully proposed, debated, and voted on during the Senate's consideration of PRWORA.[15] A review of amendments proposed and amendments finally accepted for debate will identify the dominant gender paradigm by linking ideas with authors.

The data we collected on House and Senate amendments include the name of the amendment's author and the author's party identification, committee affiliation, and leadership role. Further, we identify the text of each amendment as either gender-related or non-gender-related. Gender-related amendments are those that dealt with child care, child support, teenage pregnancy, out-of-wedlock births, domestic violence, family caps, paternity reporting requirements, maternal health, and fatherhood. Non-gender-related amendments, such as the manner of federal payments to states, were coded with the conventional paradigm labels *liberal, moderate,* and *conservative;* the gender-related amendments were coded with the gender paradigms we have identified: egality, individuality, and complementarity.[16]

House Amending Patterns

Out of the 148 amendments that Congress members proposed to the Committee on Rules, sixty-five were filed by Democrats, who attempted to amend the bill designed by Republican majorities inside committee rooms. The content of the proposed amendments shows that Democratic legislators were generally more willing to offer compromise amendments than to challenge the bill.[17] Only 34 percent of the non-gender-related amendments proposed by Democrats could be considered liberal amendments, 60 percent were moderate, and 6 percent were conservative. Instead of offering amendments in opposition to welfare reform, amendments to protect benefits for welfare recipients, or amendments to question proposals for time limitations on benefits, Democratic Congress members were more likely to offer proposals to support individual workers under a reformed system with tax credits, health coverage, and child custody arrangements.

The Democrats were even less likely to challenge reform with the proposed gender-related amendments. Only 29 percent of the gender-related amendments proposed by Democrats could be considered to be egality amendments. For example, Democratic Congress members did not offer amendments to establish child support assurance, a proposal to guarantee a minimal amount of financial support to all children in single-parent families.[18] Instead, they designed amendments that tried to support welfare recipients by working incrementally within the proposed reform. For example, Cleo Fields (D-LA), a liberal African American representative, proposed amendments to improve child nutrition under the new reform proposal; Barbara Kennelly (D-CT), a woman who considers herself a liberal feminist, proposed an amendment to require the suspension of drivers' licenses for "deadbeat dads" who refused to pay child support; and Gerald Kleczka (D-WI), a mainstream Democrat, proposed an amendment that would allow states to decide if they would grant or deny benefits to teenage mothers, rather than requiring them to deny these mothers aid. All three proposals would provide indirect support to recipients, but they did not challenge the compound gender ideology behind the bill.

Several Democrats undoubtedly opted not to challenge the bill, knowing that the Republican majority on the Rules Committee would not grant a rule. Nevertheless, a few Democrats did challenge the basic premise of this reform, with the hope that they might be offered a chance just to debate egality ideas. Sheila Jackson-Lee (D-TX), a newly elected African American woman, proposed an egality amendment with the hope that she could add job assistance, educational assistance, and two years of transitional child care for all recipients.[19] Her proposal would have changed the tenor of the entire bill. Her amendment, of course, was not accepted. Her proposal, however, exemplifies how women of color were more likely to oppose a reform plan that was not grounded in egality or civic individuality approaches.

Ultimately, the Republican majority on the House Rules Committee discarded most of these compromise proposals offered by Democrats, and only thirty amendments were ultimately selected for debate on the floor. The patterns that emerge from the set of amendments accepted for debate reveal exactly how gender paradigms became embedded in the welfare reform package. The data show that more gender-related amendments were accepted for debate than non-gender-related amendments. Moreover, the gender-related amendments accepted for debate tended to fall within the complementarity paradigm.

Table 8.4 displays the numbers of non-gender-related and gender-related amendments, both those proposed and those accepted for debate on the House floor. Although more non-gender-related amendments were proposed for debate, over 50 percent of the amendments finally accepted for debate on the House floor were gender-related. Moreover, 69 percent of the gender-related amendments actually debated on the floor were either corporative individuality or complementarity amendments (19 percent corporative and 50 percent complementarity), whereas the non-gender-related amendments tended to be more moderate in nature. In fact, none of the non-gender-related amendments in this analysis could be considered to be conventionally conservative amendments.

This kind of evidence emphasizes two important findings about the gender ideology strands and the gender paradigms central to welfare reform. First, it shows us that moderate conservatives dominated the general non-gender-related debate time on the House floor. But, more important, it shows us that advocates of a complementarity gender paradigm dominated the gender-related amendment debates. Second, this evidence dispels any argument that Democrats will support primarily liberal or egality amendments and that Republicans will primarily support conservative or complementarity amendments. The evidence, in fact, suggests that as a body, the House was willing to reform welfare without questioning perspectives on traditional gender roles and relationships. These results help to confirm that gender ideology and support for a gender paradigm is not always correlated with conventional ideology because party cannot always be used to explain behavior on gender-related proposals and voting decisions.

Table 8.4 Non-Gender-Related and Gender-Related Amendments "Proposed" and "Made in Order" by House Rules Committee for PRWORA

Conventional Paradigms	Non-Gender Proposed % (N)	Non-Gender Made in Order % (N)	Gender Paradigm % (N)	Gender Proposed % (N)	Gender Made in Order % (N)
Liberal	32.1 (26)	7.1 (1)	Egality	22.4 (15)	12.5 (2)
Moderate-liberal	32.1 (26)	28.6 (4)	Civic individuality	37.3 (25)	18.8 (3)
Moderate-conservative	33.3 (27)	64.3 (9)	Corporative individuality	19.4 (13)	18.8 (3)
Conservative	2.5 (2)	0.0 (0)	Complementarity	20.9 (14)	50.0 (8)
Total	n = 81	n = 14		n = 67	n = 16

Source: Committee on Rules, House Report 104-85, "Providing for the Further Consideration of H.R. 4, The Personal Responsibility Act of 1995," 104th Congress, 1st sess.
Note: The House Rules Committee reviewed a total of 148 amendments for consideration on the floor.

A review of the actual content of the gender-related amendments (both proposed and made in order on the floor) shows that the House was especially interested in debating issues surrounding mother-only families. A large percentage of the gender-related amendments was designed to regulate family structure, marriage, and pregnancy in ways that bolstered private patriarchy. These amendments pursued more masculinist than feminalist priorities and preferences. More than 83 percent of the proposed amendments dealt strictly with family caps, teenage pregnancy, out-of-wedlock births, abortion, and child support enforcement rather than child care, health insurance, and nutrition. Further, the gender-related amendments made in order and passed on the floor were all designed to regulate family, marriage, and pregnancy. For example, James Talent (R-MO) succeeded in adding the "sense of Congress" preamble about marriage and out-of-wedlock births to the bill, emphasizing that the purpose of the bill was to promote marriage and to prevent out-of-wedlock births; Henry Hyde (R-IL) added a provision limiting funds for abortions; and Chris Smith (R-NJ) wrote a proposal that limited cash payments but approved of vouchers for children of teenage mothers.

Senate Amending Patterns

Out of the eighty-six amendments debated on the floor of the Senate, Democrats who were trying to soften welfare reform offered 63 percent. Unlike in the House, however, both the Republican and Democratic senators debated many more liberal and moderate non-gender-related amendments and civic and corporative individuality gender-related amendments than conservative or complementarity amendments.

Additionally, fewer gender-related amendments were offered and debated in the Senate than in the House. Only 37 percent of the Senate amendments were gender-related, whereas 45 percent of the proposed amendments and 53 percent of the amendments accepted for debate in the House were gender-related. In other words, the senators spent less time debating gender issues like family caps, child support, and out-of-wedlock births. Further, the gender-related amendments debated by senators were specifically designed to toughen child support, moderate paternity reporting requirements, and ease out-of-wedlock birth restrictions. They focused on making fathers "responsible" and restoring some autonomy to women. Many of the Senate gender-related amendments resembled those offered by Paul Wellstone (D-MN), which included domestic violence exemptions on work participation requirements,[20] and by Pete Domenici (R-NM), which struck down the mandatory family cap requirements that were strongly supported in the House.[21]

Table 8.5 clearly shows that out of all the gender-related amendments debated in the Senate, only 19 percent were complementarity amendments, and as many as 28 percent were egality amendments. As noted above, Table 8.4 shows that House members had proposed and accepted for debate a majority of complementarity and corporative individuality amendments. In fact, over one-half of the gender-related amendments were individuality amendments in the House.

Even more noteworthy, the individuality amendments were much more likely to succeed in the Senate than in the House. Table 8.6 highlights the success rate for each gender strand in both the House and the Senate for the pool of gender-related amendments. Only 19 percent (n = 4) of the complementarity amendments offered in the Senate were successful, whereas 57 percent (n = 8) of the complementarity amendments offered in the House were successful. The Senate's complementarity amendments were less punitive than those passed in the House. The Senate refused to pass two complementarity amendments by Lauch Faircloth (R-NC) that would have denied assistance for out-of-wedlock births to minors or to teens who lived with guardians who had received welfare. Instead, the Senate approved of amendments that insisted on strict child support and adult supervision of teenage parents. For example, John Kerry (D-MA) succeeded in adding an amendment that requires minor applicants to enter into a parental responsibility contract, and Kent Conrad (D-ND) added a similar amendment that provides assistance to unmarried teens only if they live in an adult-supervised setting.

Gender Ideology of House and Senate Activists

The analysis of House and Senate amending patterns has shown that the dominant gender paradigm adopted in the House was the complementarity paradigm, with strong influence from the individuality (corporative) paradigm. In the Senate, the dominant gender paradigm adopted was the individuality paradigm, with less influence from the complementarity paradigm. Thus, the final emphasis of the welfare reform package had to be determined by the conference committees ultimately responsible for reconciling House and Senate versions of H.R. 4 and H.R. 3734, since the House and the Senate held different visions of the outcome of reform.

Identification of the sets of amendments proposed and supported by the activists who ultimately sat on the conference committees from the House and the Senate will help us to see how several strands of gender ideology and gender paradigms central to welfare reform converged. The welfare policy activists, who were invited to sit on the welfare reform conference committees, borrowed from several gender paradigms to frame an approach that would ultimately be supported by a majority in

Table 8.5 Non-Gender-Related and Gender-Related Amendments Heard on the Senate Floor for PRWORA

Conventional Paradigm	Non-Gender-Related Amendments % (N)	Gender Paradigm	Gender-Related Amendments % (N)
Liberal	11.2 (6)	Egality	28.1 (9)
Moderate-liberal	44.4 (24)	Civic individuality	25.0 (8)
Moderate-conservative	44.4 (24)	Corporative individuality	28.1 (9)
Conservative	0.0 (0)	Complementarity	18.8 (6)
Total	n = 54		n = 32

Source: Lexis-Nexis. 1996. "Bill Tracking Report, H.R. 4, Personal Responsibility Act of 1995."
Note: The Senate debated a total of 86 amendments on the Senate floor.

Table 8.6 Total Number of Successful Gender-Related Amendments in the House and Senate on PRWORA

	Gender-Related Senate Amendments		Gender-Related House Amendment	
Gender Paradigm	Pass % (N)	Fail % (N)	Pass % (N)	Fail % (N)
Egality	23.8 (5)	36.4 (4)	14.3 (2)	0.0 (0)
Civic	14.3 (3)	45.5 (5)	7.1 (1)	100.0 (2)
Corporative	42.9 (9)	0.0 (0)	21.4 (3)	0.0 (0)
Complementarity	19.0 (4)	18.2 (2)	57.1 (8)	0.0 (0)
Total	n = 21	n = 11	n = 14	n = 2

Source: Lexis-Nexis. 1996. "Bill Tracking Report, H.R. 4, Personal Responsibility Act of 1995."

Note: There were 48 successful gender-related amendments.

Congress. The activists in the House knew a complementarity approach would not satisfy the Senate, and the Senate could not impose their egality approach in the House.

Conferees Clay Shaw, Nancy Johnson, Jennifer Dunn, Gerald Kleczka, and Dick Zimmer (R-NJ), Marge Roukema, Dale Kildee, and Steve Gunderson were the most active members of the House Ways and Means and Economic and Educational Opportunities committees. The previous analysis of voting behavior identified each of these legislators as adherents of gender universality ideology and advocates of policies consistent with the individuality paradigm. But analysis of amending behavior allows us to see how individuality and complementarity approaches actually combined to influence their thinking. For example, Nancy Johnson, a Connecticut Republican on the Ways and Means Committee, authored six gender-related amendments for debate on the House floor. Two of these amendments were corporative individuality amendments that attempted to cut costs and encourage responsible fatherhood by requiring fathers to pay child support, and two were civic individuality amendments that would have limited work requirements when child care was not available. Clearly, this evidence suggests that Johnson was interested in an individuality approach that cut costs but included some state support to allow women time to go to work. It is interesting, however, that one of the only egality amendments allowed on the House floor was actually authored by Johnson, a Republican woman. With the aid of four other congresswomen, Johnson guided an amendment through the floor debate that would have increased the amount of funding for the child care block grant for low-income families.[22]

Two other House conferees and committee activists exemplify a similar convergence of approaches. First, Gerald Kleczka, a Wisconsin Democrat on the Ways and Means Committee, authored five amendments for the floor debate and worked hard for their passage. The voting studies suggested that Kleczka had a mixed egality/individuality voting record (see Table 8.2). His gender-related voting score was ranked as gender left, but his welfare voting score was ranked as individuality. The amendment data presented here confirm this convergence. Kleczka supported egality proposals to remove provisions denying benefits to minor parents and civic amendments to improve Supplemental Security Income (SSI) benefits for children. However, the only one of his amendments accepted for debate on the floor was an individuality amendment that supported reform but that put federal restrictions on state welfare budget allocations.[23] This example demonstrates how some ideas were filtered through the legislative process and others were tossed aside. Kleczka's gender-related egality proposals did not survive the Rules Committee, but his individuality amendments did survive. Next, Marge Roukema, a New Jersey Republican and activist on the Economic and Educational Opportunities Committee, authored several gender-related amendments in committee and on the floor. The data show that she wrote primarily individuality amendments; however, her amendments accepted for debate showed a mixed paradigmatic approach. One was a corporative amendment requiring child support enforcement, and the other was an egality amendment improving cost containment systems for infant formula.[24] Both attempted to provide better conditions for children and their mothers.

Similar scrutiny of committee and floor amendment activists during the Senate floor debate gives us insight into who was most involved in the Senate welfare reform process. The amendment data indicate that three welfare reform committee members were among the most active during the Senate debate. Unlike the House activists, however, these senators wrote only egality or civic individuality amendments. For example, Paul Wellstone, a member of the Democratic-Farmer-Labor party from Minnesota, authored two egality amendments that both passed on the Senate floor. One of those amendments allowed a domestic violence exemption for recipients who did not meet the welfare work requirements. Similarly, Carol Moseley Braun, a Democrat from Illinois, authored two egality amendments and one civic individuality amendment. The only amendment of hers that passed, however, was an egality amendment that included provisions to modify and expand job opportunities for low-income individuals. Finally, Diane Feinstein, a Democrat from California, authored more amendments than any other senator. Although Feinstein supported more civic and corporative approaches than the other Senate activists discussed here, her amending patterns most accurately represent the entire set of Senate amendment data. Feinstein authored one corporative, one civic, and three egality amendments. Both of her corporative and civic amendments passed, requiring paternal grandparents to pay child support and allowing California to develop welfare reform demonstration projects.

In summary, the patterns of House and Senate amending data uncover the legislative origins of the gender ideology embedded in welfare reform. The amendment data reveal that the corporative individuality gender paradigm, and to some extent the civic individuality gender paradigm, were both supported throughout the entire policymaking process in both the House and the Senate. In other words, more corporative and civic individuality amendments were allowed to filter through the system successfully. Still, it is important to remember that some of the activists often supported amendments from the complementarity paradigm in their attempt to ensure that marriage and family were not forgotten in the greater effort to cut costs and to require women as well as men to work for benefits. In the Senate we saw that complementarity approaches were rarely supported, which helped to temper the House's desire to emphasize complementarity when final versions were ironed out in conference committee meetings.

■ Stage Three: The Role of Congresswomen in Creating Gender

Empirical research on women legislators indicates that they are more interested in working on and voting for legislation concerning women, children, child welfare, and the family than are their male counterparts.[25] Yet these findings do not explain the voting record for PRWORA, in which Democratic women generally voted against welfare reform proposals and Republican women generally voted for welfare reform proposals. Those looking for quick, simple descriptions of the policy design process use this kind of voting record. These explanations fail to uncover the complex relationships between conventional ideology and gender ideology, leading to the assumption that conventional ideology is the only significant influence on national policy design.

Identifying a legislator's sex for the amendment data presented here helps to uncover the particular role played by congresswomen in framing welfare reform policy. It also helps to explain how congresswomen of color use a compound gender ideology in distinct ways.[26] In this final stage of analysis, we first look at the kinds of proposals offered by congresswomen as compared to congressmen. The data show that female Democrats and

Republicans tended to vote for civic and corporative individuality proposals rather than the complementarity proposals supported by their male colleagues, with few exceptions. Second, we show how the women in Congress often worked collaboratively in committees and on the House and Senate floors, before the final votes were taken, to modify welfare reform to include more child care programs, ensure child support enforcement for mothers, soften paternity reporting requirements, and remove restrictions from benefits for teenage parents. In other words, their orientation is more accurately construed as feminalist, rather than liberal, because it concentrated on issues associated with females. Liberal women offered quite different approaches than did conservative women to the same set of issues. Although certainly these women share views with their male colleagues, we also uncover a particular emphasis upon concerns of interest to women that is rare to find among congress-*men*. This discovery of a relationship between sex and choice of paradigms helps to underscore the argument that conventional ideology and gender ideology converged to frame the welfare reform package.

Amendments Made by Congresswomen

In the House, women legislators proposed 39 percent of the gender-related amendments to the Rules Committee for debate. Of the gender-related amendments accepted by the Rules Committee for debate on the floor, 37 percent were offered by women legislators, and of the gender-related amendments ultimately debated and successfully passed on the House floor, 36 percent were offered by women legislators. These findings indicate that the women legislators were consistently involved in the amending process and that they offered a substantial number of gender-related amendments, given that they held only 12 percent of the congressional seats in the 104th Congress.

An interesting feature of these data is that Republican women proposed more gender-related amendments than Democratic women. Republican women proposed fourteen and Democratic women proposed twelve of the gender-related amendments. Moreover, Republican women proposed gender-related amendments that were more similar to those written by Democrats and unlike those written by Republican men. Where Republican men proposed more complementarity amendments, Republican women proposed more egality and individuality amendments. In fact, Republican women proposed more individuality amendments and fewer complementarity amendments than did the Democratic women! The only exception to this observation of Democratic congresswomen is that the Democratic congresswomen of color were consistently more likely to offer egality amendments than individuality or complementarity amendments.

The white congresswomen were much more likely to support a combination of egality and individuality amendments.

More specifically, 21 percent of the amendments proposed by Republican congresswomen were egality amendments, 36 percent were civic individuality amendments, and 29 percent were corporative individuality amendments. Most notably, Republican women were also responsible for the only two egality amendments made in order and passed on the House floor. In fact, Republican women not only wrote the only egality amendments eventually passed on the floor, but they also wrote the few civic and corporative individuality amendments eventually passed as part of the welfare reform bill. For example, Marge Roukema offered a successful egality amendment that improved cost containment systems for infant formula for low-income families, and Nancy Johnson spearheaded an egality amendment that expanded the funding for child care programs.[27] These observations of women legislators further bolster the argument that gender ideology operates in tandem with a conventional governing ideology, especially when combined with knowledge of the feminale orientation of many of the amendments and when compared with the marked difference in amending patterns between male and female legislators.

Women Collaborating

A review of the kinds of amendments proposed may let us identify the gender focus of congressmen and women during the floor debates, but a close examination of the committee activity and the collaborative efforts of congresswomen allows us to see that gender ideology is at work during the entire legislative process.[28] The few women on the committees with welfare reform jurisdiction began to offer proposals for altering the legislation as soon as welfare reform was referred to committee and subcommittee. In subcommittee meetings, women legislators offered approximately 10 percent of all amendments made during the markup sessions on H.R. 4. For example, Barbara Kennelly offered the only four gender-related amendments that would improve child care funding, enforce child support payments, and omit strict paternity reporting requirements during a markup meeting of the Ways and Means Subcommittee on Human Resources. Although the subcommittee accepted none of her amendments, similar proposals were offered by Republican women during the full committee meeting and were adopted in part.

In the full committee markup meetings, women legislators offered 33 percent of all amendments in the Ways and Means and 10 percent of all amendments in the Economic and Educational Opportunities committees. That is a notable amount of amendment activity by women, simply because women comprised only 8 percent of each of these committees. The amendments offered by the Democratic women again failed in full committee, but the Republican women were quick to reword and reintroduce the amendments so that the efforts of Democratic women would not be discarded entirely. These "rewordings" often changed the approach from egality to civic or corporative individuality, but they still indicate the desire to consider the lives of women and their families in policymaking. Republican women proposed to limit rather than omit paternity requirements, increase child care funding rather than expand child care programs, and allow optional rather than mandatory state family caps. For example, Kennelly attempted to cut the paternity reporting requirements in committee and on the floor as she had in subcommittee. Her concern was for women who could be victims of abuse if paternity were established or who simply might not be able to comply with the requirements. Her amendment failed, but Nancy Johnson and Jennifer Dunn offered an alternative proposal that would stop women from being penalized if paternity were not established yet the women cooperated with state requirements to identify the child's father.[29]

Not only did women legislators in the House work together to make subtle changes, but they counted on collaboration with women in the Senate. During the Ways and Means full committee meetings, Kennelly and Johnson supported an amendment that would have required states to make child care available.[30] Although this amendment failed, Johnson and Kennelly knew that Nancy Landon Kassebaum (R-KS) would support a similar proposal in the Senate's version of the welfare reform legislation. In fact, Johnson stated that she withheld some of her amendments because she knew Kassebaum would add those amendments later in the Senate.[31]

The House and Senate floor amendment process similarly demonstrates the efforts that congresswomen made to collaborate with and support each other in committee. During the floor debate over a Roukema-Kennelly amendment in the House, those who rose in support included Patricia Schroeder (D-CO), Constance Morella (R-MD), Jane Harman (D-CA), Nita Lowey (D-NY), and Anna Eshoo (D-CA). Just before the vote was taken on the amendment, Eshoo stood to acknowledge the work of Roukema and Kennelly. She also credited the bipartisan representatives of the Women's Caucus for collaborative efforts at improving this bill:

> Mr. Chairman . . . I rise in support of the Roukema amendment. I would like to salute the gentlewoman from New Jersey for her decade-long effort on this as well as the gentlewoman from Connecticut (Mrs. Kennelly) and the women that have worked long before me in the House of Representatives through the bipartisan Women's Caucus. Mr. Chairman, this bipartisan measure would put real teeth in the enforcement of child support payments.[32]

All the debates over the amendments offered by women, in fact, showed some bipartisanship among women legislators interested in improving PRWORA for women welfare recipients. Nancy Pelosi (D-CA) acknowledged that the Johnson amendment to improve funding for child care was a step in the right direction, although she was opposed to relying on state funding for child care rather than federal funding:

> Now the amendment offered by our colleagues, the gentlewoman from Connecticut (Mrs. Johnson), the gentlewoman from Ohio (Ms. Pryce) and the gentlewoman from Utah (Mrs. Waldholtz) is a step in the right direction, and I commend the sponsors for offering it. . . . In my State of California, H.R. 4 cuts 35,000 child care slots. This amendment would restore 9,000 of those. That, as I said, is a step in the right direction.[33]

Even when a majority of the Democratic women was not strongly supportive of the amendments offered by Republican women, they reluctantly endorsed them. Patricia Schroeder stood in support of a second amendment offered by Roukema that was intended to improve cost containment systems for infant formula provided through the Women, Infant, and Children (WIC) program, despite her misgivings about the entire bill.[34]

Congressional Quarterly Weekly Report confirms findings of collaboration among women legislators involved in the floor amending process.[35] For example, a 1995 report indicates that Nancy Johnson was unconcerned when the Rules Committee disallowed a floor amendment to guarantee child care to welfare recipients who were required to work.[36] As noted, Johnson stated that she was unconcerned because she knew that Kassebaum had promised to discuss the matter in the Senate.

The Republican Party moderates in the Senate who helped redesign the House version of PRWORA were led on the Senate floor in part by Nancy Kassebaum and by Olympia Snowe (R-ME).[37] Snowe worked on civic and egality amendments designed to bolster funding for child care, increase state contributions to the program, delete the family cap, and allow checks for unwed teenage mothers.[38] Although Snowe did not formally offer any of the eighty-six amendments, her handiwork is apparent in the design of both successful and unsuccessful egality, civic, and corporative individuality amendments. For example, she worked on one of the civic amendments offered by Nancy Kassebaum to significantly improve child care funding and another corporative individuality amendment offered by Barbara Boxer to cut benefits for fathers who did not provide child support.[39]

Although women may have collaborated across the aisle, an important caveat to this evidence of collaboration is documented by Hawkesworth in her analysis of the racing and gendering of welfare policy. Hawkesworth concludes that congresswomen of color were ignored as they pursued welfare reform that would address the structural causes of poverty.[40] She reports that these women had their positions misrepresented, amendments blocked, and authority challenged by their Democratic colleagues and their Republican adversaries alike. This kind of evidence suggests that women of color may have been excluded from collaboration because of their race. We cannot determine whether race caused this exclusion here. Still, it is important to note that we similarly found that congresswomen of color were most likely to support egality amendments that would eliminate poverty, improve wages, and provide health care. Those kinds of issues are important to all low-income people but are especially important to poor black constituents, who, as we discuss in Chapter 6, face significant challenges to advancement through employment. However, our analysis using the lens of the gender paradigms does show that a strong majority of Congress members from both sides of the aisle avidly pursued individuality approaches, whereas those supporting egality, regardless of race, were in the minority and most often lost.

In summary, both the House and Senate women legislators, on the whole, worked to redesign PRWORA in a more feminale direction by making work easier for women and their children. Although they supported a range of gender paradigms, they concentrated their efforts on gender-related additions to the bill, efforts arguably made necessary because the masculinist positions were embedded in the original version of the bill. They typically adopted the individuality approach that women should work, but they made an effort to emphasize civic individuality by including fathers through child support enforcement and some state-sponsored support through child care services. Overall, their activity at all steps of the legislative process further demonstrates that both gender and sex make a difference in the design of national legislation. Without these women in Congress, the normal masculine orientation and masculinist preferences would have reigned unnoticed and unchallenged. Precisely because masculinism exists as gender normality, the feminalist proposals become obvious.[41]

◼ Conclusion

The three stages of analysis presented here demonstrate how gender ideology influenced the gender paradigms central to the design of PRWORA. First, we saw that a legislator's sex and gender ideology influenced twenty welfare votes held in the House committees with welfare reform jurisdiction. More specifically, we saw that the key committee activists shared common voting patterns on both gender and welfare legislation. Further, the activists with the most success at amending the legislation with their own provisions tended to share preferences for one paradigm—the individuality paradigm.

In the second stage of analysis, we went beyond establishing a relationship between welfare policy and gender ideology by studying the amendment proposals offered on the House and Senate floors during debate over H.R. 4. A review of the successful and unsuccessful amendment proposals helped us to identify more precisely the gender paradigms debated during the design of PRWORA. The data analysis revealed that not all gender paradigms were represented equally during the House and Senate floor debates. The individuality paradigm, both civic and corporative, was the most likely to be debated and passed on both the House and Senate floors. The complementarity paradigm, and the egality paradigm to a lesser extent, were used by these activists in their attempt to find a coalition that would pass a new welfare reform package. This record of amending patterns clearly demonstrates how several ideologies converged and one dominant paradigm emerged and was embedded in PRWORA.

Finally, the analysis of voting behavior and amendment patterns in the first and second stages of analysis allowed us to look at the role played by congresswomen in welfare reform. Women worked in collaboration during committee meetings, floor debates, and across chambers to influence the design of welfare reform. They collaborated in pursuit of feminalist policies against the backdrop of masculinist preferences. Although the women shared conventional ideological patterns with their male colleagues, they were still more likely to take a civic individuality approach over a corporative individuality or complementarity approach, and to do so in a feminalist manner. Again, these patterns bolster evidence of the independence of gender and governing ideologies.

The analysis of the compound model of gender ideology and gender paradigms in this chapter clearly shows that gender influenced the passage of an important national policy, despite the fact that it was passed with a partisan vote. The welfare reform debate may have been overshadowed by election year rhetoric in 1996, and members of Congress and candidates may have debated deficit reduction and returning social policy to the states. But we still found that the most active legislators shared a vision of childbearing and childrearing that would reshape a national policy for the indefinite future.

■ Notes

1. Personal Responsibility and Work Opportunity Reconciliation Act of 1996 (PROWRA), Public Law 104-193, 42 USC 601, Sec. 101 {5}c.

2. See Fenno, *The Power of the Purse;* Shepsle, "Institutional Arrangements and Equilibrium in Multidimensional Voting Models"; and Shepsle and Weingast, "The Institutional Foundations of Committee Power."

3. "Presidential Veto of Welfare Reform Bill—H.R. 4, 1996-01-09"; Jeffrey L. Katz, "Ignoring Veto Threat, GOP Links Welfare, Medicaid," *Congressional Quarterly Weekly Report,* May 25, 1996, 1465–1467.

4. See Fenno, *Congressmen in Committees;* Hall, *Participation in Congress;* Hall and Grofman, "The Committee Assignment Process and the Conditional Nature of Committee Bias"; Kingdon, *Congressmen's Voting Decisions;* Maltzman, "Meeting Competing Demands"; Maltzman and Smith, "Principals, Goals, Dimensionality and Congressional Committees"; Norton, "Committee Influence over Controversial National Policy"; Weingast, "Floor Behavior in the U.S. Congress."

5. Welfare reform votes included in the "welfare index" from H.R. 4: amendment on tax cuts by Archer (R-TX); amendments en bloc by Archer (R-TX); amendment for work hour increase by Talent (R-MO); amendment for vouchers for teenagers by Bunn (R-OR); amendment for newborn vouchers by Smith (R-NJ); amendment for housing preference by Moran (D-VA); amendment for food stamp block grant by Hostettler (R-IN); amendment for child support liens by Salmon (R-AZ); amendment for license suspension for late child support by Roukema (R-NJ); substitute amendment by Deal (D-GA); adoption of the rule for H.R. 4; motion to rise by Kennedy (D-MA); and welfare overhaul previous question by Solomon (R-NY). Votes included in the "welfare reform index" from H.R. 3734: instruction to conferees; vote on conference report; adoption of the rule for H.R. 3734; amendment requiring able-bodied recipients to work twenty hours a week for food stamp eligibility by Ney (R-OH); amendment for food stamps by Tanner (D-TN); motion to recommit by Tanner (D-TN); final vote on H.R. 3734.

6. Norton, "Uncovering the Unidimensionality of Gender Voting in Congress."

7. Fenno, *Congressmen in Committees;* Hall, "Participation and Purpose in Committee Decision Making"; and Hall, *Participation in Congress.*

8. See Committee on Rules, House Report 104-85, "Providing for the Further Consideration of H.R. 4, Personal Responsibility Act of 1995," 104th Cong., 1st sess., March 21, 1995.

9. To make interpretations of the table as clear as possible, the women's issue voting index (proxy for gender ideology) was collapsed and labeled with only three of the compounded gender ideology variants. However, all the gender variants are still being considered in the analysis. The label *gender left* overlaps with intersectors for this part of the analysis; the label *universalists* overlaps with intersectors and similarists; and the label *gender traditionalists* overlaps with patriarchalists. Note that the collapse of the compounded model is done only to improve clarity during empirical analysis of voting behavior.

10. Jeffrey Katz, Alissa Rubin, and Peter MacPherson, "Major Aspects of Welfare Bill Approved by Subcommittee," *Congressional Quarterly Weekly Report,* February 18, 1995, 525–532.

11. See list of en bloc amendments offered by Talent and Archer expressing the "sense of Congress" about marriage and family in PRWORA in the Committee on Rules, House Report 104-85, "Providing for the Further Consideration of H.R. 4, Personal Responsibility Act of 1995," 104th Cong., 1st sess., March 21, 1995.

12. Herrera, Epperlein, and Smith, "The Stability of Congressional Roll-Call Indexes," 403; Krehbiel, *Information and Legislative Organization;* Krehbiel, "Why Are Congressional Committees Powerful?"; Poole and Rosenthal, *Congress.*

13. Norton, "Uncovering the Unidimensionality of Gender Voting in Congress"; Norton, "Committee Influence over Controversial National Policy."

14. See Committee on Rules, House Report 104-85, "Providing for the Further Consideration of H.R. 4, The Personal Responsibility Act of 1995," 104th Congress, 1st session, March 21, 1995. Technically, 161 amendments were filed with the Committee on Rules and reported in this report. However, several of these amendments were duplicates or withdrawn. Thus, only 148 of the amendments were used for this data set.

15. Only the amendments to Senator Robert Dole's (R-KS) "amendment in the nature of substitute" (amendment No. 2280) to H.R. 4 were included in the data set for the Senate. This version of the bill was amended and passed by the Senate as PRWORA.

16. As discovered in the first stage of analysis, the gender left tend to support gender-related egality approaches to welfare reform, universalists tend to support individuality approaches, and the gender traditionalists tend to support complementarity approaches. Similarly, we assume here that conventional liberals will support non-gender-related liberal approaches to welfare reform, moderates will support moderate approaches, and conservatives will support conservative approaches. Further review of these relationships in this second stage of the analysis, however, does show that these expected correlations do not entirely explain welfare reform legislative outcomes. Many conventional moderates were willing to accept complementarity approaches to gender-related welfare reform in an effort to get the bill passed. We found that to be especially true in the House of Representatives. Additionally, to further clarify and distinguish the moderate non-gender-related amendments and the individuality gender-related amendments, the moderate amendments were coded in two categories: liberal moderate and conservative moderate. Similarly, the individuality amendments were coded as the civic individuality and corporative individuality versions, as previously discussed in Chapter 2. These distinctions allow us to evaluate more precisely the ways in which conventional ideology and gender ideology converged to become a part of the welfare reform package.

17. See Committee on Rules, House Report 104-85, "Providing for the Further Consideration of H.R. 4, The Personal Responsibility Act of 1995," 104th Congress, 1st session, 8–18.

18. Garfinkel, "Bringing Fathers Back In."

19. See proposed amendment number 49, Committee on Rules, House Report 104-85, "Providing for the Further Consideration of H.R. 4, The Personal Responsibility Act of 1995," 104th Congress, 1st session, 10.

20. 104th Cong., 1st sess. *Congressional Record* 141 (September 14, 1995): S13561.

21. 104th Cong., 1st sess., *Congressional Record* 141 (September 13, 1995): S13489.

22. 104th Cong., 1st sess., *Congressional Record* 141 (March 23, 1995): H3592.

23. 104th Cong., 1st sess., *Congressional Record* 141 (March 22, 1995): H3515.

24. 104th Cong., 1st sess., *Congressional Record* 141 (March 23, 1995): H3592 and H3633.

25. See Bratton and Haynie, "Agenda Setting and Legislative Success in State Legislatures"; Dodson, "Making a Difference"; Dodson, *The Impact of Women in Congress;* Mansbridge, "Should Blacks Represent Blacks and Women

Represent Women?"; Phillips, *The Politics of Presence;* Swers, *The Difference Women Make;* and Thomas, *How Women Legislate.*

26. See Hawkesworth, "Congressional Enactments of Race-Gender."

27. See proposed amendment numbers 13 (Nancy Johnson, R-CT) and 15 (Marge Roukema, R-NJ), made in order on the floor, Committee on Rules, House Report 104-85, "Providing for the Further Consideration of H.R. 4, The Personal Responsibility Act of 1995," 104th Congress, 1st session, 25–26.

28. See Carroll and Casey, "Welfare Reform," for an excellent qualitative account of this collaboration, based upon interviews with congresswomen and their staff members.

29. Jeffrey Katz and Alissa Rubin, "House Panel Poised to Approve GOP Welfare Overhaul Bill," *Congressional Quarterly Weekly Report,* March 4, 1995, 691.

30. Ibid., 689.

31. Jeffrey Katz, "GOP Moderates Central to Welfare Overhaul," *Congressional Quarterly Weekly Report,* March 18, 1995, 813–814.

32. 104th Cong., 1st sess., *Congressional Record* 141 (March 23, 1995): H3631.

33. Ibid., H3583.

34. Ibid., H3591.

35. That lends even more evidence to our own findings and those of Carroll and Casey, "Welfare Reform."

36. Jeffrey Katz, "House Passes Welfare Bill; Senate Likely to Alter It," *Congressional Quarterly Weekly Report,* March 25, 1995, 873.

37. The House and Senate moderates working on welfare reform had named themselves the "Mod Squad," Carroll and Casey, "Welfare Reform," 126.

38. Jeffrey Katz, "GOP Moderates Flex Muscles," *Congressional Quarterly Weekly Report,* September 16, 1996, 2805.

39. "Bill Tracking Report," 104th Cong., 1st sess., US House of Representatives, H.R. 4, Personal Responsibility Act of 1995," Lexis-Nexis, 1996, 8–44.

40. Hawkesworth, "Congressional Enactments of Race-Gender," 540.

41. These findings have significant implications for those committed to an inclusive democracy, descriptive representation, and the "politics of presence," in Ann Phillips's term. This analysis of congresswomen's participation in welfare reform emphasizes that a legislator's sex can have a notable influence on national policymaking outcomes. Further, these findings reinforce arguments supporting legislative institutions that adopt gender quotas or "parity" systems, where the number of women legislators or women running for office is fixed by statutory or constitutional mandate, because the policy product is likely to be shaped with an intersection of a compound gender ideology and governing ideology that is sensitive to the lives women lead.

9

Recognizing the Sexual Politics of Policy

THE NOMINEE'S REMARKS WERE BRIEF. THE SENATORS' QUESTIONS were pro forma. And the hearing ended not long after it began. But behind this quiet, even boring, hearing was a contentious discussion about the direction of future policy and the government's power to create gender.

Nominated by President George W. Bush in 2001 to be the assistant secretary of family support for the Department of Health and Human Services, Wade Horn included in his comments a revocation of a previous position. An unabashed advocate of complementarity, Horn earlier had written a briefing paper recommending that the government refashion its social welfare policies to discourage single-parent families and reward two-parent heterosexual ones. When such programs as Head Start, public housing, financial aid for education, and job training were limited and could not be extended to all who were eligible, he argued in 1997, married couples should receive benefits first. Only after all such families were offered the benefits would single parents be able to receive them, and then only if funding were still available. In the 2001 hearings, however, Horn explained that he had listened to his critics and rewritten the paper to remove this recommendation. It was divisive, he realized.[1]

Indeed, it was. Division was crucial to the proposal. Distinguishing people, holding up some as commendable and others as unworthy of support, was the means by which marriage would be advanced and unwed parenthood discouraged. According to Horn's proposals, government would use rewards to induce men and women to adopt the traditional gender roles of husband and wife and castigate those who did not hew to these standards of good family values.

Although the transparent use of state power to differentiate people and then reward some and penalize others marshaled a firestorm of protest

219

in this particular case, Horn's revocation of this recommendation should not blind us to the observation that other policies do the same, even when the consequences are initially ambiguous or appear benevolent.[2] In the attempt to change behavior, policies extend benefits—whether economic, psychological, or procedural—to some and deny them to others. They legitimize certain roles and behaviors, upholding them as exemplary and worthy of imitation. They ignore some behaviors and actions, rendering them invisible, unrecognized, and valueless. They rebuke others, marking them as undesirable and the persons engaged in them as unworthy.

When the behaviors, roles, and actions at stake determine the types of gender that people may adopt or "perform," the government creates gender through policy. First the Wisconsin legislature and Governor Tommy Thompson and then the 104th Congress and President Bill Clinton established a national policy that redrew gender with new ideas about mothers, fathers, work, and family. Through policy that often is ostensibly about other subjects, government contests and legitimizes gender options, the roles, expectations, and valued behaviors that men and women are supposed to adopt to be good citizens. If individuals choose unauthorized modes of gender, the government has the capacity to deem them bad citizens. Through such delegitimation, these people may not receive the benefits of citizenship, including access to the full benefits offered by the state and recognition of the ways in which they contribute to the community.[3]

Importantly, policy often creates gender seemingly without an explicit agenda or direct debate because the gender outcome is a by-product of an agenda, formulation, and deliberation about some other policy. As a result, the process of creating gender is masked. Although some decisionmakers and attuned members of the public may be aware of the sexual politics of policy and realize that gender is being created, most are not. This book has attempted to raise this awareness of the processes involved, to measure the presence of gender ideology in policymaking, and to provide a framework that can ultimately be adapted to analyze gender creation in any policy area.

The paradigms of complementarity, individuality, and egality expose the normative standards of good behavior that vie for legitimacy. Paradigms also reveal the patterns and practices of gender promoted cumulatively through a welter of policies that appear in any one issue area. Thus, they allow us to identify major shifts in the direction of public policy, the emergence of a dominant approach to government-sanctioned gender, and how some proposals continue to challenge this dominance. Paradigms result from contests among policymakers whose ideological viewpoints share some elements but not others. Introducing gender and compounding it with conventional governing ideologies help to predict and explain why some policy proposals—but not others—succeed politically. The gendered ideological framework helps us explain the common interests of strange bedfellows, who share overlapping interests in a policy target or outcome despite great differences on why a policy should proceed. For example, our analysis of congressional decisionmaking shows that in welfare reform, even liberal feminists allied with traditional conservatives because they both sought means to enhance women's employment; the new right and the gender left agreed on programs to employ poor men despite their substantial disagreements concerning the importance of two-parent families to society.

The adoption and implementation of the Personal Responsibility and Work Opportunity Reconciliation Act (PRWORA) denotes a breaking point long in the making. It marks the ascendancy of the individuality paradigm over the complementarity paradigm as the dominant policy approach to gender. The policy activists in Congress who succeeded in shaping the PRWORA were clearly those who advocated individuality approaches to reform. Our analysis shows that egality approaches met with negligible success and complementarity approaches with nominal recognition. Thus, the ground upon which women stand as they stake their claims to be good citizens has shifted, for the welfare reforms of the 1990s have decimated care work as a valuable contribution to the commonweal. Not only did these reforms devalue women's care for their own children, but also they undermined their care of their communities, such as welfare recipients' leadership of community organizations in black and Latino neighborhoods.[4] Republican motherhood has been driven out by economic citizenship in the "achieved" elements of citizenship. As a result, Judith N. Shklar's observation that real citizens are taxpayers denies unremunerated care work any value toward citizens' obligations to contribute to the "civic minimum." And without that contribution, individuals are not deemed deserving citizens who should expect fair reciprocity from the state.[5]

Thus, a good citizen can only be a successful worker, one whose paid labor is supposed to provide autonomy, independence, self-esteem, and dignity. Whether one's worthiness as a citizen depends on the fact that one labors and not on the monetary success of those labors is still a contested issue, played out in an ongoing battle over the civic and corporative versions of the individuality paradigm. Over time, various compromises continue to be reached concerning the government's responsibility to support individuals in their role as workers—whether government should provide subsidies for child care, extend health care to uninsured workers, offer education and training to workers with low wages, or subsidize low earnings through programs such as the earned income tax credit. These are important battles, and the resolution of these disputes matters for the economic well-being of many women, men, and children. But even generous policies grounded in the civic version of the individuality paradigm still recognize as valuable, as worthy, as commendable only those working-age individuals who labor for wages.

Despite the influence of masculinity on the individuality paradigm, the success of masculinism has led many to be troubled about the implications for men. The extension of the individuality paradigm to women prompted concerns about the proper behavior of and place for good men. If women assume important masculine tenets through paid employment and transmit them to their children by acting as good breadwinning role models, then men no longer occupy a unique place in the family or the polity. Even though demands for child support from noncustodial fathers appease many policymakers, others remain concerned that to create good men, government should insist on more than just a check. Most initiatives in response to this observation have focused on renewing the male role in families by creating fathers, husbands, and male breadwinners. Initial efforts to renew complementarity through punitive measures intended to reduce out-of-wedlock childbearing floundered on the grounds of unfairness and infringements on state flexibility. Subsequent proposals to rejuvenate fatherhood through a host of social services met more political success but had little tangible outcome. Moreover, the fatherhood programs highlighted the fact that many men had low earnings and that increasing their earnings so they could provide a middle-class standard of living for children, let alone a wife, was no easy matter. The myth of the male breadwinner was challenged by these programs, and they quickly lost political appeal.

Despite these early political and policy failures, the quest to revive complementarity continues through policy proposals designed to renew marriage and thus reinstate men as husbands. Powerful legislators continue to support proposals similar to those offered by Bill Archer (R-TX) and Jim Talent (R-MO) in the 104th Congress, which proclaimed the value of marriage, female caregivers, and male breadwinners. Similarly, executive branch officials like Wade Horn have not abandoned the belief that children too seldom fared well when raised by single mothers, that the absence of fathers in their lives was a central cause of their difficulties, and that the primary way to create fathers was to first create husbands. Horn's faith in these claims led him to back the use of state power to promote marriage and to search for policies that would engender less opposition to state intervention, a position that acquired some financial backing during the reauthorization of PRWORA. The Department of Health and Human Services inventoried states for policies that promoted marriage in ten areas, from tax incentives and marriage education to marriage campaigns and youth education.[6] The state marriage inventory shows clearly that many in the government are willing to use a variety of means to reassert traditional gender roles, especially those consistent with patriarchal ideology and the complementarity paradigm. Overall, these observations suggest that the complementarity proposals given secondary status in 1996 remain part of the larger debate about the creation of gender at both the state and national level.

The insistence that women be treated like men offers the hope of stronger standing for women as citizens. Yet the individuality paradigm's failure to incorporate feminale realities and preferences creates masculine mothers with little ground on which to demand that government recognize and value care work. In addition, this emphasis on masculine values has prompted a return to the complementarity paradigm in order to shore up men's standing as citizens. A genuine chance to strengthen fathers' roles as caregivers never received serious attention as legislators shied away from the policies in the egality paradigm needed to shift masculinity itself and unhinge care work from sexed bodies. Only a few elite men will benefit, and nearly all of us will suffer as a consequence of this masculinist success.

■ A Happy Marriage of Masculinism and Capitalism: Semi-Autonomous Women and Tamed Men

With the passage of W-2 in Wisconsin and adoption and implementation of PRWORA, the ideal of republican motherhood that provided the justification for AFDC has been replaced by the ideal of masculine mothers. Advocates from the center to the left who supported the policy changes that led to this shift argued that if women and men worked, they would be able to claim full citizenship status and thus could demand and justify social welfare programs on their behalf. But to what extent and in what ways could the ideal of masculine mothers challenge prevailing understandings of workers and citizenship status?

The similarist argument that policy needed to "make work pay" offers the potential to undermine the prevailing understanding of work and citizenship. After all, if existing jobs do not pay, if work is not compensated sufficiently and government must intervene to subsidize child care, health care, and low wages, certainly the claim that work leads to independence is problematic. Conservatives have recognized this challenge, at least implicitly, and they fight the very notion that government must intervene to make work pay. Good workers succeed and do not require government's help; "making people struggle a little bit is not necessarily the worst thing," declared Senator Rick Santorum (R-PA).[7]

The difficulty with similarist positions is that programs perceived as supporting or enabling work are more politically palatable than programs that directly increase the monetary rewards of work. Work-support policies, such as child care assistance and health care coverage, are understood as devices that remove barriers, open opportunities, and persuade hesitant women that they too can compete in the labor market. These aids were pushed heartily by Democrats—neo-liberals and social liberals as well as social Democrats—during the debate over passage of the original bill and again during the reauthorization debate. Indeed, during reauthorization the two main items Democrats asked for were child care assistance and extended health care coverage. Lack of child care was successfully portrayed by liberal feminism as a barrier to work, a position attractive to proponents of corporative feminalism who seek to remove this barrier so women, too, can make it in the labor market on the same footing as men. Lack of health care was also positioned as a barrier to work, although the costs discouraged much action, despite the fact that the middle class felt changes in health care policy were essential.

Income subsidies that directly increase the monetary rewards of work stand on precarious political footing, for they fly too directly in the face of the autonomous, independent citizen. The very fact of income supplements taints the image. Because good workers are by definition autonomous and independent, they should not need such income supplements. The need for supplements implies that the individuals are not good workers and therefore not deserving. Just as it was not sufficient to "be" a mother when PRWORA was passed, it is not sufficient to "be" a worker. Instead, it is the act of working that matters. Arguments by proponents of similarism and even intersector thought give no reason to revise the notion of what constitutes a good worker. Thus, the idea of using income subsidies to make work pay does not have strong political legs because it does not displace the claim that the act of working is itself meritorious and alone will lead to better citizens.

Through the lens of gender ideology, by far the strongest political potential lies in a revamped notion of a family wage system, a system that allows an adult—whether male or female—to earn enough to support a family. Such a system would give women greater autonomy because they too must work and earn, but under that system, presumably they would do so at better wages; hence it could appeal to everyone from advocates of traditionalism to the gender left. A revised family wage system also offers men the promise of respectable wages, appealing to proponents of traditional conservatism who seek breadwinning men and to proponents of patriarchalism who seek married men. Because poor men have a greater incentive to work if wages can bring a modicum of dignity and because better wages increase the likelihood of stable marriages and thus help to "tame" men, this notion could appeal to everyone from proponents of the gender left to proponents of patriarchalism. However, reconstituted as a "living wage" campaign, with a self-sufficiency standard, such a family wage system proves very threatening to the prevailing labor market and wage system. Moreover, such a system exposes the myth of male breadwinner. Earnings needed under the self-sufficiency standard reach about $40,000 in most areas of the United States. Currently, too large a percentage of all workers have earnings below this level, even when paired as a family unit.

Gender ideology, however, compounds with governing ideology, so ideas about fiscal policy, market economics, and the like also drive policy. Given current political realities, a more likely scenario rests in a conservative rendition that can be supported by advocates of an array of gender ideologies. The notion of a family wage system now includes the idea that both people will and should work. A two-earner family compensates for the low earnings of women and the low earnings of men. A two-earner family also provides protection from the vagaries of the market; when one is unemployed, the other will still be working. In addition, it allows for care functions through such strategies as "tag-team child care," in which one adult provides care while the other works. Most mother-only households will continue to struggle financially. These contingencies all fit nicely with the emphasis traditional conservatives place on pragmatism, the idea that people should "marry or cope."

This conservative rendition of the family wage system differs from the focus on marriage by proponents of patriarchalism because the importance of marriage is rooted in economic security for both men and women. Moreover, it accepts the idea that men do not necessarily provide for their families, at least on the basis of their wages alone. It also handles nicely demands for child support enforcement; in fact, it encourages such demands and gives them an important niche, an element attractive to proponents of feminalism across the spectrum. Such a revamped family wage system arguably will prove very powerful politically because it serves as a compromise among many of the different gender ideologies we highlight, appeasing many of their proponents. Women gain more autonomy but do not threaten major societal institutions because they remain ensconced in some version of private patriarchy. Men can fulfill the provider role even if they no longer are sole providers, so they cast off the parts of deadbeat and scofflaw. By entering into nuclear family arrangements, men also become more respectable and have greater potential to become good guys or promise keepers to their mates and children. Its political strength lies in the fact that it supports rather than threatens ideas about the labor market and capitalism, family, and even individual autonomy. It does not have explicit policy constraints on individual choices about marriage, divorce, or employment, pleasing the center to left of the ideological continuum. It allows policymakers to ignore low earnings generally, especially the precipitous decline in male wages, which has garnered remarkably little attention politically.

The ideal of the masculine mother created by the adoption and implementation of the PRWORA emphasizes the masculine more than mothering. Because the status of citizen is that of worker and not much else, it relies on and fosters an attenuated notion of citizenship and community more generally. Failure to recognize mothering—mother-work—as grounds for citizenship means individuals have no alternative to their status as workers. Without an alternative to ground a challenge, no entrée exists for other claims to access to benefits. It produces a "happy marriage between masculinism and capitalism" by creating semiautonomous women who pair up with tamed men.[8]

■ Making Gender Protoideology More Meaningful in Political Representation

Several factors contribute to a growing awareness that gender ideology is at play in policymaking, despite the fact that policy analysis seldom explicitly acknowledges or measures the influence of ideology beyond the traditional liberal-conservative continuum. Scholarly theorizing about gender, including masculinity, has grown substantially since the 1970s, to the point at which it largely has been mainstreamed on most college campuses, even if it is still subject to attack by those who challenge "gender feminists." Although few in the political world use a nuanced articulation of ideology or of gender, seemingly awareness of gender has risen.

Awareness of gender ideology also can be used strategically. The right has found ways to use gender ideology to its own advantage, such as promoting complementarity in a variety of policy areas, from welfare and the military to Title IX and workplace rules. Proponents of universalism and traditionalism also have found ways to co-opt similarist and intersector positions, for example, by deploying the principle of the "same" treatment to roll back policies such as affirmative action. Finally, the fact that men have gender too and do not simply constitute some universal norm is becoming more evident in politics. No place has this been on greater display than in the 2004 presidential election as George W. Bush and John Kerry strove to make themselves the more manly of the men, to project the most dominant of masculinities. Hence, it is time to acknowledge that both male and female policymakers use gender as well as conventional governing ideologies to shape public policy decisions about gender paradigms.

Such awareness is a critical first step to making the conflicts over the creation of gender visible and to approaching in conscious and deliberate ways the changes in gender that occur through changes in other policies. Most important, by systematically analyzing gender implications in welfare policy, the attack on feminale work becomes apparent. Without such analysis, policy seemingly targeted at a small number of poor, irresponsible, dependent mothers might have been seen only under the frame of the undeserving poor.

With theoretical and empirical analysis based upon the gender ideology framework, these policy actions can be understood as much larger contests between the protoideological masculinist and feminalist values, not only the conservative and liberal aspects of ideology. The Hobbesian notion of an atomistic citizen, an individual who achieves alone in the world and can exist only with the denial of "(m)other," becomes *the* only valid model of citizen.[9] The less prominent gestures toward marriage do little to relieve this masculinist victory because they generally seek to reinstitute private patriarchy to the detriment of feminale heteronomy— of being both connected and independently strong. Such denial has profound implications for the type of civil society the government fosters. It also undermines one of women's most important traditional sources of political power—mothering, the care and raising of future citizens and workers. If scholars raise the consciousness of gender protoideology, then when females and their male allies in elected office attempt to represent their constituents, they can better challenge the masculinist dominance of politics and the masculinist assumptions of policy proposals. Granting legitimacy to gender protoideology would enable policymakers to frame public problems in feminalist terms without disloyalty to liberal or conservative positions. It would confer more value on feminality and the policies and activities associated with it. It would enrich and enhance the representation of all Americans by allowing a full range of female-based perspectives, as well as by broadening the scope of possible modes of masculinity in policy.

■ Extending Gender Analysis to Policymaking

No analysis of policy is complete without an assessment of its effects upon gender because policy creates gender. Even as they shape what is considered private and what public, analysts need to attend to the gendered implications of public problems, to consider the ways in which gender is created when problems are framed on the public agenda, solutions formulated, and deliberations held. Routine analysis of policy should consider the ways it allocates values and resources and hence determines differential gender opportunities by race and class or according to individual situations. Awareness of gender paradigms and their ideological roots improves the capacity to analyze the contests under way, to predict unlikely alliances and potential points of compromise. Large swaths of public power are at stake. *Nothing less than the capacity of women to achieve equal representation is implicated in the unwillingness to recognize masculinism as the founding protoideology that has guided governing since the American Revolution.* Without recognition, the difficulty of operating from feminalist positions within the policy environment can be cast as failure on the part of individual women rather than the systemic and structural disadvantage that it is.

The gender framework presented here is ripe for adaptation to other policy areas. In our introduction we emphasized that welfare reform provides an important case study. Welfare reform has substantial consequences for men, women, and children, and major gender battles have been fought over social welfare policy. However, we also note that a compound gender ideology framework could help further the understanding of how liberal and conservative policymakers construct gender through the adoption of employment, sexual harassment, surrogacy, or gender identity politics. We also suggest that this gender analysis could be applied to policy arenas that at first glance seem to have little to do with gender, such as foreign affairs and military operations. In addition, the framework presented here could be adapted to uncover different elements that help form the core of ideology, especially to explore the roots of ideological perspectives centered on race and the ways in which they compound with the left-right governing ideological spectrum. In short, we invite scholars to adapt this approach to other policy and other elements. No longer should gender remain submerged, implicit rather than explicit.

Politics, in David Easton's classic terms, is about the authoritative allocation of resources and values, including those that make gender. We need to make ordinary the analysis of gender in policymaking. The sexual politics of policy demands awareness by students of policy, policymakers, and citizens alike because the consequences have enormous implications for us all.

■ Notes

1. *Nominations of Allen Frederick Johnson, William Henry Lash III, Brian Carlton Roseboro, Kevin Keane, and Wade Horn,* Hearing before the Committee on Finance, United States Senate, 107th Cong., 1st sess., June 21, 2001, 12–17. Horn did not repudiate all punitive recommendations. For example, in the original briefing paper, Horn suggested that schools return to stigmatizing teens who have children, actions they stopped because they thought it would be discrimination under Title IX. Horn argued that schools should stigmatize male teens who had children to avoid charges of discrimination. The original briefing paper is

Wade Horn and Andrew Bush, "Fathers, Marriage, and Welfare Reform," Hudson Institute Report, March 1997, http://www.welfarereformer.org/articles/father.htm. The revised version is Wade Horn and Andrew Bush, "Fathers, Marriage, and the Next Phase of Welfare Reform," Acton Institute Policy Forum, Spring 2003, http://www.acton.org/ppolicy/forum/no3.html.

2. For newspaper reports on Horn's nomination, see Jessica Thompson and Rob Hotakainen, "In Marriage Debates, No Love Is Lost," *Minneapolis Star Tribune,* August 13, 2001, A1. For a discussion on opposition from women's groups, see Sarah Stewart Taylor, "Wade Horn Says in Senate Hearing He Was Wrong," June 25, 2001, Women's Enews, http://www.now.org/eNews/june2001/062501horn.html.

3. Katz, in *The Price of Citizenship,* especially in the Epilogue, makes a similar argument rooted in T. H. Marshall's framework of civil, social, and political citizenship.

4. Jenning, "Welfare Reform and Neighborhoods."

5. From White, *The Civic Minimum.* For a discussion of concepts about citizenship, see also Katz, *The Price of Citizenship;* Shklar, *American Citizenship;* and Schudson, *The Good Citizen.*

6. Karen N. Gardiner, Michael E. Fishman, Plamen Nikolov, Asaph Glosser, and Stephanie Laud, *State Policies on Marriage: Final Report Submitted to the U.S. Department of Health and Human Services,* September 2002. http://aspe.hhs.gov/hsp/marriage02f/.

7. Elizabeth Shogren, "Tighter Rules Likely for Welfare Families: A Senate Panel Approves a Bill That Would Force More Recipients to Find Jobs, Work Longer Hours," *Los Angeles Times,* September 11, 2003, A18.

8. Our words here play on Hartman, "The Unhappy Marriage of Marxism and Feminism."

9. The concept of "(m)other" comes from Di Stefano, *Configurations of Masculinity.*

Appendixes

■ **Appendix A: Political Beliefs and Legislative Decisionmaking Survey of Wisconsin State Legislators, 1995–1996**

Noted below are the survey questions included in the "Political Beliefs and Legislative Decisionmaking Survey of the Wisconsin State Legislators, 1995–1996," and the variables created for analysis from the survey questions.

Ideological Variables

Ideological variables were created from two survey questions asking respondents to identify their policy priorities, first as (1) fiscally liberal, (2) fiscally moderate, or (3) fiscally conservative; and second as (1) socially liberal, (2) socially moderate, or (3) socially conservative. These variables were coded to identify the following broad ideological priorities: (1) strongly liberal policy priorities, (2) moderately liberal policy priorities, (3) moderately conservative policy priorities, or (4) strongly conservative policy priorities.

Political Beliefs Scale

Legislators were asked to place themselves on a ten-point continuum on eight sets of political beliefs. The eight continua include the following sets of beliefs: (1) taxation scale: from "provide services that meet needs" to "keep taxes low," (2) market regulation scale: from "government must regulate the market" to "the market produces good results," (3) race discrimination scale: from "we need to enforce civil rights laws" to "race discrimination is not a problem," (4) government support scale: from "government does good things" to "government power should be feared," (5) government entitlement scale: from "many people need a helping hand" to "individual effort determines success," (6) female gender role scale: from "women need to support themselves" to "traditional gender roles are best," (7) male gender role scale: from "men need to care for home and family too" to "traditional gender roles are best," (8) family structure scale: from "good families come in many forms" to "traditional families are best." These eight belief scales were coded into one scale used to identify the following broad political beliefs: (1) progressive, (2) moderate, (3) traditional.

Gender Ideological Variables

Women's Role Beliefs Scale. This variable was created from one of the political belief questions asked in the survey. The continuum used for this variable ranged from "women need to support themselves" to "traditional gender roles are best."

Men's Role Beliefs Scale. This variable was created from one of the political belief questions asked in the survey. The continuum used for this variable ranged from "men need to take care of home and family too" to "traditional gender roles are best."

Gender Beliefs Scale. Three of the gender-related political belief continua were used to create this variable. The continua used for this variable included the following: (1) from "women need to support themselves" to "traditional gender roles are best," (2) from "men need to care for home and family too" to "traditional gender roles are best," (3) "from good families come in many forms" to "traditional families are best." This variable was recoded into a four-point "gender beliefs" scale, ranging from very progressive to very traditional.

■ Appendix B: Key Vote Index

Ten key votes taken in the Wisconsin State Assembly and Senate during the 1995–1996 legislative session were used to create a legislative voting index. Legislators were ranked from 0 to 100 depending on how many times they voted with the conservative position on each vote. A 100 percent vote score indicates a conservative legislator, and a 0 percent score indicates a liberal legislator. The key vote index was recoded into three values for use in this analysis: (1) liberal—0 through 33 percent, (2) moderate—34 through 66 percent, (3) and conservative—67 through 100 percent. The key votes used to create the index were obtained from the Wisconsin Legislative Reference Bureau and included the following votes:

1. Limit medical malpractice pain and suffering clause (AB 36)
2. Limit liability in tort reform (SB11)
3. Limit financial obligations for custody of mentally ill (SB 244)
4. Set standards for commitment of dangerously mentally ill (SB 270)
5. Reform auto insurance (SB 6)
6. Reform welfare (W-2) (SB 591)
7. Institute twenty-four-hour waiting period before abortions (AB 441)
8. Amendment to twenty-four-hour waiting period on abortions (AB 441a)
9. Require school uniforms (AB 824)
10. Repeal and renew Child Protective Services law (SB 501)

■ Appendix C: Variables Used in the Regression Analysis, Table 8.1

Dependent Variable:
Welfare Reform Preference Index

This index makes use of votes on twenty amendments to H.R. 4 and H.R. 3734; 0 = no votes on all twenty welfare reform proposals; 100 = yes votes on all twenty welfare reform proposals. Scores range from 0 to 100 percent. Serves as a proxy measure of a member's welfare reform preferences.

Independent Variables, Gender-Related

Women's Issue Voting Index. American Association of University Women (AAUW) Voting Index. 0 = no votes in favor of AAUW women's issues, ranging from abortion to educational equity; 100 = yes on all votes in favor of AAUW women's issues. Scores range from 0 to 100 percent. Serves as a proxy measure of a member's gender ideology.

Sex. 1 = male; 0 = female.

Partial birth abortion ban. 1 = yes vote on "Partial Birth Abortion Ban;" 0 = no on ban.

Number of children. Serves as indicator of family responsibility or child care knowledge/experience (range = 1–10).

Independent Variables, Non-Gender-Related

Party. 1 = Republican; 0 = Democrat.

Nonwhite district. Percentage of district residents who are nonwhite, including black, Hispanic, and Asian residents. Scores range from 0 to 100 percent, with 100 percent indicating no whites in the district.

Religion. 1 = fundamentalist (i.e., Evangelical, Baptist, conservative Catholic); 0 = nonfundamentalist (i.e., Protestant, Jewish, Catholic).

Bibliography

Abramovitz, Mimi. 1988. *Regulating the Lives of Women: Social Welfare Policy from Colonial Times to the Present.* Boston: South End Press.

Auletta, Ken. 1982. *The Underclass.* New York: Vintage Books.

Bederman, Gail. 1995. *Manliness and Civilization: A Cultural History of Gender and Race in the United States, 1880–1917.* Chicago: University of Chicago Press.

Bell, Winifred. 1965. *Aid to Dependent Children.* New York: Columbia University Press.

Beller, Andrea H., and John W. Graham. 1993. *Small Change: The Economics of Child Support.* New Haven: Yale University Press.

Blankenhorn, David. 1995. *Fatherless America: Confronting Our Most Urgent Social Problem.* New York: Basic Books.

Boris, Eileen. 1999. "When Work Is Slavery." In *Whose Welfare?* edited by Gwendolyn Mink, 36–55. Ithaca, NY: Cornell University Press.

Bratton, Kathleen A., and Kerry L. Haynie. 1999. "Agenda Setting and Legislative Success in State Legislatures: The Effects of Gender and Race." *Journal of Politics* 61:658–679.

Brod, Harry, and Michael Kaufman, eds. 1994. *Theorizing Masculinities.* Thousand Oaks, CA: Sage Publications.

Brown, Wendy. 1988. *Manhood and Politics: A Feminist Reading in Political Theory.* Totowa, NJ: Rowman and Littlefield.

———. 1995. *States of Injury: Power and Freedom in Late Modernity.* Princeton, NJ: Princeton University Press.

Bryner, Gary C. 1998. *Politics and Public Morality: The Great American Welfare Reform Debate.* New York: W. W. Norton.

Buker, Eloise. 1999. *Talking Feminist Politics: Conversations on Law, Science, and the Postmodern.* Lanham, MD: Rowman and Littlefield.

Burke, Vincent J., and Vee Burke. 1974. *Nixon's Good Deed: Welfare Reform.* New York: Columbia University Press.

Butler, Judith P. 1993. *Bodies That Matter: On the Discursive Limits of "Sex."* New York: Routledge.

———. 1999. *Gender Trouble: Feminism and the Subversion of Identity.* New York: Routledge.

Califano, Joseph. 1981. *Governing America.* New York: Simon and Schuster.

Carlson, Robert B., and Kevin R. Hopkins. 1981. "Whose Responsibility Is Social Responsibility?" *Public Welfare* 39:8–17.

Carroll, Susan J., and Kathleen J. Casey. 2001. "Welfare Reform in the 104th Congress: Institutional Position and the Role of Women." In *Women and Welfare: Theory and Practice in the United States and Europe,* edited by Nancy J. Hirschmann and Ulrike Liebert, 111–132. New Brunswick, NJ: Rutgers University Press.

Carver, Terrel. 1996. *Gender Is Not a Synonym for Women.* Boulder, CO: Lynne Rienner.

Clatterbaugh, Kenneth. 1997. *Contemporary Perspectives on Masculinity.* Boulder, CO: Westview.

Connell, R. W. 1987. *Gender and Power: Society, the Person, and Sexual Politics.* Stanford, CA: Stanford University Press.

———. 1995. *Masculinities.* Berkeley: University of California Press.

Corbert, Thomas J. 1995. "Welfare Reform in Wisconsin: The Rhetoric and the Reality." In *The Politics of Welfare Reform,* edited by Donald F. Norris and Lyke Thompson, 19–54. Thousand Oaks, CA: Sage Publications.

Cox, Gary W., and Mathew D. McCubbins. 1994. *Legislative Leviathan: Party Government in the House.* Berkeley: University of California Press.

Crittenden, Ann. 2001. *The Price of Motherhood.* New York: Henry Holt.

Crowley, Jocelyn Elise. 2003. *The Politics of Child Support in America.* Cambridge: Cambridge University Press.

Danziger, Sheldon H., and Daniel H. Weinberg. 1994. "The Historical Record: Trends in Family Income, Inequality, and Poverty." In *Confronting Poverty: Prescriptions for Change,* edited by Sheldon H. Danziger, Gary D. Sandefur, and Daniel H. Weinberg, 18–50. New York: Russell Sage Foundation.

Davies, Gareth. 1996. *From Opportunity to Entitlement: The Transformation and Decline of Great Society Liberalism.* Lawrence: University Press of Kansas.

Davis, Martha F. 1993. *Brutal Need: Lawyers and the Welfare Rights Movement, 1960–1973.* New Haven, CT: Yale University Press.

Dawson, Michael C. 2001. *Black Visions: The Roots of Contemporary African-American Political Ideologies.* Chicago: University of Chicago Press.

Di Stefano, Christine. 1991. *Configurations of Masculinity: A Feminist Perspective on Modern Political Theory.* Ithaca, NY: Cornell University Press.

Dodson, Debra. 2005. "Making a Difference: Behind the Scenes." In *Women and Elective Office: Past, Present, and Future,* edited by Sue Thomas and Clyde Wilcox, 129–151. New York: Oxford University Press.

———. 2006. *The Impact of Women in Congress.* New York: Oxford University Press.

Duerst-Lahti, Georgia. 1989. "The Government's Role in Building the Women's Movement." *Political Science Quarterly* 104:249–268.

———. 1998. "Competing Gender Ideologies: The Case of Welfare Reform." Paper presented at the Midwestern Political Science Association annual meeting, April 23–25.

———. 2001. "Conservative Women's Political Thought, Gender Ideology, and the Necessity of Feminism." Presented at the annual meeting of the Western Political Science Association, Las Vegas, Nevada, March 15–17.

———. 2002. "Governing Institutions, Ideology, and Gender: Toward the Possibility of Equal Political Representation." *Sex Roles* 47:371–389.

———. 2002. "Knowing Congress as a Gendered Institution." In *Women Transforming Congress,* edited by Cindy Simon Rosenthal, 20–49. Norman: University of Oklahoma Press.

Duerst-Lahti, Georgia, and Noelle Norton. 1999. "Gender Ideologies in Welfare Reform: The Case of Wisconsin Works." Presented at the annual meeting of the Western Political Science Association, Seattle, Washington, March 25–27.

Duerst-Lahti, Georgia, and Rita Mae Kelly, eds. 1995. *Gender Power, Leadership, and Governance.* Ann Arbor: University of Michigan Press.

Duncan, Greg. 1984. *Years of Poverty, Years of Plenty.* Ann Arbor, MI: Institute for Social Research, University of Michigan.

Easton, David. 1965. *A Systems Analysis of Political Life.* New York: Wiley.

Edin, Kathryn, and Laura Lein. 1997. *Making Ends Meet: How Single Mothers Survive Welfare and Low-Wage Work.* New York: Russell Sage Foundation.

Edsall, Thomas Byrne, and Mary D. Edsall. 1991. *Chain Reaction: The Impact of Race, Rights, and Taxes on American Politics.* New York: W. W. Norton.

Eisenstein, Zilla. 1981. *The Radical Future of Liberal Feminism.* Boston: Northeastern University Press.

Elshtain, Jean Bethke. 1981. *Public Man, Private Woman: Women in Social and Political Thought.* Princeton, NJ: Princeton University Press.

Feldstein, Ruth. 2000. *Motherhood in Black and White: Race and Sex in American Liberalism, 1930–1965.* Ithaca, NY: Cornell University Press.

Fenno, Richard F., Jr. 1966. *The Power of the Purse: Appropriations Politics in Congress.* Boston: Little Brown.

———. 1973. *Congressmen in Committees.* Boston: Little Brown.

Ferguson, Ann. 1989. *Blood at the Root: Motherhood, Sexuality, and Male Dominance.* London: Pandora Press.

Ferguson, Kathy E. 1993. *The Man Question: Visions of Subjectivity in Feminist Theory.* Berkeley: University of California Press.

Fossett, James W., and Thomas L. Gais. 2002. "A New Puzzle for Federalism: Different State Responses to Medicaid and Food Stamps." Presented at the annual meeting of the American Political Science Association, Boston, Massachusetts, August 29–September 1.

Frankel, Noralee, and Nancy S. Dye, eds. 1991. *Gender, Class, Race and Reform in the Progressive Era.* Lexington: University of Kentucky Press.

Freeman, Jo. 1995. "From Seeds to Harvest: Transformations of Feminist Organizations and Scholarship." In *Feminist Organizations,* edited by Myra Marx Ferree and Patricia Yancey Martin, 397–408. Philadelphia: Temple University Press.

Gais, Thomas, and R. Kent Weaver. 2002. "State Policy Choices Under Welfare Reform." In *Welfare Reform and Beyond,* edited by Ron Haskins, Andrea Kane, Isabel V. Sawhill, and R. Kent Weaver, 33–40. Washington, DC: Brookings Institution Press.

Garfinkel, Irwin. 1992. "Bringing Fathers Back In: The Child Support Assurance Strategy." *American Prospect* 9:74–83.

Gavanas, Anna. 2004. *Fatherhood Politics in the United States: Masculinity, Sexuality, Race, and Marriage.* Urbana: University of Illinois Press.

Gilder, George. 1973. *Sexual Suicide.* New York: Quadrangle.

———. 1981. *Wealth and Poverty.* New York: Basic Books.

Gillespie, Ed, and Bob Schellhas, eds. 1994. *Contract with America.* New York: Random House.

Goodwin, Joanne. 1997. *Gender and the Politics of Welfare Reform: Mothers' Pensions in Chicago, 1911–1929.* Chicago: University of Chicago Press.

Gordon, Linda. 1994. *Pitied But Not Entitled: Single Mothers and the History of Welfare, 1890–1935.* Cambridge, MA: Harvard University Press.

————, ed. 1990. *Women, the State, and Welfare.* Madison: University of Wisconsin Press.

Grant, Judith. 1993. *Fundamental Feminism: Contesting the Core Concepts of Feminist Theory.* New York: Routledge.

Hall, Richard L. 1996. *Participation in Congress.* New Haven, CT: Yale University Press.

Hall, Richard L., and Bernard Grofman. 1990. "The Committee Assignment Process and the Conditional Nature of Committee Bias." *American Political Science Review* 84:1149–1166.

Handler, Joel F. 1995. *The Poverty of Welfare Reform.* New Haven, CT: Yale University Press.

Hartman, Heidi. 1981. "The Unhappy Marriage of Marxism and Feminism: Towards a More Progressive Union." In *Women and Revolution,* edited by L. Sargent, 1–41. Boston: South End Press.

Hartsock, Nancy C. M. 1983. *Money, Sex, and Power: Toward a Feminist Historical Materialism.* Boston: Northeastern University Press.

Hawkesworth, Mary. 1997. "Confounding Gender." *Signs* 22:649–685.

————. 2003. "Congressional Enactments of Race-Gender: Toward a Theory of Raced-Gendered Institutions." *American Political Science Review* 97: 529–550.

Hearn, Jeff. 1992. *Men in the Public Eye.* London: Routledge.

Herrera, Richard, Thomas Epperlein, and Eric R. A. N. Smith. 1995. "The Stability of Congressional Roll-Call Indexes." *Political Research Quarterly* 48:403–416.

Hirschmann, Nancy J., and Ulrike Liebert, eds. 2001. *Women and Welfare: Theory and Practice in the United States and Europe.* New Brunswick, NJ: Rutgers University Press.

Hochschild, Arlie. 1989. *The Second Shift: Working Parents and the Revolution at Home.* New York: Viking Press.

Hoover, Kenneth. 2000. *Ideology and Political Life.* Belmont, CA: Wadsworth.

Jackson, John E., and John W. Kingdon. 1992. "Ideology, Interest Group Scores, and Legislative Votes." *American Journal of Political Science* 36:805–823.

Jenning, James. 2002. "Welfare Reform and Neighborhoods: Race and Civic Participation." In *Lost Ground: Welfare Reform, Poverty, and Beyond,* edited by Randy Albelda and Ann Withorn, 129–144. Cambridge, MA: South End Press.

Jonasdottir, Anna. 1994. *Why Women Are Oppressed.* Philadelphia: Temple University Press.

Jones, Kathleen B. 1993. *Compassionate Authority: Democracy and the Representation of Women.* New York: Routledge.

Josephson, Jyl J. 1997. *Gender, Families, and State: Child Support Policy in the United States.* Lanham, MD: Rowman and Littlefield.

Kann, Mark E. 1991. *On the Man Question: Gender and Civic Virtue in America.* Philadelphia: Temple University Press.

————. 1998. *A Republic of Men.* New York: New York University Press.

————. 1999. *The Gendering of American Politics: Founding Mothers, Founding Fathers, and Political Patriarchy.* Westport, CT: Praeger.

Kaplan, Thomas. 2000. "Wisconsin Works." In *Managing Welfare Reform in Five States: The Challenge of Devolution,* edited by Sarah F. Liebschutz, 103–121. Albany, NY: Rockefeller Institute Press.

Katz, Michael B. 2001. *The Price of Citizenship: Redefining America's Welfare State.* New York: Henry Holt.

Kaus, Mickey. 1992. *The End of Equality.* New York: Basic Books.

Kerber, Linda. 1980. *Women of the Republic: Intellect and Ideology in Revolutionary America.* Chapel Hill: University of North Carolina Press.

———. 1998. *No Constitutional Right to Be Ladies: Women and the Obligations of Citizenship.* New York: Hill and Wang.

Kessler-Harris, Alice. 1982. *Out to Work: A History of Wage-Earning Women in the United States.* New York: Oxford University Press.

———. 1995. "Designing Women and Old Fools: The Construction of the Social Security Amendments of 1939." In *U.S. History as Women's History,* edited by Linda K. Kerber, Alice Kessler-Harris, and Kathryn Kish Sklar, 87–106. Chapel Hill: University of North Carolina Press.

Kiewiet, D. Roderick, and Mathew D. McCubbins. 1991. *The Logic of Delegation: Congressional Parties and the Appropriations Process.* Chicago: University of Chicago Press.

Kimmel, Michael S. 1996. *Manhood in America: A Cultural History.* New York: Free Press.

———. 2000. "Saving the Males: The Sociological Implications of the Virginia Military Institute and the Citadel." *Gender and Society* 14:494–516.

———, ed. 1995. *The Politics of Manhood.* Philadelphia: Temple University Press.

Kingdon, John W. 1989. *Congressmen's Voting Decisions.* Ann Arbor: University of Michigan Press.

———. 1995. *Agendas, Alternatives, and Public Policies.* New York: HarperCollins.

Krehbiel, Keith. 1987. "Why Are Congressional Committees Powerful?" *American Political Science Review* 81:929–935.

———. 1991. *Information and Legislative Organization.* Ann Arbor: University of Michigan Press.

Kritzer, Herbert M. 1978. "Ideology and American Political Elites." *Public Opinion Quarterly* 42:484–502.

Lasswell, Harold. 1958. *Politics: Who Gets What, When, How.* Cleveland: Meridian Books.

Lieberman, Robert C. 1998. *Shifting the Color Line: Race and the American Welfare State.* Cambridge, MA: Harvard University Press.

Lorber, Judith. 1993. "Believing Is Seeing: Biology as Ideology." *Gender and Society* 7:568–581.

———. 1994. *Paradoxes of Gender.* New Haven, CT: Yale University Press.

Lorde, Audre. 1983. *Sister Outsider.* Freedom, CA: Crossing Press.

Lowi, Theodore J. 1972. "Four Systems of Policy, Politics, and Choice." *Public Administration Review* 32:298–310.

Lurie, Irene. 1992. "JOBS Implementation in 1991: The Progress of Ten States." *Publius* 22:79–91.

Maltzman, Forrest. 1995. "Meeting Competing Demands: Committee Performance in the Postreform House." *American Journal of Political Science* 39:653–682.

Maltzman, Forrest, and Steven S. Smith. 1994. "Principals, Goals, Dimensionality, and Congressional Committees." *Legislative Studies Quarterly* 19:457–476.

Mansbridge, Jane. 1999. "Should Blacks Represent Blacks and Women Represent Women? A Contingent Yes." *Journal of Politics* 61:628–657.

Mason, Mary Ann. 2000. *The Custody Wars: Why Children Are Losing the Legal Battle and What We Can Do About It.* New York: Basic Books.

Mead, Lawrence. 1986. *Beyond Entitlement: The Social Obligations of Citizenship.* New York: Free Press.

———. 1992. *The New Politics of Poverty: The Nonworking Poor in America.* New York: Basic Books.

———, ed. 1997. *The New Paternalism: Supervisory Approaches to Poverty.* Washington, DC: Brookings Institution Press.

Mettler, Suzanne. 1998. *Dividing Citizens: Gender and Federalism in New Deal Public Policy.* Ithaca, NY: Cornell University Press.

Meyer, Jack A. 1984. "Budget Cuts in the Reagan Administration: A Question of Fairness." In *The Social Contract Revisited,* edited by D. Lee Bawden, 33–64. Washington, DC: Urban Institute.

———. 1986. "Social Programs and Social Policy." In *Perspectives on the Reagan Years,* edited by John L. Palmer, 65–89. Washington, DC: Urban Institute.

Mezey, Susan. 2003. *Elusive Equality: Women's Rights, Public Policy, and the Law.* Boulder, CO: Lynne Rienner.

Mink, Gwendolyn. 1995. *The Wages of Motherhood: Inequality in the Welfare State, 1917–1942.* Ithaca, NY: Cornell University Press.

———. 1998. *Welfare's End.* Ithaca, NY: Cornell University Press.

———, ed. 1999. *Whose Welfare?* Ithaca, NY: Cornell University Press.

Minogue, Kenneth, ed. 1996. *Conservative Realism: New Essays in Conservatism.* London: HarperCollins.

Monson, Renee. 2002. "Ties That Bind: Child Support Enforcement and Welfare Reform in Wisconsin." In *Work, Welfare, and Politics: Confronting Poverty in the Wake of Welfare Reform,* edited by Frances Fox Piven, 227–240. Eugene: University of Oregon Press.

Moynihan, Daniel Patrick. 1967. "The Negro Family: The Case for National Action." In *The Moynihan Report and the Politics of Controversy,* edited by Lee Rainwater and William L. Yancey, 39–124. Cambridge: Massachusetts Institute of Technology.

———. 1973. *The Politics of a Guaranteed Income: The Nixon Administration and the Family Assistance Plan.* New York: Random House.

Murray, Charles. 1984. *Losing Ground: American Social Policy, 1950–1980.* New York: Basic Books.

———. 1985. "Have the Poor Been 'Losing Ground'?" *Political Science Quarterly* 100:427–445.

———. 1996. "Keeping Priorities Straight on Welfare Reform." *Society* 33:10–12.

Nathan, Richard P., and Thomas L. Gais. 1999. *Implementing the Personal Responsibility Act of 1996: A First Look.* Albany, NY: Rockefeller Institute of Government.

Neubeck, Kenneth J., and Noel A. Cazenave. 2001. *Welfare Racism: Playing the Race Card Against America's Poor.* New York: Routledge.

Newman, Louise Michele. 1999. *White Women's Rights.* New York: Oxford University Press.

Noble, Charles. 1997. *Welfare as We Knew It: A Political History of the American Welfare State.* New York: Oxford University Press.

Norton, Noelle H. 1995. "Women, It's Not Enough to be Elected: Committee Position Makes a Difference." In *Gender Power, Leadership, and Governance,* edited by Georgia Duerst-Lahti and Rita Mae Kelly, 115–140. Ann Arbor: University of Michigan Press.

———. 1999. "Committee Influence over Controversial National Policy: The Reproductive Policy Case." *Policy Studies Journal* 27:203–216.

———. 1999. "Uncovering the Unidimensionality of Gender Voting in Congress." *Legislative Studies Quarterly* 24:65–86.

Offen, Karen. 1998. "Defining Feminism: A Comparative Historical Approach." *Signs* 14:119–157.

Pateman, Carole. 1988. *The Sexual Contract.* Stanford, CA: Stanford University Press.

Patterson, James T. 1994. *America's Struggle Against Poverty, 1900–1994.* Cambridge, MA: Harvard University Press.

Pavetti, LaDonna, and Dan Bloom. 2001. "State Sanctions and Time Limits." In *The New World of Welfare,* edited by Rebecca Blank and Ron Haskins, 245–270. Washington, DC: Brookings Institution Press.

Phillips, Anne. 1995. *The Politics of Presence: The Political Representation of Gender, Ethnicity, and Race.* New York: Oxford University Press.

Piven, Frances Fox, and Richard A. Cloward. 1993. *Regulating the Poor: The Functions of Public Welfare.* New York: Vintage.

Poole, Keith T., and R. Steven Daniels. 1985. "Ideology, Party, and Voting in the U.S. Congress." *American Political Science Review* 79:373–399.

Poole, Keith T., and Howard Rosenthal. 1991. "On Dimensionalizing Roll Call Votes in the U.S. Congress." *American Political Science Review* 85: 955–975.

———. 1997. *Congress: A Political-Economic History of Roll Call Voting.* New York: Oxford University Press.

Popenoe, David. 1996. *Life Without Father: Compelling New Evidence That Fatherhood and Marriage Are Indispensable for the Good of Children and Society.* New York: Martin Kessler Books.

Quadagno, Jill, and Catherine Fobes. 1995. "The Welfare State and the Cultural Reproduction of Gender: Making Good Girls and Boys in the Job Corps." *Social Problems* 42:171–190.

Rector, Robert. 2001. "Comment." In *The New World of Welfare,* edited by Rebecca Blank and Ron Haskins, 264–267. Washington, DC: Brookings Institution Press.

Roberts, Dorothy. 1997. *Killing the Black Body: Race, Reproduction, and the Meaning of Liberty.* New York: Pantheon Books.

———. 1999. "Welfare's Ban on Poor Motherhood." In *Whose Welfare?* edited by Gwendolyn Mink, 152–170. Ithaca, NY: Cornell Unversity Press.

Roper, Pamela Forrestal. 1997. "Hitting Deadbeat Parents Where It Hurts: Punitive Mechanisms in Child Support Enforcement." *Alaska Law Review* 14:41–76.

Rosenthal, Cindy Simon. 1998. *When Women Lead: Integrative Leadership in State Legislatures.* New York: Oxford University Press.

Ruddick, Sara. 1989. *Maternal Thinking: Toward a Politics of Peace.* Boston: Beacon Press.

Sapiro, Virginia. 1983. *The Political Integration of Women.* Urbana: University of Illinois Press.

Sartorius, Rolf, ed. 1983. *Paternalism.* Minneapolis: University of Minnesota Press.

Schon, Donald A., and Martin Rein. 1994. *Frame Reflection: Toward the Resolution of Intractable Policy Controversies.* New York: Basic Books.

Schram, Sanford F. 2000. *After Welfare: The Culture of Postindustrial Social Policy.* New York: New York University Press.

Schram, Sanford F., Joe Soss, and Richard C. Fording, eds. 2003. *Race and the Politics of Welfare Reform.* Ann Arbor: University of Michigan Press.

Schudson, Michael. 1998. *The Good Citizen: A History of American Civic Life.* Cambridge, MA: Harvard University Press.

Shaeffer, William R. 1983. "Rating Congress—The Convergence of Objectivity and Subjectivity." *Political Methodology* 9:329–340.

Shepsle, Kenneth A. 1979. "Institutional Arrangements and Equilibrium in Multidimensional Voting Models." *American Journal of Political Science* 23:27–59.

Shepsle, Kenneth, and Barry Weingast. 1987. "The Institutional Foundations of Committee Power." *American Political Science Review* 81:85–104.

Shklar, Judith N. 1991. *American Citizenship: The Quest for Inclusion.* Cambridge, MA: Harvard University Press.

Skocpol, Theda. 1992. *Protecting Soldiers and Mothers: The Political Origins of Social Policy in the United States.* Cambridge, MA: Harvard University Press.

Smith, Eric R. A. N., Richard Herrera, and Cheryl Herrera. 1990. "The Measurement Characteristics of Congressional Roll-Call Indexes." *Legislative Studies Quarterly* 15:283–295.

Solinger, Rickie. 1998. "Dependency and Choice: The Two Faces of Eve." *In Whose Welfare?* edited by Gwedolyn Mink, 7–35. Ithaca, NY: Cornell University Press.

———. 2001. *Beggars and Choosers: How the Politics of Choice Shapes Adoption, Abortion, and Welfare in the United States.* New York: Hill and Wang.

Stacey, Judith. 1996. *In the Name of the Family: Rethinking Family Values in the Postmodern Age.* Boston: Beacon Press.

Steiner, Gilbert. 1966. *Social Insecurity.* Chicago: Rand McNally.

Stone, Deborah. 1997. *Policy Paradox: The Art of Political Decision Making.* New York: W. W. Norton.

Swers, Michele L. 2002. *The Difference Women Make.* Chicago: University of Chicago Press.

Tamerius, Karen. 1995. "Sex, Gender, and Leadership in the Representation of Women." In *Gender Power, Leadership, and Governance,* edited by Georgia Duerst-Lahti and Rita Mae Kelly, 93–112. Ann Arbor: University of Michigan Press.

Teles, Steven M. 1998. *Whose Welfare? AFDC and Elite Politics.* Lawrence: University of Kansas Press.

Thomas, Sue. 1994. *How Women Legislate.* New York: Oxford University Press.

Thomas, Sue, and Susan Welch. 1991. "The Impact of Gender on Activities and Priorities of State Legislators." *Western Political Quarterly* 44:445–456.

Walby, Sylvia. 1990. *Theorizing Patriarchy.* Oxford: Basil Blackwell.

———. 1997. *Gender Transformations.* London: Routledge.

Waters, Malcolm. 1989. "Patriarchy and Viriarchy: An Exploration and Reconstruction of Concepts of Masculine Domination." *Sociology* 23:193–212.

Weingast, Barry. 1989. "Floor Behavior in the U.S. Congress: Committee Power Under the Open Rule." *American Political Science Review* 83:795–815.

White, Stuart. 2003. *The Civic Minimum: On the Rights and Obligations of Economic Citizenship.* New York: Oxford University Press.

Wood, Gordon S. 1991. *The Radicalism of the American Revolution.* New York: Vintage Books.

Yates, Gayle Graham. 1975. *What Women Want: The Ideas of the Movement.* Cambridge, MA: Harvard University Press.

Young, Iris Marion. 1997. *Intersecting Voices: Dilemmas of Gender, Political Philosophy, and Policy.* Princeton: Princeton University Press.

Index

About the Book

SELDOM DO WE NOTICE, LET ALONE EXPLICITLY ACKNOWLEDGE, that public policies set distinct parameters for gender. But as *Creating Gender* compellingly demonstrates, in reality governments *do* use policy to legitimize and support some gender-based behaviors while undermining others.

Looking in depth at the case of welfare reform but considering a wide range of policy arenas, the authors examine how government policy-making in essence defines the "proper" nature of males and females. At the heart of their analysis is an effort to resolve questions about how policies determine what women and men must do to be granted standing as good citizens and what benefits they can subsequently accrue. The result is a clear yet sophisticated exploration of the troublesome, sometimes insidious, ways in which gender ideology works in tandem with conventional political ideologies in the United States today.

Cathy Marie Johnson is professor of political science and the Schumann Faculty Fellow in Democratic Studies at Williams College. Her research interests center on social welfare policy and the representation of children in US politics. She is the author of *The Dynamics of Conflict Between Bureaucrats and Legislators* and has published several articles on bureaucracy and public policy.

Georgia Duerst-Lahti is professor of political science at Beloit College, where she has held many administrative posts, including associate dean. Her research interests revolve around gender theory related to US political institutions, public leadership, and election campaigns. She is currently researching changes in gender and leadership in public organizations, based on a twenty-year comparison, and gender in presidential elections, with a special focus on manifestations of masculinity. Her best-known work is *Gender Power, Leadership, and Governance,* with Rita Mae Kelly.

Noelle H. Norton is professor of political science and international relations at the University of San Diego, where she also directs the honors program. Her research interests focus on Congress, congressional committees, women in Congress, and institutional gender analysis. Her current projects include an exploration of gender and executive branch reorganization strategies. She has published several articles on analyzing gender and congressional roll call voting and on women in Congress in *Legislative Studies Quarterly, Political Research Quarterly,* and *Policy Studies.*